Criminal Fraud and Election Disinformation

OXFORD MONOGRAPHS ON CRIMINAL LAW AND JUSTICE

Series Editor:
Jeremy Horder LLD, FBA, Professor of Criminal Law, London School of Economics

This series aims to cover all aspects of criminal law and procedure including criminal evidence. The scope of this series is wide, encompassing both practical and theoretical works.

OTHER TITLES IN THIS SERIES

Policing the Borders Within
Ana Aliverti

Criminalizing Sex
A Unified Liberal Theory
Stuart P. Green

Reasons to Doubt
Wrongful Convictions and the Criminal Cases Review Commission
Carolyn Hoyle and Mai Sato

Fitness to Plead
International and Comparative Perspectives
Ronnie Mackay and Warren Brookbanks

Criminal Misconducts in Office
Law and Politics
Jeremy Horder

The Preventive Turn in Criminal Law
Henrique Carvalho

Criminal Justice and Taxation
Peter Alldridge

In Search of Criminal Responsibility
Ideas, Interests, and Institutions
Nicola Lacey

Preventive Justice
Andrew Ashworth and Lucia Zedner

Character in the Criminal Trial
Mike Redmayne

Homicide and the Politics of Law Reform
Jeremy Horder

The Insecurity State
Vulnerable Autonomy and the Right to Security in the Criminal Law
Peter Ramsay

Manifest Madness
Mental Incapacity in the Criminal Law
Arlie Loughnan

The Ethics of Plea Bargaining
Richard L. Lippke

Prosecuting Domestic Violence
A Philosophical Analysis
Michelle Madden Dempsey

Abuse of Process and Judicial Stays of Criminal Proceedings
Second Edition
Andrew L.-T. Choo

A Philosophy of Evidence Law
Justice in the Search of Truth
H. L. Ho

Excusing Crime
Jeremy Horder

Criminal Fraud and Election Disinformation

Law and Politics

JEREMY HORDER

OXFORD
UNIVERSITY PRESS

OXFORD
UNIVERSITY PRESS

Great Clarendon Street, Oxford, OX2 6DP,
United Kingdom

Oxford University Press is a department of the University of Oxford.
It furthers the University's objective of excellence in research, scholarship,
and education by publishing worldwide. Oxford is a registered trade mark of
Oxford University Press in the UK and in certain other countries

First Edition published in 2022

Impression: 1

Published in the United States of America by Oxford University Press
198 Madison Avenue, New York, NY 10016, United States of America

British Library Cataloguing in Publication Data

Data available

Library of Congress Control Number: 2021950162

ISBN 978–0–19–284454–5

DOI: 10.1093/oso/9780192844545.001.0001

Printed and bound by
CPI Group (UK) Ltd, Croydon, CR0 4YY

Preface

This book is about what our approach should be to fraudulent claims and distortion of the truth in politics, especially during elections. Why should that approach be a matter of legal or political concern? After all, lies, dishonesty, and misleading statements have always been a factor in politics. Demonizing and mischaracterization of political opponents, and of their policies, together with myth-making about past events and current controversies, form a more or less substantial part of many party political programmes, and of much vigorous, partisan political debate online. Does that not suggest that toleration of such practices, albeit reluctant, is the right attitude?

Arguably, not. Dishonesty and distortion of the facts are morally wrong. Moreover, they may lead to setbacks to important political interests. Reliance on a false election claim may lead me to vote in a way I would not otherwise have done. A false political claim widely publicized about me as a candidate may lead me to lose an election I might otherwise have won. A false claim that an election was marred by fraud may lead me (if I am an election official) to allocate resources to a recount of votes that is in fact unwarranted. So, does—and should—the law seek to provide protection from the risk that these kinds of setbacks occur, by directly prohibiting the making of false or misleading political or electoral claims, or by making internet platforms censor such content? In this book, I elaborate on and defend an answer to that question.

In that regard, I draw a key distinction between what I call 'political viewpoint' fraud, and what I call 'electoral participation' fraud. Broadly speaking, in the interests of protecting freedom of speech, false or known-to-be-misleading claims (disinformation) involving political viewpoint content should be tolerated, not only by the criminal law but also by key actors with responsibility for hosting political content such as internet platforms. By contrast, in the interests of preserving the integrity of the electoral process (in the face of an increasingly partisan approach by some political parties to that process) disinformation involving electoral participation information should be prohibited by the criminal law, and censored by internet platforms.

In Chapters 1 and 2, I explore and defend the distinction between the two categories of political disinformation, and explain how it should in general shape the law (criminal law in particular) and internet platform policy. I then go on in Chapters 3 and 4 to explain how UK law (and to some extent, law in the Commonwealth) wrongly uses the criminal law to prohibit false or misleading political claims falling into both categories of disinformation. The criminal law should be used only to prohibit false or misleading electoral participation claims.

Acknowledgements

The global pandemic of 2020 made finding opportunities for discussion of ideas with others more challenging, and we have all been the poorer for that. However, I would like to thank members of the Criminal Law Discussion group at the LSE, and John Child (Birmingham University) for their willingness to comment on parts of an earlier draft. I must also thank Jacob Rowbottom (University College, Oxford), whose ground-breaking article in the 2012 *Oxford Journal of Legal Studies*, addressing many of the issues tackled in this book, initially inspired me to think I could make a contribution to this area of law and policy. Most of all, I should like to thank my wife, Naomi-Jiehua, whose love, patience, and support have been my 'rod and staff' throughout.

Jeremy Horder
Saint Bertrand's Day, 2021

Contents

Table of Cases

AUSTRALIA

CANADA

ECHR

GERMANY

IRELAND

SINGAPORE

UK

USA

Table of Legislation

MALAYSIA

NEW ZEALAND

REPUBLIC OF IRELAND

SCOTLAND

SINGAPORE

UNITED KINGDOM

UNITED STATES OF AMERICA

General Introduction

This book seeks to explore and defend in depth a simple proposition in relation to the regulation, whether through the criminal law or otherwise, of known-to-be-false or misleading political speech ('disinformation'). This is that Governments, regulators, and platform moderators should make central to their approach a distinction between what I call 'electoral participation disinformation' and what I call 'political viewpoint disinformation'.[1] I defend the view that restrictions on free speech (criminal offences, internet platform take-down requirements, and so on) are necessary and fully justified in the case of electoral participation disinformation. This is false or misleading information concerning (say) where to vote, about qualifications to vote or stand as a candidate, and about requirements for voting or vote-counting.[2] By contrast, I argue that placing such restrictions on political viewpoint disinformation (outlined below) is unnecessary and unjustified, unless this disinformation also involves wrongdoing that *is* justifiably targeted with such restrictions.[3] The best response to political viewpoint disinformation is a form of counter-speech: persuading people, non-coercively, to engage critically with such content.

The distinction between the two kinds of disinformation is not just one designed to assist in the principled rationalization of criminal and regulatory law as it applies to elections, even though that is my main concern. It raises a fundamental question in political theory. To what extent can one have a relatively untrammelled, passionate, and partisan politics, within a political and electoral system that passionate and partisan political activists on all sides accept on a *non*-partisan basis? On the one hand, criminalization of, and the placing of other kinds of restrictions on, the dissemination of electoral participation disinformation, reflect a commitment to non-partisanship in the conduct of (and in the rules governing) elections. On the other hand, tolerance of political viewpoint disinformation acknowledges that there are limits, in a democracy, to the extent to which one can or should seek to extend the interpretation and reach of the non-partisan state. An appeal of

[1] The proposition I am defending is not a new one, but so far as I am aware, no one has gone into it in depth or drawn out the full implications of defending it. See Richard Hasen (2013).

[2] See Chapter 1, section 1.2 for fuller exposition of the distinction.

[3] Examples of such harms (which I will for the most part not be considering in detail) are hate speech, intimidation, incitement to commit crime or to become involved in terrorist organizations, causing disabling emotional distress, or other kinds of harmful or harm-threatening speech such as false health advice that poses dangers to those who follow it.

Criminal Fraud and Election Disinformation. Jeremy Horder, Oxford University Press. © Jeremy Horder 2022.
DOI: 10.1093/oso/9780192844545.003.0001

non-partisan features of the state is that these features promise medium- to long-term benefits for all (or nearly all) that outweigh the allure of short-term partisan advantage (for some). A fairly conducted election may hand ruling Party X a defeat it could have avoided by changing the election rules beforehand to its (partisan) advantage; but then, Party X may also hope to regain power from its opponents under those self-same rules at some point in the future, if its opponents also stick by those rules when they are in power (avoiding their own version of partisan meddling). So, there is a common interest in suppressing conduct, such as participation disinformation, that threatens the fairness of elections. When elections take place, with broad recognition of that common interest in place, participants are in effect treating each other as political 'adversaries' and not as political 'enemies'.[4]

However, the fragile nature of such 'zero-sum' political settlements,[5] once they cease to be shored up by deep-rooted and widely shared commitments or 'constitutional patriotism',[6] is in this respect illustrated by the drift of US politics towards a more partisan form of 'democracy'. Following President Trump's repeated (and wholly unjustified) attacks on the US electoral system in the 2020 Presidential election, no less than 361 bills had been introduced by April 2021 seeking to restrict ballot access.[7] That signifies the extent to which some American politicians—Republicans in particular—regard their opponents not as (legitimate) political adversaries but as political enemies, to be kept out of power by any means Republican supporters themselves will tolerate.[8] Against that background, it is important to recognize that there are risks to the stability and legitimacy of the non-partisan dimensions of the state as a whole, in seeking to extend its interpretation and hence its reach into the substance (as opposed to the form) of electoral politics. Prohibitions on the substance of what people may say are certainly necessary and proportionate in some cases, as when people engage in the politics of (say) race hate or in intimidation;[9] but these should not be seen as instances of overreach. In the context of electoral politics, race hate and intimidation involve attempts to

[4] For this distinction, see Chantal Mouffe (2005).

[5] Settlements in which the degree to which X benefits from the rules broadly matches the degree to which Y benefits from them.

[6] Jurgen Habermas (1996), 286.

[7] https://thevotingnews.com/ (last accessed 12/04/2021). See, further, William D. Hicks et al. (2015). In a less dramatic way, such a trend can also be detected in the UK, with the proposal for introducing a requirement to show ID at the polling station: see https://www.theguardian.com/politics/2021/feb/28/using-photo-id-in-british-elections-will-harm-democracy-say-us-civil-rights-groups (last accessed 11/05/2021). We should note, though, that in the US most democratic voters have supported the need to show ID at the polls: https://news.gallup.com/poll/194741/four-five-americans-support-voter-laws-early-voting.aspx (last accessed 13/04/2021). Depending on how such a requirement is implemented and managed over time, it may not, as such, be a requirement sustained solely or mainly by partisan considerations.

[8] https://www.theguardian.com/commentisfree/2021/jun/28/republicans-gerrymandering-congress-elections (last accessed 28/06/2021).

[9] Committee on Standards in Public Life (2017); Cabinet Office (2019). See also the discussion in Chapter 3.

silence people by denying them freedom (from fear) in political expression, conduct that ought to be condemned on a non-partisan basis in any liberal democracy worthy of the name.[10]

By contrast, overreach is involved in the use of coercion to ensure that people, whatever their political leanings, engage publicly only in evidence-based political argument: rationalist politics. The aim of such coercive measures is to silence or restrict the speech of those whose politics stems from their attachment to, for example, charismatic leaders, conspiracy theories, or political narratives constructed largely from emotive content. This constitutes overreach because (as we will see) to pursue such an aim is, in part, to try systematically to exclude people from public political debate merely on the grounds that their style of politics is distasteful to mainstream politicians, difficult or impossible to engage with on mainstream terms, and a threat to the political legitimacy of mainstream officials, whatever their traditional party political allegiances. In other words, the pursuit of the aim is in a way itself an engagement in partisan politics. It is motivated by the wish to privilege mainstream forms of political discourse, and hence shield (mainstream) politicians from denunciation based on political arguments falling outside this form of discourse. The partisan element in attacks by mainstream politicians on populist and emotive political speech is often masked by the fact that political viewpoint fraud can certainly lead to harm (in a political sense). Two examples of political harm that may be caused by viewpoint fraud are the waste of a vote by a deceived voter, or the loss of electoral support for a candidate that would—were it not for the fraud—have seen them elected.[11] However, for a variety of reasons discussed in due course, to suffer such a harm as a result of viewpoint fraud is to not to be subject to a denial of one's civil rights, by way of contrast with cases in which such harms are brought about by electoral participation fraud.

1 Explaining the Key Distinction in Outline

Unlike electoral participation information, political viewpoint information is a broad category, although it is not to be equated with political opinions (even though opinions will commonly be based on political viewpoint information). For example, political viewpoint information includes information—factual claims—about the personal and political lives of candidates, and the attributes and policies of political parties. To give two examples that have been the subject of litigation (as we will see), a claim that an election candidate has never lived in the constituency is

[10] See the discussion in Chapters 2 and 3, and in Jeremy Horder (2021a). We should note that the claim here is not that issues of race or intimidation are 'non-political' issues. They are deeply political issues: John Crowley (1993).

[11] I touch on the issue of harm at the end of this chapter, and consider it in more depth in Chapter 1.

a claim based on political viewpoint information, as is a claim that a political candidate or party has Nazi associations. Beyond these issues, political viewpoint information extends to information about matters of social policy, economic policy, law, justice, and rights, together with claims about how politically important events should be described.[12] So, to give an example that sparked an official rejection (rare Government counter-speech), a false claim that recently arrived asylum seekers had all tested positive for COVID-19 is a claim based on political viewpoint information.[13]

All such political viewpoint claims, in virtue of having supposedly factual content, are distinct from simple opinions such as 'Candidates who haven't lived in the constituency don't deserve to be elected', 'John Doe's extremist pronouncements make him unfit for public office', or 'It is too risky to allow more asylum seekers into the country'. Nonetheless, on my account, in spite of their alleged factual content, when political viewpoint claims involve disinformation they should be treated in the same way as the expression of political opinion, and protected from restrictions.[14] In Chapters 1 and 2, I argue that the right approach to political viewpoint disinformation is counter-speech of a particular kind: speech designed to encourage people to engage critically with political viewpoint content. This is counter-speech that, in the case on online speech, involves the attachment to false or misleading content of unreliability warnings and of links to other viewpoints. Such an approach is not a cure-all. For example, although unreliability warnings have proven effective in deterring many users from accessing material,[15] there is evidence that some people tend to believe falsehoods (other than very obviously fake material) even if warnings about the reliability of such material do accompany their spread.[16] Nonetheless, such a less-than-perfect 'more speech' solution is to be preferred to less-than-perfect solutions involving censorship.

For Jurgen Habermas:

> [W]e understand a speech act when we know the kinds of reasons that a speaker could provide in order to convince a hearer that he is entitled in the given circumstances to claim validity for his utterance—in short, when we know what makes it acceptable.[17]

[12] See further Chapter 1 for more detailed examination of political viewpoint information.

[13] https://www.independent.co.uk/news/uk/home-news/farage-covid-home-office-b1808726.html (last accessed 08/04/2021).

[14] ECHR, Article 10: 'Everyone has the right to freedom of expression. This right shall include freedom to hold opinions and to receive and impart information and ideas without interference by public authority and regardless of frontiers.'

[15] Department for Digital, Culture, Media and Sport, and Home Office (2020), para 5.32.

[16] G. Pennycook, T. D. Cannon, and D. G. Rand (2018).

[17] Jurgen Habermas (1998), 232.

Whatever the merits of this claim, it is not part of the legitimate function of governments, regulators, and platform moderators and their algorithms to shore up this kind of rationalistic account of the comprehensibility of (political) speech acts, by coercing us into thinking and acting only on the basis of—supposedly—adequately grounded political viewpoint information. That is what can be called the 'rationalistic political fallacy'. Pursuing such a policy threatens to deny political breathing space to political movements sparked and sustained by raw emotion. That would be wrong, because (for example):

> Anger in politics can play a particularly vital role, motivating some people to participate in ways they might ordinarily not—even if they have the ability and opportunity to do so.[18]

In that regard, I reject what I call, in Chapter 2, 'militant' democratic thinking: the use of the rationalistic fallacy to justify the use of coercion and restriction, on the grounds that false political viewpoint speech threatens democratic government. Those motivated to engage in politics through absorbing or championing conspiracy theories and other false political narratives should not face free speech barriers when they do so. The role of agencies such as governments, regulators, and platform moderators, in that regard, is simply to encourage us to sift political content to find political truths for ourselves.

This approach to political viewpoint information involves a willingness to tolerate the spread of content that is undoubtedly perverse, partisan, hurtful, spiteful, valueless, or needlessly divisive. One example would be a fake claim that a mass shooting was in fact organized by gun-control activists as part of their gun-control agenda.[19] Another example, subject to what I will say in a moment, is the claim that President Barack Obama was not born in the USA.[20] Ridiculous and outrageous though these claims may be, they do not, as such, involve or threaten harm. However, as indicated above, when political viewpoint disinformation edges into harmful or harm-threatening speech, it need not and should not be tolerated. So, in fact, some known-to-be-false claims about the ineligibility of President Obama (and Vice-President Harris[21]) to hold high office are properly construed not simply as political dirty tricks but as motivated by and designed to stoke race hate. Accordingly, when they take such a form (and it will be a matter of construction, in context), such claims can be banned, restricted, and targeted with sanctions.

To consider a different example, further discussed in Chapter 1, President Trump made frequent claims that the legitimacy of the 2020 presidential election

[18] Nicholas A. Valentino (2011), 168; Debra Thompson (2017).

[19] https://www.businessinsider.com/marjorie-taylor-greene-conspiracy-theories-mass-shootings-parkland-vegas-2021-1?r=US&IR=T (last accessed 22/03/2021).

[20] https://www.bbc.co.uk/news/election-us-2016-37391652 (last accessed 22/03/2021).

[21] https://www.bbc.co.uk/news/world-us-canada-53774289 (last accessed 22/03/2021).

was undermined by widespread fraud. For reasons I will give, this is a political viewpoint claim, even though it is obviously about the election process. It is not an electoral participation claim—a concept which I construe narrowly—because it is not connected to the potential involvement of any individual participant or group of participants in the existing electoral process, in the way that they use (or fail to use) the process itself.[22] Accordingly, the President should have been permitted to continue making this (absurd) claim, in the interests of free speech. However, he could legitimately have been silenced if there came a point when repeating it in a certain way or at a key point became, in the circumstances, an incitement to engage in violence: that is clearly a kind of unlawful speech justly prohibited.[23]

We will see that the distinctions between electoral participation disinformation, political viewpoint disinformation, and perverse opinion are clear enough to support legal and policy approaches that draw on the distinctions. Even so, there will sometimes be a need for interpretive analysis and fine line-drawing, as the examples just given illustrate. In the area of free speech, that is a familiar enough and inevitable problem. The European Court of Justice, for example, has seen fit to rule on whether an accusation that someone is a 'thief' was a factual claim, or alternatively a piece of general abuse (mere opinion).[24] As we will see, UK election candidates are protected by a criminal law offence, under section 106 of the Representation of the People Act 1983 Act ('the 1983 Act'), from false statements about their 'personal' conduct or character, if the statements were intended to affect their vote return. However, that protection does not extend to false statements about a candidate's 'political' conduct or character.[25] So, English courts have been asked to rule on whether the following false accusations about a candidate are *purely* personal in nature, or involve a political element: that the candidate associates with violent terrorists, that they have never lived in the constituency, and that they hate Muslims.[26] The gist of my argument, though, is that a focus on the personal/political distinction shines light in the wrong place. Whether personal or political in nature, and whether or not about an individual's character or conduct, these kinds of false statements all involve political viewpoint disinformation. Consequently, they should not be restricted from the 'top down' by criminal or regulatory law, or through platform moderator policy.[27] Instead, they should be vigorously opposed by counter-speech of different kinds.

[22] A proposition defended in detail in Chapter 4.
[23] Whether his claims ever did cross that line may be doubted: see the discussion in Chapter 1.
[24] *Vitrenko & Others v Ukraine* (Application no.) 23510/02, 16 December 2008.
[25] Representation of the People Act 1983, s. 106, discussed further in Chapters 1 and 3.
[26] See the discussion of these examples in Chapter 3.
[27] A 'top-down' remedy is a remedy that can be justified without a necessary link to a complaint made by an individual about a violation of their rights. If and when a wronged candidate seeks to show that they have been defamed, they seek a 'bottom-up' remedy, to which civilized legal systems and platforms must provide some appropriate response. See further Cass Sunstein (2021). I say more about this in the next section.

2 Private and Public Law Remedies for Political Disinformation

I will not be concerned with actions in private law focused on political viewpoint disinformation—'bottom-up' initiatives— even though they may obviously exercise at least some deterrent effect on those disposed to circulate damaging and false or misleading political claims about individuals. Neither will I discuss the important development whereby internet platforms take responsibility for handling individual complaints about defamatory content.[28] My concern will be with the policies that are or should be pursued through initiatives from the 'top down', namely from governments, regulators, or internet platforms, in relation to a broader range of political falsehoods than those which are defamatory. Nonetheless, actions for defamation do offer a way in which those actively involved—or caught up—in politics may seek to take action to claim compensation for false claims made about them in the course of campaigns, or (exceptionally) to prevent such false claims being circulated or spread.[29] For example, in 2021, Dominion Voting Systems Corporation sued a pro-Trump attorney, Sidney Powell, for $1.3 billion, claiming defamation in virtue of Powell's false claims that the company's voting systems were created in Venezuela to rig the election, and that the company deleted or changed votes.[30] In another 2021 case, Arlene Foster, Northern Ireland's First Minister, was awarded £125,000 following the posting of a tweet, at an especially politically sensitive time, falsely claiming that she had been engaged in an extra-marital affair.[31] A particularly instructive English example is *Waterson v Lloyd and Carr*.[32]

In the run-up to the general election in 2010, as part of their campaign literature, the local Liberal Democrat party published statements in the *Sussex Courier* about the claims made for parliamentary expenses by the sitting MP for Eastbourne, Nigel Waterson. Under a front-page headline, 'Expenses scandal MP faces defeat', the Liberal Democrats said that Waterson had been paid almost £70,000 during the last four years towards the cost of his Kent family home over 60 miles away from his constituency. Amongst other things, there was also a claim that he had spent

[28] See e.g. The Defamation (Operators of Websites) Regulations 2013. For a fresh examination of defamation in political contexts, see Cass Sunstein (2021).

[29] Jacob Rowbottom (2012), 508–9. Representation of the People Act 1983, s. 106(3), 'A person making or publishing any false statement of fact as mentioned above may be restrained by interim or perpetual injunction by the High Court or the county court from any repetition of that false statement or of a false statement of a similar character in relation to the candidate and, for the purpose of granting an interim injunction, prima facie proof of the falsity of the statement shall be sufficient.'

[30] https://www.wsj.com/articles/pro-trump-lawyer-sidney-powell-seeks-to-dismiss-defamation-suit-over-election-claims-11616468931; https://www.theguardian.com/us-news/2021/mar/23/sidney-powell-trump-election-fraud-claims (both last accessed 24/03/2021). Powell defended her claim by claiming that her statements were ones of opinion, and that no reasonable person would in any event have believed them.

[31] https://www.bbc.co.uk/news/uk-northern-ireland-57268308 (last accessed 01/06/2021).

[32] [2013] EWCA Civ 136. See https://www.kingsleynapley.co.uk/insights/blogs/dispute-resolution-law-blog/defamation-defence-honest-comment-or-statement-of-fact (last accessed 23/03/2021).

over £1,000 of taxpayers' money to have his garage door redecorated. Crucially, in the comment section of the paper, the Liberal Democrats made a link with the 'expenses scandal' of 2009: 'Local residents have delivered their verdict on the MP's expenses scandal. […] Eastbourne Conservative MP Nigel Waterson who has come under fire in recent months for his own scandalous expenses claims.' In another publication, the *Eastbourne and Willingdon Express*, the Liberal Democrats doubled down on the forging of the link, by saying 'Voting Labour here in Eastbourne and Willingdon will just let our expenses scandal MP off the hook.'

Having lost his seat at the election, Waterson sued his opponent (Lloyd) and Lloyd's campaign agent (Carr) for libel. He did so on the basis that, by forging an association in voters' minds between the 2009 expenses scandal, involving some criminally wrongful claims made by MPs for expenses, and Waterson's own (legitimate) use of the expenses system, Lloyd and Carr were wrongly implying that Waterson himself had been involved in impropriety.

In a split decision, overturning the judgment at first instance, the Court of Appeal found against Waterson. They did so on the basis that the overall impression being given by the publications was an honest opinion, and so not actionable. In the Court of Appeal's view, the 'scandal' being alleged in the publications, albeit emanating from the revelations in 2009 about MPs' expenses, was that someone could—*ex hypothesi*, legitimately—claim so large a sum as £70,000 to spend on a domestic property that was far from the MP's constituency. The majority in the Court of Appeal found no explicit or implicit defamatory association as a matter of fact between Waterson and the making of *unlawful* expense claims. The decision shows how judges may be divided amongst themselves (here, effectively, two versus two) on the justiciability of allegedly false or misleading political speech: a threat to the perception that the judges remain impartial in cases where such issues are at stake, which is a matter taken up in Chapters 1 and 4. The decision also demonstrates, though, that the courts will generally seek to construe political speech as the expression of opinion (and thus protected by Article 10). They do this in the interests of preserving a wide margin for the promulgation of content that is hyper-partisan, unfair, hurtful, and mud-slinging: in other words, the very stuff of deeply committed and passionate electoral politics.[33]

Alongside private law actions, there are also public law remedies available in cases where an election has allegedly been influenced by fraud. Under the 1983 Act, someone found guilty of the section 106 offence (mentioned above) of making a false statement about the personal conduct or character of a candidate with the intention of affecting the candidate's vote return will be barred from standing for Parliament and from holding elective office for three years.[34] If the person making

[33] See further, *Otegi Mondragon v Spain* 1(Application no. 2034/07) 15th March 2011; Chantal Mouffe (2005).

[34] Representation of the People Act 1983, ss. 160 and 173.

the false statement was the candidate elected, the election is also declared void, and the individual will not be permitted to stand again.[35] In Chapter 3, I consider this 'election candidate defamation offence' in depth. However, moving beyond defamation cases, the courts also have a general power to intervene in elections undermined by fraud (amongst other things). Under section 164 of the 1983 Act:

> Where on an election petition it is shown that corrupt or illegal practices . . . committed in reference to the election for the purpose of promoting or procuring the election of any person at that election have so extensively prevailed that they may be reasonably supposed to have affected the result— (a) his election, if he has been elected, shall be void.

For this purpose, corrupt or illegal practices will, under section 115 of the 1983 Act, include the use of any 'fraudulent device' that impedes or prevents, or is intended to impede or prevent, the free exercise of the franchise of an elector, or which induces or prevails—or is intended to induce or prevail—on an elector (not) to vote.

This broad-ranging discretion given by section 164 to the courts to overturn elections seriously tainted by fraud (or by other corrupt or illegal practices) was described by Benjamin Disraeli as a constitutional principle of 'vast importance'.[36] It is further considered in Chapter 4, where my focus will be the scope of the criminal fraud offence created by section 115. A crucial question that arises is: is it, or should it be, open to the courts to overturn an election under section 164, as well as to convict an individual of the section 115 offence, when the fraud in question was a political viewpoint fraud, rather than an electoral participation fraud? To give a hypothetical example of the difference that is made by giving a positive answer to this question, we could consider the UK's 2016 referendum on leaving the EU.[37] Suppose that section 164 applied to referendums as well as to elections (it does not, even though the section 115 offence has such an application[38]). Then, if section 164 encompassed political viewpoint fraud as well as participation fraud, it would have been possible (as it is in Switzerland) to challenge the validity of the referendum in the courts on the grounds that, for example, it was tainted by fraud brought about by, amongst other things, a Russian disinformation campaign.[39] So far as it concerns election results, my response to that kind of possibility is that the courts' powers under section 164, and the scope of the section 115 offence, should be confined to electoral participation frauds.

[35] Representation of the People Act 1983, ss. 159(1) and 164.
[36] Benjamin Disraeli to Queen Victoria, 31 January 1868, in Michael Pharand et al. (1982), 40, cited by Kathryn Rix (2017), 65.
[37] Further discussed in Chapter 1.
[38] For discussion, see Jeremy Horder (2021a).
[39] Ewan McGaughey (2018).

3 Criminal and Regulatory Restrictions on Political Disinformation

Alongside private and public law remedies, there is the use of the criminal law to deter and punish election (or more broadly, political) fraud. For example, Article 1, section 18500 of the California Elections Code (Chapter 6) creates an offence in the following circumstances:

> Any person who commits fraud or attempts to commit fraud … in connection with any vote cast, to be cast, or attempted to be cast, is guilty of a felony, punishable by imprisonment for sixteen months or two to three years.

In my terms, this provision is, like many other similar provisions around the world, ambiguous concerning whether or not it covers political viewpoint fraud alongside electoral participation fraud. Do I commit an offence under this provision not only when I falsely tell a would-be voter that the polls have closed (electoral participation fraud), but also when I knowingly give false reassurance to a voter that a candidate the voter is minded to favour is a decorated veteran (political viewpoint fraud)?

The US Supreme Court has proved sceptical concerning the constitutional validity of such offences under the First Amendment, when they extend beyond frauds involving defamatory statements about election candidates.[40] A focus on defamatory statements has the attraction of limiting the scope for political controversy arising from the application of such offences, by concentrating as much (or more) on the personal wrong done to the candidate as on the political distortion of the voting process.[41] Such statements are the focus of the offence in section 106 of the 1983 Act (mentioned above and discussed in Chapter 3), and in a number of common law jurisdictions which historically drew on UK law.[42] Here is a modern example. Section 61 of the Elections Modernization (Canada) Act 2018 now creates the following offence:

> No person or entity shall, with the intention of affecting the results of an election, make or publish, during the election period,
>
> (a) a false statement that a candidate […] has committed [or been charged with or is being investigated for] an offence …; or

[40] *The State of Washington on the relation of Public Disclosure Commission v 119 Vote No! Committee* (1998) 135 Wn 2d 618, 629. See the discussion in ch. 4 of Cass Sunstein (2021).

[41] This theme is pursued in Jacob Rowbottom (2012), and Jeremy Horder (2021a).

[42] See Chapter 3.

(b) a false statement about the citizenship, place of birth, education, professional qualifications or membership in a group or association of a candidate […].

As we will see in Chapter 3, and as I indicated earlier, controversy has arisen in relation to the interpretation of the UK equivalent of section 61 (section 106 of the 1983 Act), because of the vagueness inherent in the notion of a false statement made about someone's 'personal' conduct or character. Section 61 seeks to minimize the scope for such controversy, by specifying a limited number of aspects of character or reputation that it will be an offence to make a false statement about (with a view to affecting the result of an election): broadly, these are criminality, nationality, educational qualifications, and formal associations. This introduces a greater degree of certainty, but at the cost of opening up many gaps in the protection offered to (would-be) office-holders engaged in elections. Whilst a false allegation that someone has committed an offence is covered, a false claim that they have *not* committed one falls outside its scope. Similarly, a false allegation that a candidate held racist views, or had stood for an opposing party in a previous election, would fall outside the protection offered. By contrast, candidates do enjoy the security of knowing that a false allegation that they are members of the Canadian Association of Railway Modellers ('membership in a group') is covered. With greater legal certainty comes greater moral arbitrariness.

In general, I am doubtful about whether there can be a justification for criminal offences touching on any kind of political viewpoint disinformation, even defamatory disinformation, for reasons that will be explored in Chapters 1, 3, and 4. Such offences threaten to chill provocative political speech, to make martyrs of outspoken and hot-headed political critics, and to draw criminal courts or regulators into unwanted and potentially damaging political controversy.[43] For related reasons, in Chapter 2, I also take a restricted view of what internet platforms, through their moderators and algorithms, should be doing to limit the posting and spread of political viewpoint disinformation. Like the legislature and the criminal courts, they should come down hard on the dissemination of electoral participation disinformation; and they generally do. Here, for example, is Facebook's policy on the matter:

We prohibit:

- Explicit and implicit misrepresentation of the dates, locations, times and methods for voting or voter registration.

[43] For similar arguments, see Cass Sunstein (2021).

- Misrepresentation of who can vote, qualifications for voting, whether a vote will be counted, and what information and/or materials must be provided in order to vote.
- Misrepresentation of whether a candidate is running or not.
- Calls for coordinated interference that would affect an individual's ability to participate in an election.
- Content stating that voting participation may or will result in law enforcement consequences.
- Content claiming that the US Immigration and Customs Enforcement (ICE) is at a voting location.
- Explicit claims that people will be infected by COVID (or another communicable disease) if they participate in the voting process.
- Offers to buy or sell votes with cash or gifts.
- Statements that advocate, provide instructions or show explicit intent to illegally participate in a voting process.[44]

Unlike courts, though, platforms are in a position to take a sophisticated approach to political viewpoint disinformation, rather than simply banning or (contrariwise) permitting it. They can implement 'more speech' solutions, such as warning users about the potential unreliability of certain kinds of claim, whilst refraining from interference with the reach of such disinformation.[45] I argue that such a policy is the right one because it encourages users to engage critically with political claims and statements, rather than taking on the far more contentious task of deciding which political claims and statements are to be restricted or banned, and which (perhaps) are to be promoted.

4 What Issues this Book Does and Does Not Address

In Chapter 1, I will explain why the dissemination of false political viewpoint disinformation should be tolerated, and not subject to restriction (*a fortiori*, when restriction takes the form of criminal penalties), and why spreading electoral participation disinformation should not be tolerated and should in fact be made subject to criminal penalties. Unlike electoral participation information, political viewpoint disinformation often forms part of authentic but hyper-partisan political narratives that, unlike many mainstream political narratives, engage a range of people in adversarial political argument who might otherwise be politically apathetic. Mainstream politicians should thus not seek to skew the political agenda in

[44] Facebook (2020).

[45] See Cass Sunstein (2021), 133, '[S]ome of the most promising tools do not involve censorship or punishment; they involve more speech-protective approaches, such as labels and warnings.'

their favour by using law or regulation to stifle political viewpoint misinformation, wherever it comes from. In any event, the regulatory and (even more so) the criminal processes are unsuited to litigation over political viewpoint matters.

In Chapter 2, I turn my attention to the specific issue of political disinformation online. The discussion is set in the context of a distinction between having a legal doctrine of toleration, and demonstrating a tolerant moral outlook. An attitude of legal and moral intolerance towards political viewpoint disinformation is characteristic only of authoritarian or militant democratic regimes. So, on the one hand, I argue that, as well as following the legal doctrine of toleration, internet platforms should generally adopt a tolerant moral outlook towards political viewpoint disinformation. However, they should nonetheless seek to encourage sceptical or enquiring engagement on the part of users with potentially false and misleading (or anonymous) content. On the other hand, platforms ought positively to be intolerant of hate speech, intimidatory speech, incitement to commit crimes, and other harmful content such as electoral participation misinformation. What we find is that the major internet platforms in fact often adopt a more sophisticated and nuanced approach to these issues than the governments that seek to regulate them.

In Chapters 3 and 4, I turn my attention to a detailed examination of English (and to some extent Commonwealth) criminal law, in historical perspective, as it bears on false or misleading claims aimed at influencing elections. Consistent with the thesis developed in Chapters 1 and 2, I argue the law is insufficiently attentive to the distinction between political viewpoint and electoral participation disinformation. I also develop a theme outlined in Chapter 1, namely that political viewpoint disputes are ill-suited to resolution in the (criminal) courts.

In a book of readable length, it is obviously impossible to do justice to the full range of issues that might usefully have been addressed. One omission (well covered by other writers[46]) is broadcasting. Do 'broadcasters', in virtue simply of engaging in the act of broadcasting, have a responsibility not to peddle false viewpoint information (let alone electoral participation information), that ordinary laypeople using the internet do not have? For what it is worth, in stable democracies,[47] I do not think that they necessarily do have such a responsibility, unless they are holding themselves out, expressly or impliedly, as presenting news in an unbiased manner. If they are not doing that, then so long as viewers are consistently made aware of where—as the phrase goes—the broadcaster is 'coming from' (perhaps quite literally, in the case of foreign states), the broadcasting of political viewpoint disinformation should be tolerated, regrettable though we ought to find such a practice. Of course, a politically responsible state will seek to ensure that

[46] Article 19 (2019b).

[47] Different considerations may apply in very fragile democracies. See Kofi Annan Commission on Elections and Democracy in the Digital Age (2020).

broadcast consumers have free or low-cost access to at least some broadcasting that aspires to present a broad range of news issues in a fair and unbiased way, but that is another matter.

This book is about political disinformation—information known or suspected to be false or misleading when it is spread. It has not been possible to cover the issues raised by the dissemination of misinformation—information that is false or misleading but which is passed on unwittingly. More significantly, to maintain a clear and simple focus on disinformation, I have largely set on one side a consideration of hate speech and intimidation, even though there is no doubt that these practices have a significant impact—quite possibly even more of an impact than disinformation—on the electoral process.[48] However, I argue, in Chapter 2, that one reason for adopting an intolerant attitude—morally and legally—to political hate speech is broadly the same reason for adopting such an attitude towards electoral participation disinformation. This is that both are political 'silencing' techniques, practices that undermine the equality conditions for democratic citizenship that we are entitled to see honoured and respected.

What that means, though, is that I do not explore here the complex relationship between hate speech and political viewpoint disinformation, as it affects hyper-partisan political individuals and groups. If—as I argue—these individuals' and groups' freedom to disseminate viewpoint disinformation should be respected, but their freedom to spread hate should not, what scope, in practice, does that leave them to develop and spread their political agenda? After all, evidence indicates that the more detached from reality political disinformation is, the more likely it is to contain intimidatory or hate speech.[49] Even so, that will have to be a subject for another time; but we should note that the Canadian Supreme Court has seen no difficulty in upholding the right to spread false political viewpoint narratives (even when highly inflammatory),[50] whilst also defending the constitutionality of criminal laws prohibiting hate speech.[51]

Finally, something should be said about the mode of analysis. Clearly, a major concern (especially in Chapters 3 and 4) is with the criminal law, and the justification for using it to deter and punish political liars and truth-distorters. However, the discussion does not follow the traditional path of seeking to shed light on the law by analysing it in terms of *actus reus*, *mens rea*, and justification and excuse, coupled with consideration of the harm principle, even though it would have been possible to proceed in that way. The reason for this is that using such a prism through which to view the relevant rules and principles unduly narrows or limits

[48] See for example ch. 5 of Committee on Standards in Public Life (2017). Moreover, some of the issues raised by hate speech, such as the possibility that the courts will become embroiled in politicized legal disputes, are similar to those raised by the juridification of political viewpoint disinformation.

[49] Michael Hameleers et al. (2021).

[50] *R v Zundel* [1992] 2 SCR 731.

[51] *R v Keegstra* [1990] 3 SCR 697.

the range of issues that would otherwise come naturally into focus. For example, consider the case of a false factual claim about the state of the economy contained in a party election manifesto, which leads some people to cast their vote in favour of the party: a classic case of political viewpoint disinformation at work. In Chapter 1, we will consider a range of reasons why it would be undesirable to make such a false claim subject to legal action, even if the falsehood was unjustifiably and inexcusably included in the manifesto quite deliberately. That being so, questions about the false claims concerning the *actus reus* or *mens rea*, or about justification and excuse, largely become side issues.

Nonetheless, would it be right to say that the voters who relied on the truthfulness of the manifesto claim when casting their votes have been harmed? That question might still seem important. Clearly, if someone's vote is denied or stripped of its intrinsic value, as a form of political expression, when they arc induced to rely on false electoral participation information, then an important civil right has been denied or undermined. They have been harmed 'politically'. Is the same thing true in the party manifesto case? A seemingly significant difference between such a case and other examples of political viewpoint disinformation, such as a false claim that a mass shooting was staged by anti-gun activists, is that the manifesto claim (unlike the mass shooting claim) is more commonly directly intended to persuade people to exercise a civil right, by voting in a particular way. Consequently, those misled by the false manifesto claim endure a setback to their political interests, when the claim leads them to cast their vote in a way that they would not otherwise have done, had they known or suspected the truth. As we will see in Chapter 1, for that reason, militant democrats draw no distinction between electoral participation disinformation and political viewpoint disinformation. In their view, both may lead to harm done of an equivalent kind, and thus, the dissemination of both kinds of disinformation should be restricted or banned.

One problem with that approach, whether or not we say that there was 'harm done' in the manifesto case, is that it leaves far too little scope for free viewpoint speech in election campaign contexts. False political viewpoint speech, especially during election periods, is very commonly aimed at persuading people to vote in a particular way, or to enhance or (contrariwise) to do damage to the electoral prospects of a particular candidate or party. So, to regard as punishable harms (or as harms worthy of regulatory restriction) either damage done by false viewpoint claims to one's electoral prospects, or the waste of one's vote when cast on a false viewpoint basis, is necessarily to countenance stifling far too much speech that is simply intemperate, provocative, or controversial.[52] Consequently, citizens must be trusted to avoid such harms by the use of their own judgement, rather than through state efforts to deter the harms' occurrence. An example from a different

[52] See the discussion in Chapter 1, and in Jeremy Horder (2021a). See also Cass Sunstein (2021).

context might be psychological harm caused (to an adult) by watching a deeply disturbing feature film or a highly distressing news story. Too much that is of great value, in terms of artistic expression or news reporting, would be lost by using coercive measures to shield adults from the risk of suffering such a harm in this way. Consequently, they must be trusted to take their own avoiding action. Harm done by political viewpoint disinformation needs to be analysed in a similar way.

In (relatively) open democracies, a whole variety of political narratives and counter-narratives abound in public space. In such a democratic environment, part of what it means to treat 'citizens' as such is to treat them as adequately capable of forming as well as acting on their own conception of a (political) good.[53] Accordingly, when they are misled by viewpoint disinformation to their detriment, although citizens suffer harm, their political rights are not violated.[54] In any event, even if we do not trust citizens to avoid this harm, what makes us think that we can, by contrast, trust those who would be thrust into the spotlight by their role in deciding what viewpoint speech is to be banned and which speakers silenced?[55] As one US court has put it, 'the state does not possess an independent right to determine truth and falsity in public issues'.[56] Regulators and platform moderators would be taking on a modern version of the discredited role of the Lord Chamberlain, whose function it was until 1968 to license only dramatic productions that conformed to standards of decency.[57] By contrast, there are few, if any, free speech-based countervailing considerations to take into account when seeking to justify prohibitions or restrictions on the dissemination of electoral participation disinformation. So, it is justified and proportionate to target with restrictions the harm—and the interference with civil rights–to which such disinformation may lead.

[53] See the discussion of the 'autonomy principle' in ch. 1 of Frederick Shauer and Richard H. Pildes (1999), 1812 and 1814.

[54] As we will see in Chapter 1, there is more to the argument than this, important though this argument is.

[55] See the discussion of the 'scepticism principle', in Chapter 1; Cass Sunstein (2021).

[56] *State of Washington v 119 Vote No! Committee* 957 P 2nd 691 (1998), 698.

[57] The role of the Lord Chamberlain in censoring dramatic productions was abolished by the Theatres Act 1968.

1
Political Disinformation: Law, Elections, and Partisan Politics

1.1 Introduction

(i) (In)tolerance of political disinformation: some overarching considerations

Lies and known-to-be-misleading statements are, and always have been, an enduring feature of (election) politics and political argument. So, what matters about these practices is not simply whether they can be justified or excused (I will not be much concerned with this). What matters extends to the circumstances in which we should tolerate such practices, even when engaging in them lacks justification or excuse.[1] In that regard, a key issue is the subject matter of the lie or misleading statement. Let me start with an easy case for non-toleration, but one that is central to the argument in this book. We should be intolerant of lies or known-to-be-misleading statements (disinformation) concerning what I called in the General Introduction 'electoral participation' information. This is disinformation about the bureaucratic process involved in voting, standing as a candidate, or officiating in the process. I will say more about it shortly. In general, most jurisdictions rightly adopt an intolerant standpoint towards such disinformation. When statements are intended to deceive or mislead people about participation in the voting process, criminalizing the making of such statements, or in some other way restricting them, is fully justified.

Of course, we are all entitled to express views about how the electoral process *ought* to be conducted. In that regard, there will always be people disposed to peddle falsehoods or misleading claims to back up their opinions on (say) who ought to be entitled to vote or stand for election. However, false or misleading claims aimed at influencing the possible shape of future election rules and procedures is (as we will see shortly) 'political viewpoint' disinformation. For that reason, my argument will be that it should be tolerated. The category of electoral

[1] I will say a good deal more about the notion of 'toleration' in Chapter 2, when the distinction between toleration as a political doctrine, and toleration as a moral outlook, will be important.

Criminal Fraud and Election Disinformation. Jeremy Horder, Oxford University Press. © Jeremy Horder 2022.
DOI: 10.1093/oso/9780192844545.003.0002

participation disinformation, disinformation that should be banned or restricted, is very important but it is also narrow. Principally, it concerns false or known-to-be-misleading information bearing principally on normative features of the existing electoral process itself, such as eligibility to take part, conditions that must be satisfied if one is to take part, or the proper way to take part—whether as a voter, a candidate, or an election administrator. However, electoral 'participation' is not an exclusively normative concept. So, non-normative disinformation about how—say—to reach a polling station, is also electoral participation disinformation.

By contrast, the position is different when disinformation takes the form of what I call 'political viewpoint' disinformation.[2] This is also a highly significant category of disinformation, but by way of contrast with electoral participation disinformation, it is very broad in scope. Political viewpoint disinformation involves lies or known-to-be-misleading statements about, for example, facts bearing on the personal histories or beliefs of people involved in politics, about what political parties stand for, about how politically charged events came about or concerning what was said or done at them, and so on. I will say more about it in due course. When addressing political viewpoint disinformation, as we will see, the law is commonly far less clear about what its message is and should be. Further, the guidance given to internet platforms and their moderators on what, if anything, to do about such information has been both more equivocal and more controversial. No one argues against the case for permitting—even encouraging—vigorous and impassioned political speech; but the moral case for tolerating political viewpoint disinformation may seem opaque and fragile, not least (say) when it comes from outside a jurisdiction. Nonetheless, there is a free-speech case, explored and defended in this chapter, for toleration of lies and (known-to-be-) misleading statements amounting to political viewpoint disinformation. Before making that case, though, I will start with some brief remarks about what difference it might make that a particular kind of person, namely a politician, is the person responsible for a political lie or misleading statement. That gives us a way of introducing some of the wider issues I will be addressing, in this chapter and in Chapter 2.

There have long been Machiavellian efforts to normalize lying as a tool of statecraft.[3] Further, there are certainly some (relatively weak) strategic considerations standing in the way either of seeking in some formal way to deter officials from propagating political disinformation, or of holding them to account when they do it. We may worry that fear of being punished or held too closely to account will lead officials effectively to conceal sources of disinformation, or in some other way to put themselves beyond the reach of accountability systems. Even so, in a

[2] See Jeremy Horder (2021a); Joshua Sellers (2018).

[3] See, for example, the discussion in Martin Jay (2010), Introduction; Peter Oborne (2005). It has been argued that lying and dishonesty are simply a counterpoint to truthfulness and honesty in politics, the one helping to define and shape the character of the other: Michael A. Peters (2015).

politically flourishing state, officials must accept that they are elected or appointed on the basis that they will act—other than in wholly exceptional circumstances—in a transparent and honest way in the performance of their functions,[4] because 'the state acts legitimately only if it furthers the "common good" of the political community'.[5] However instrumentally useful it may seem, it adds nothing of intrinsic value to one's life as an official to be free to lie or mislead in the course of one's duties (quite the opposite).[6]

At a constitutional level, this point is made manifest in, for example, rules providing that, if a Minister knowingly makes a false statement in Parliament, then Parliament may hold him or her accountable for the lie by requiring their resignation. The Ministerial Code in Scotland says: 'It is of paramount importance that Ministers give accurate and truthful information to the Parliament, correcting any inadvertent error at the earliest opportunity. Ministers who knowingly mislead the Parliament will be expected to offer their resignation to the First Minister.'[7] In terms of the criminal law's role in relation to lies told by officials more generally, it is notable that the criminal offence of misconduct in public office applies to instances in which an official has (without excuse or justification) told a lie in the course of performing their functions.[8]

Even so, beneath these rules and codes lies a more complex picture. As we will see, disinformation may form part of a broader political narrative which has substantial public support, making toleration of that disinformation perfectly comprehensible.[9] Further, when elected officials are carrying out their duties, they probably have a good deal of scope in practice to push, without fear of sanction, at the limits of legal and ethical tolerance of dishonesty, dissembling, and so forth, in the interests (as they see it) of party and of government.[10] Unelected police and prosecutorial bodies may prove reluctant to investigate cases at these limits, for fear of politicizing their own role. Opposition parties may be concerned about the scope they will themselves have for manoeuvre in Government, if they protest too loudly now. So, judgements about dishonest politicians will come, if they come at all, at the next election.[11] Yet, understanding when it is permissible to threaten

[4] Subject, in the case of transparency, to restrictions legitimately generated by national security concerns.

[5] Mark Seidenfeld (1992), 1528.

[6] That is not to say that there can never be a reason to say something false or misleading, in one's official capacity. For example, a political leader might be justified in falsely saying publicly that they have no objection to meeting a rival to search for common ground on some important issue, even though they secretly detest the rival and would rather have no contact with them at all.

[7] Scottish Ministerial Code (2018), para 1.3(c).

[8] https://www.thelawpages.com/court-cases/Keith-Wallis-12790-1.law (last accessed 09/04/2021).

[9] https://www.upi.com/Top_News/Voices/2019/12/19/Why-people-vote-for-politicians-they-know-are-liars/6591576760843/ (last accessed 27/04/2021).

[10] Even if the same degree of tolerance would not be shown to dishonest conduct motivated by financial self-interest. See, generally, Eric Alterman (2020).

[11] Even then, incidents of proven dishonesty or misleading statements are unlikely to be judged in isolation, but set by voters into the context of a political party's overall political record. See the discussion in section 1.5(i) below.

officials with sanctions of some kind, if they disseminate disinformation in the course of performing their formal functions, is the (relatively) easy part.

More problematic is the fact that officials—elected politicians in particular, because they must engage ceaselessly with broadcast and social media—may tell political lies, or (even more frequently) knowingly may make misleading political claims, other than in the course of performing an official function. These statements will simply be contributions to ongoing political debate, much like those made by any other person. No doubt, in virtue of the public position they hold, engaging in such conduct should be regarded as especially morally reprehensible. It is a measure of people's strength of feeling on this issue that in 2017–18, 14,771 people signed a petition to Parliament demanding that it should be made illegal, 'for any UK politician to lie or mislead the public'. Even so, when political viewpoint disinformation is in issue, there is no reason to prohibit or even to restrict such conduct through legal means. On the contrary, seeking to prohibit or restrict such conduct in that way damages a free-speech culture.

First, whilst lies and misleading statements may not, in themselves, add anything of value to public debate—indeed they may poison or degrade it—I will suggest that participation and engagement in political activism more broadly can have intrinsic value, even if the narrative on which it is focused is constituted by false or misleading claims. That is as true for continuing speech-activism on the part of serving politicians as it is for such activism when engaged in by anyone else. Moreover, we should recognize the real risk that partisan motives, rather than some more neutral concept of the public good, may be behind many calls for action to be taken against particular politicians for 'lying'.[12] The ever-present threat of politicization of a process giving formal redress for lying in politics means that such a cure is especially vulnerable to turning out to be worse than the disease. By contrast, in a flourishing free-speech culture, one may reasonably hope that vigorous counter-narratives will spontaneously develop in opposition to significant political lies or misleading statements. In Chapter 2, I will explain what internet platform moderators, as *de facto* guardians of public space, are entitled to do to assist users to engage with that process.

However, the desirability of tolerating the dissemination of political viewpoint disinformation does not imply an automatic right to conceal the source of that disinformation. 'Who' is saying something may matter as much or even more than 'what' they are saying. Should one not, for example, be entitled to know that one is receiving information from or debating with a chat-bot rather than a human being? To give a different kind of example, for some people, that a source of political disinformation is associated with a foreign jurisdiction is something that

[12] See the discussion of the case brought against Boris Johnson MP by the 'Brexit Justice' campaign in section 1.2(ii), and the discussion of *Rickert v Public Disclosure Commission* 161 Wn 2d 843 (2007) below.

ought to be disclosed.[13] Going back, though, to the discussion above, what ought—surely—in all cases to be disclosed is when information comes ultimately from an official source (whether the information is true, false, or misleading). Then, the case for disclosure of the source is very strong, whether or not the official source is based overseas. We are entitled to know when state officials are trying to inform or influence us, whatever view we take about the nature of that information or influence. All of these themes are pursued at different points through this book, and in this chapter in particular.

(ii) The potentially penal consequences of lying in politics

Many jurisdictions around the world use the criminal law, alongside a variety of regulatory and preventative or other discouraging measures (such as official 'reprimands'[14]), to deter and prevent the publication and dissemination of false or misleading political information, especially when such disinformation is designed to influence elections or referendums.[15] Sometimes, these measures are direct, and involve the threat of criminal sanctions. An example from a US state code is the following 'gross misdemeanour' in Minnesota:

> (a) A person is guilty of a gross misdemeanor who intentionally participates in the preparation, dissemination, or broadcast of paid political advertising or campaign material with respect to the personal or political character or acts of a candidate, or with respect to the effect of a ballot question, that is designed or tends to elect, injure, promote, or defeat a candidate for nomination or election to a public office or to promote or defeat a ballot question, that is false, and that the person knows is false or communicates to others with reckless disregard of whether it is false.[16]

An analogous offence in English law, focusing on falsehoods about the personal character and conduct of election candidates, discussed in detail in Chapter 3, can be found in section 106 of the Representation of the People Act 1983 ('the 1983 Act'). Section 106 makes it an 'illegal practice', and a summary offence, to publish a false statement of fact about an election candidate's personal conduct or character, in order to affect the candidate's vote return.[17]

[13] The strength of the case for this will be assessed in section 1.3(i) below.

[14] See the discussion in Richard Hasen (2013).

[15] Daniel Funke and Daniela Flamini (2018).

[16] Statutes 211B.06.

[17] Unlike the Minnesota provision, section 106 excludes from its scope false claims about a candidate's 'political' character. See the discussion in Chapter 3. One noticeable contrast between the Minnesota provision and English law, is that English law provides specifically for a defence of honest (and reasonable) belief in the truth of the statement made. For further discussion, see Chapter 3, and *R (on the application of Woolas) v The Parliamentary Election Court* [2010] EWHC 3169 (Admin).

By contrast, restrictive or discouraging measures are sometimes indirect, such as threats of regulation or sanction directed at social media platforms, should platforms fail to provide an adequate means for challenging or for removing false or misleading political content posted by platform users. An example of indirect measures of this kind, designed to prevent the spread of false political information online, can be found in Germany's Network Enforcement Act 2017, considered in detail in Chapter 2. A major concern about indirect measures is that when they are over-intrusive or involve disproportionate threats, they may encourage 'collateral' censorship: 'when one private party, like Facebook, has the power to control speech by another private party, like a Facebook user'.[18] From a free-speech perspective, that may be just as objectionable as the use by the state of direct measures of the sort just cited.

The use of all such measures, whether direct or indirect, may have different aims, aims which will almost invariably be controversial. On the one hand, such measures may have an ostensibly benign purpose, in political contexts, such as creating a positive environment in which candidates can conduct their campaigns, although acting for such a purpose will not by itself make the taking of such measures justified.[19] On the other hand, whilst presenting such measures as intended to secure such a benign purpose, a state may in fact intend to use them in an improperly authoritarian way to suppress criticism of the government itself.[20] An example, discussed in detail in Chapter 2, comes from section 7 of Singapore's Protection from Online Falsehoods and Manipulation Act 2019. Under section 7, 'a person must not do any act in or outside Singapore in order to communicate in Singapore a statement, knowing or having reason to believe that ... it is a false statement of fact', when that communication of the statement is likely to 'diminish public confidence in the performance of any duty or function of, or in the exercise of any power by, the Government, an Organ of State, a statutory board, or a part of the Government, an Organ of State or a statutory board'.

One problem about having laws that permit the suppression of false or misleading political viewpoint information is that it can be difficult in some instances to disentangle the two kinds of intent (benign; authoritarian). For example, in any democratic country, a prime minister must continue to take responsibility for running the government, whilst simultaneously him or herself standing for election at the appropriate time. In that situation, what scope, if any, should there be to take action against false claims made about the prime minister as a candidate (the supposedly benign purpose), if one is also trying to uphold the principle that people should be free to circulate information—whether false or not—about the

18 Michael I Meyerson (1995), 118.

19 *Rickert v Public Disclosure Commission* 161 Wn 2d 843 (2007), 3.

20 A common complaint, in relation to the persistence in many countries, of the offence of criminal defamation as it applies to Government officials: see e.g. Council of Europe (2003).

government (avoiding authoritarianism)? This chapter, and indeed this book, seek to answer that question. In subsection 1.1.(iii) I will set out the basic framework, within which I will provide the answer.

(iii) The proper approach to limiting sanctions on political lies

As we will see in Chapter 2, for an authoritarian regime, a wide-ranging coercive and deterrent response to the propagation of allegedly false or misleading political claims—whether those claims relate to electoral participation or viewpoint information—is relatively easy to justify.[21] A hallmark of such regimes is that they claim the right to set the key terms on which citizens engage (if at all) in politics, including in political debate, and can be expected to shape those terms—including what is to count as a 'false' political claim that may be suppressed—to serve their own ends.[22] However, in democracies, a 'militant' democratic approach to the dissemination of false or misleading information can also involving advocating a coercive response to the dissemination of political viewpoint (as well as electoral participation) disinformation.[23] Although narrower in scope than the approach characteristic of an authoritarian regime, a militant democratic state sees political viewpoint disinformation as capable of causing harm equivalent to (say) hate speech or intimidation, and thus regards the dissemination of such disinformation as a threat to democracy. Accordingly, on the militant democratic account, restrictions on its publication and spread, even including criminal sanctions, are necessary and proportionate. A militant democratic approach to deterring the spread of false political information may—exceptionally—be justified, when a democracy is fragile, and the spread of such information is designed wholly or substantially to undermine it.[24] However, as we will see in due course, such an approach has also been adopted in stable, flourishing democracies, as a means of seeking to maintain a certain quality in political discourse, a far more controversial development.

By contrast, the liberal-democratic approach defended here involves distinguishing between, and treating differently, the two basic kinds of false or misleading political information outlined earlier: electoral participation disinformation, and political viewpoint disinformation (whether or not it is disseminated during an election or referendum period). An example of the former (electoral participation disinformation) is a false claim intentionally spread online that the polls are closing early because of a bomb scare. Examples of the latter (political viewpoint disinformation) would be false claims that 'candidate X broke all her

[21] This section draws on Jeremy Horder (2021b).
[22] Gábor Attila Tóth (2017) para 34.
[23] See Jan-Werner Muller (2012), ch. 59.
[24] See, for example, the report of the Kofi Annan Commission on Elections and Democracy in the Digital Age (2020).

promises when she was last in office', that 'party Y's policies have been endorsed by the Pope', or that a riot was instigated by an *agent provocateur*. Legislatures that employ the criminal law to deter and punish the dissemination of false political claims sometimes fail to draw clearly a distinction between the two kinds of information. For example, under Ohio law, it is an offence to: '[p]ost, publish, circulate, distribute, or otherwise disseminate a false statement concerning a candidate, either knowing the same to be false or with reckless disregard of whether it was false or not, if the statement is designed to promote the election, nomination, or defeat of the candidate'.[25] On the face of it, this looks like a prohibition directed at false political viewpoint claims about a candidate. This dimension to the offence has led to its being challenged as constitutionally inconsistent with the protection of free (political) speech provided by the First Amendment to the US Constitution.[26] However, the prohibition is capable of extension beyond political viewpoint matters, to false statements bearing on electoral participation issues. For example, false statements that a candidate has died or withdrawn, or that a candidate has changed their name (e.g. to that of another candidate on the ballot), are false statements 'concerning a candidate'. However, they are not the kind of false political viewpoint statements prohibitions on which raise difficult constitutional questions under the First Amendment. They are statements aimed at affecting participation in the election process by candidates and voters, and for that reason are—or ought to be—far less vulnerable to constitutional challenge. As we shall see in Chapter 2, the failure to draw a distinction between the two kinds of false or misleading statement is also characteristic of a number of proposals to make internet platforms responsible for failing to censor false political content (indirect coercion). However, the distinction is morally and politically fundamental.

Prohibitions on (false) political viewpoint information impinge on a key element of freedom of speech in politics: the freedom to say what one thinks important about candidates, parties, policies, and events, and to communicate those views to others. It can certainly be argued that the 'right to lie' is not a protected freedom.[27] In *R (on the application of Woolas) v The Parliamentary Election Court*,[28] the High Court held that 'the right to freedom of expression under Article 10 does not extend to a right to be dishonest and tell lies'.[29] However, as a justification for enforced censorship of political viewpoint disinformation, such a view gains traction only by decontextualizing the promulgation of particular political falsehoods and pieces of misleading information. We will see below that such promulgation may be inextricably bound up with the development of hyper-partisan, anti-establishment political narratives that citizens have every right to develop, however

[25] Ohio Revised Code 3517.21(10).

[26] *Susan B Anthony List v Ohio Elections Commission* 45 F Supp 3d 765, 769 (2014).

[27] *Reynolds v Times Newspapers* [2001] 2 AC 127; *Gertz v Robert Welch* 418 U.S. 323 (1974).

[28] [2010] EWHC 3169 (Admin).

[29] Ibid., para 106.

distasteful such narratives may appear to traditional politicians and activists. These narratives commonly make central to their themes a challenge to militant democratic claims to arbitrate on matters of political truth and, in particular, on the acceptability of political viewpoints for discussion. All the more reason, then, for tolerant liberal-democratic thinkers and activists to disavow such claims. That is so, even though evidence suggests that disinformation and conspiracy theories are more commonly adopted as part of an online political strategy on the right of the political spectrum, making the development of political narratives based on them a particular problem for centrist and centre-left politics.[30]

In this work, I will be concerned to defend a maximalist view of the scope for tolerating the dissemination of false or misleading political claims (viewpoint disinformation); but this defence will be subject to two important qualifications. One is that disinformation may justifiably be subject to prohibition or restriction, if there are grounds for prohibiting other than simply falsity, such as that it involves intimidation or hate speech.[31] The second qualification is that, to warrant protection from any kind of interference, the expression and dissemination of political viewpoint information must be 'authentic'. There must be a genuine speaker who makes the statement, and not a fake account, identity, or a 'bot', and the dissemination must not solely be motivated by making an economic gain. Even questions about authenticity may not, though, justify prohibiting or restricting the dissemination or spread of disinformation. I take up the latter issue in Chapter 2.

By contrast, I will defend the vigorous suppression of false or misleading electoral participation information, in relation to which the threat of criminal law coercion legitimately plays a central role. A good example of legislative drafting designed clearly to embody the distinction between electoral participation and political viewpoint disinformation was provided by the US Deceptive Practices and Voter Intimidation Prevention Bill 2019, aimed at extending existing federal provisions (outlawing threats and coercion in elections[32]) to the use of fraud.[33] Section 3(3) of the 2019 Bill was intended to prohibit anyone, within the 60 days preceding an election, from communicating information known, 'to be materially false', with intention of misleading voters, or of preventing or impeding them from exercising their right to vote; but, crucially, only where the information in question concerned:

[30] Deen Freelon, Alice Marwick, and Daniel Kreiss (2020). It is perhaps worth noting that the UK Conservative Party was the biggest spender on election advertising on Google platforms in the whole of Europe, spending 25 per cent more than the party in second place in that regard: https://transparencyreport.google.com/political-ads/region/EU (last accessed 10/04/2021). As Thomas Wischmeyer aptly puts it, for the (extreme) right, 'social media have become an important political playground': Thomas Wischmeyer (2019), 25.

[31] See the discussion in the General Introduction, and in Chs 2 and 3.

[32] 18 US Code 594; https://www.law.cornell.edu/uscode/text/18/594 (last accessed 11/04/2021).

[33] https://www.congress.gov/bill/116th-congress/senate-bill/1834/text (last accessed 11/04/2021).

(i) the time or place of holding any election described . . .; or
(ii) the qualifications for or restrictions on voter eligibility for any such election, including . . . any criminal penalties associated with voting . . . or information regarding a voter's registration status of eligibility.

The 2019 Bill is thus aimed at electoral participation disinformation, and does not extend to political viewpoint disinformation. Such a policy is designed to make the Bill more consistent with First Amendment jurisprudence that makes it clear that political viewpoint speech is—unless it amounts to a defamatory violation of individual rights—constitutionally protected even when it is (known to be) false.[34]

Here are three examples of such false electoral participation disinformation. The first is from the US Presidential election in 2020. Robocalls were instigated in Detroit, Philadelphia, and Pittsburgh, containing the false-but-threatening campaign message, 'If you want to vote by mail . . . your personal information will be turned over to the police and to debt collectors'.[35] The calls were a blatant attempt to use false election participation information to deter democrat-leaning voters from taking part in mail-in voting. An earlier example comes from the Maryland Gubernatorial election of 2010. Republicans organized 112,000 'robocalls' (purporting to come from a Democrat source) to voters in areas with many African Americans, falsely suggesting that the democrat candidate had already won, although the polls were in fact still open for two more hours. A senior individual involved in organizing the calls was convicted of fraud.[36] In the final example, from 2004, a number of individuals associated with the Republican party were convicted of conspiring to engage in 'telephone harassment', after they were found to have been involved in a scheme systematically to jam a Democrat-run telephone line offering voters transport to the polls.[37] The threat of coercion and the use of other measures, such as social media platform bans, to suppress these kinds of electoral disinformation practices are justified by the fact that there is what the US courts call a 'compelling Government interest' in the free and fair conduct of electoral processes.[38] That interest is underpinned by—indeed, partly constituted by—the maintenance of a complex regulatory system, the consistent enforcement of which is vital to maintenance of voter confidence in democracy.

[34] See also *Rickert v Public Disclosure Commission* 168 P 3d 826 (2007), and the discussion in Stuart P. Green (2018), 491–92.

[35] https://news.berkeley.edu/2020/09/29/stacking-the-deck-how-the-gop-works-to-suppress-minority-voting/ (last accessed 11/04/2018).

[36] https://thevotingnews.com/ex-ehrlich-campaign-manager-schurick-convicted-in-robocall-case-the-washington-post/ (last accessed 11/04/2021).

[37] https://www.justice.gov/archive/opa/pr/2004/December/04_crm_768.htm (last accessed 3/04/2021); http://archive.boston.com/news/nation/washington/articles/2006/06/10/fallen_star_blames_self_gop_tactics/ (last accessed 13/04/2021). One of those involved, Allen Raymond, a former Republican political consultant, went on to write a book about how to rig elections: Allen Raymond (2008).

[38] See e.g. *Susan B Anthony List, et al. v Ohio Elections Commission* 45 F Supp 3d 765 (2014).

Prohibitions on election participation disinformation protect an authoritative and unique scheme for electoral participation provided by government for the casting of votes. The justification for creating and enforcing such prohibitions comes, in part, from the fact that a citizen's casting of a vote, unlike their expression or dissemination of a political viewpoint, is normatively significant as an expression of their political citizenship. However, the justification also comes from the fact that there is, of course, no alternative to the official system provided for casting a vote. Just as there is only one set of rules governing standards of conduct in driving on public roads, in relation to any given election (be it local or national) there will be only one set of rules for voting in it. Even if one believes the electoral system to be compromised and untrustworthy, there is no other way to cast one's vote. By contrast, in open democracies, there is no analogy to this, where political viewpoint information is concerned. In such democracies, there are networks of more or less formal and informal practices of disseminating political information (from party manifestos, through hustings, to print media, internet blogs, and political rallies). Local authorities and government departments may also provide opportunities for citizens to debate the political merits of policies and initiatives.[39] However, there is no official and authoritative *system* for taking part in political viewpoint discussions and for forming political viewpoints. Indeed, in an open democracy, the very nature of political viewpoint development and expression, as a free practice, might be thought to depend on the absence of government orchestration.[40] As one US court put it, the state cannot 'substitute its judgment as to how best to speak for that of speakers and listeners; free and robust debate cannot thrive if directed by the government'.[41]

A flourishing culture of free political viewpoint development and expression depends, instead, on the extent to which there have emerged a diverse range of fora open to or devoted to this end, and on the extent to which such fora *voluntarily* respect and encourage truthful and respectful (albeit vigorous) political debate. Building on the remarks made above, having explained in more detail the distinction between political viewpoint disinformation and electoral participation disinformation, I will explore different reasons for advocating tolerance (in relation to the former), and the use of proportionate sanctions (in relation to the latter).

[39] See e.g. https://www.london.gov.uk/about-us/londonassembly/meetings/ieListMeetings.aspx?CatId=12932&bcr=1 (last accessed 11/04/2021).

[40] It follows that that, in a fragile democracy, in which—say—people have historically been intimidated into remaining politically silent, there might be a justification for a more prominent role for government in promoting the development and expression of political viewpoint information. See further, Kofi Annan Commission on Elections and Democracy in the Digital Age (2020).

[41] *Washington ex Public Disclosure Commission v 119 Vote No! Committee*, 957 P 2d 691 (Wash. 1998), 626.

1.2 Political Viewpoint and Disinformation Electoral Participation Disinformation

(i) Electoral participation disinformation

As I have indicated, electoral participation information is information concerning existing election processes and procedures. It is information concerning such matters as eligibility to vote or to stand as a candidate, the receipt of voting cards, attendance at the polls, the form of the ballot paper, voting, counting votes, and returning results. It thus involves the actions of citizens in seeking to exercise their right to vote, and of candidates in standing for election, but also the conduct of election administrators, and other bodies (if separate from election administrators) responsible for different parts of the election process. To preserve the integrity of the processes and procedures designed to facilitate such actions on the part of voters, candidates, and election administrators, the state is entitled to stand in judgement on the truth and falsity of claims about the election process. It is permissible directly (or indirectly) to target the dissemination of disinformation about election participation with restrictions and sanctions, including criminal sanctions, when the information is intended to influence participation or non-participation in the process. For that reason, the category of electoral participation disinformation should be understood narrowly, on an account of free-speech restrictions that prioritizes protecting freedom of political speech. It should be understood to be confined almost exclusively to what one might call 'bureaucratic process' information. So, in particular, it is not appropriate to create substantial overlap between the categories of election participation disinformation and of political viewpoint disinformation, by suggesting that someone who is misled about (say) what particular candidates and parties stand for is the victim of electoral participation disinformation. Such a person is not a victim of 'bureaucratic process' disinformation, but of political viewpoint disinformation, even if it is true in such a case that the individual was influenced by disinformation (not) to cast a vote.

One should not, though, characterize the confining of election participation information—to that which concerns the election's bureaucratic process—as an attempt to restrict it to something politically trivial or insubstantial. On the contrary, the integrity of the bureaucratic process in elections is a fundamental feature of flourishing democracies. There can be few better illustrations of that proposition than the controversies that arose in the 2020 US Presidential election, when (misguided) anger over allegations of voting fraud led to violent protests involving thousands of people, to the invasion of the capitol building in Washington, and to the deaths of some of those involved.[42] Whether the practice of vigorous electoral

[42] https://www.bbc.co.uk/news/world-us-canada-55555074 (last accessed 11/04/2021).

debate can truly be politically meaningful—irrespective of whether it is conducted in a fog of political viewpoint disinformation—depends in part on the maintenance of the vitality and integrity of the election process, and hence (in part) on the deterrence and suppression of disinformation about the process. That is true even within political movements such as populism that challenge orthodox understandings of how to distinguish truth from falsity in politics, or challenge the significance of the distinction within politics. One of the political mainstays of many versions of populism is the determination to hold elected representatives more fully and regularly accountable, through a free and fair electoral process.[43]

It is true that forms of populism focused specifically on, say, charismatic anti-establishment leaders, may be ambivalent about an electoral process that could see such leaders removed from office by votes in favour of the 'establishment' candidates. Hence, such forms of populism may be more likely to involve a partisan approach to the integrity of election procedures.[44] It is also true that in some countries even traditional ('establishment') parties, such as the Republican Party in the United States, have taken a partisan approach to parts of the electoral process.[45] The tightening of voter registration requirements, and changes in the location or operation of the polling stations,[46] are two approaches commonly designed to suppress—and often effective in suppressing—votes cast by ethnic minorities (considered more likely to vote for the rival Democratic Party).[47] That shows the degree to which the non-partisan elements of the democratic state in the USA have become threatened to a much greater extent than in most European democracies. The main rival parties are coming to regard each other as political enemies, rather than as political adversaries.[48] Consequently, they (the Republican Party, in particular) increasingly reject non-partisan constitutional rules intended to block the gaining of partisan advantages. Even so, it is notable that when deliberately misleading information has been used to suppress votes in US elections, this has been far less commonly tolerated: indeed, as we saw earlier, it has led to prosecutions of the perpetrators in the criminal courts. Whatever their views on voter ID requirements, or other voter-suppression techniques, there is scant evidence that voters

[43] Robert R. Barr (2009), 37. See also, Douglas Carswell and Daniel Hannan (2008).

[44] https://news.berkeley.edu/2020/09/29/stacking-the-deck-how-the-gop-works-to-suppress-minority-voting/ (last accessed 13/04/2021).

[45] Such an approach, spearheaded by the Conservative Party, is also taking shape in the UK: https://news.sky.com/story/labour-hits-out-at-cynical-and-ugly-voter-id-plans-ahead-of-queens-speech-12302746 (last accessed 10/05/2021).

[46] https://www.propublica.org/article/why-do-nonwhite-georgia-voters-have-to-wait-in-line-for-hours-their-numbers-have-soared-and-their-polling-places-have-dwindled (last accessed 13/04/2021).

[47] See Zoltan Hajnal et al. (2017). An irony about that is that, even as recently as 2016, a majority of Democratic Party voters also reported that they supported requirements to show ID in order to vote: https://news.gallup.com/poll/194741/four-five-americans-support-voter-laws-early-voting.aspx (last accessed 13/04/2021).

[48] Chantal Mouffe (1995).

support the partisan use of misleading information to prevent or suppress voting in individual elections.

What does the category of electoral participation disinformation *not* include? I have already indicated that it does not include information meant to support or oppose the direction of reform of electoral processes. I will return to this issue, but the need for a narrowly focused account of electoral participation disinformation—distinct from political viewpoint disinformation—also means that, even in relation to existing processes, it should not be regarded as including information aimed only at encouraging or likely to encourage people *generally* (not) to vote. Such information may simply not be about the bureaucratic process of voting. An example would be a claim that all the candidates are 'criminals' who do not deserve anyone's vote. Such a claim is really a political viewpoint claim, and thus, on my account, a protected claim from a free-speech perspective. Even if disinformation concerns, in a general sense, the bureaucratic process of voting, it may nonetheless not be aimed at influencing electoral participation by any individual or group. The dissemination of such disinformation should be tolerated, not prohibited. Consider, for example, President Trump's tweet on June 20 2020, concerning the then forthcoming Presidential election: 'RIGGED 2020 ELECTION: MILLIONS OF MAIL-IN BALLOTS WILL BE PRINTED BY FOREIGN COUNTRIES, AND OTHERS. IT WILL BE THE SCANDAL OF OUR TIMES!'[49] This might look like false electoral participation information. However, to begin with, it is very general in character, and seemingly not aimed at influencing (non-) participation by any individual or group in the election process. Secondly, it is really a kind of political viewpoint disinformation. It is disinformation about the supposedly interfering political tactics of countries seeking to influence the US election. A false claim of this kind should not, then, be subject to censorship or sanction, even if—as I will argue in Chapter 2—it is acceptable to warn those who see such tweets that the claims involved are or may be highly contestable.

By contrast, consider what may have been another of President Trump's alleged communications, this time supposedly directed at an election official, and motivated by his loss in the Presidential election of 2020. He is reported to have pressured a senior election official in Georgia to organize a recount of votes, in the light of what the President (falsely) claimed was evidence that ballots had been shredded and voting machinery had been removed from Fulton County in the state.[50] President Trump may honestly have believed the claim to be true, which would mean he was not guilty of election fraud because he lacked the fault element; but nonetheless, his claim was a false claim designed to influence the administration of the existing election process. It is thus permissibly regarded as the *actus reus* of election fraud. There might appear to be a good deal of scope for obfuscating

[49] https://www.bbc.co.uk/news/blogs-trending-55009950 (last accessed 11/04/2021), his capitals.
[50] https://www.bbc.co.uk/news/election-us-2020-55524838 (last accessed 11/04/2021).

point- and distinction-making here. However, the overarching principle of interpretation is clear, even if partisan politicking may not always fall neatly into a given category of information. As few restrictions should be placed on the dissemination of political (dis)information as are consistent with maintaining the integrity of the electoral process, and the understanding of political statements should be guided accordingly.

(ii) Political viewpoint disinformation

Few people doubt that false political viewpoint information is now spread much more widely, and more quickly, than ever before (especially at election times). A study of 126,000 news stories distributed on Twitter between 2006 and 2017 revealed that falsehoods (as established by fact-checking organizations) were 70 per cent more likely to be retweeted than true stories.[51] It has been estimated that in the 2016 US Presidential election, false stories relating to the two candidates were shared at least 38 million times on Facebook, with just over half of Americans who recalled seeing these statements believing them.[52] What, then, is political viewpoint information? In answering this question, I should begin by making clear that it is not to be equated with the mere expression of political opinion. That would make the argument far too easy. It is trite law that the expression of opinion receives a high level of protection from criminalization in the courts,[53] even if some liberal democratic states continue to have opinion-focused offences such as (for example) insulting public officials.[54] Political viewpoint disinformation should receive the same high level of protection, even though it involves (false) claims of fact and not just opinions. One advantage of such an approach is avoiding the need for over-refined distinctions between value judgements and viewpoint statements involving (implied) factual assertions. For example, as we saw in the General Introduction, the European Court has created uncertainty in relation to the margin of appreciation on this point for signatories to the ECHR, by itself pronouncing on whether, when one candidate called another a 'thief' on television, this was a simply a generalized allegation that the person was dishonest (opinion), or was instead a specific allegation that the person in question had committed theft (fact).[55]

Political viewpoint information is information about any matter bearing on who governs or wishes to govern; about institutions, groups, and individuals concerned with issues of governance, including social justice and rights; about how

[51] Soroush Vosoughi, Deb Roy, and Sinan Aral (2018), at 1148.
[52] See Hunt Allcot and Matthew Gentzkow (2017).
[53] See *Otegi Mondragon v Spain* (Application no. 2034/07) 15 March 2011.
[54] See the discussion in Chapter 2.
[55] *Vitrenko & Others v Ukraine* (Application no. 23510/02), 16 December 2008. See also the leading case of *Lingens v Austria* (Application no. 9815/82), 8 July 1986, and Jeffrey L. Kirchmeier (1988).

government is conducted, whether at home or abroad; about (instances of) participation and activism in relation to those matters; and about events—and their supposed causes—to which political significance is or ought to be attached. This definition is meant to be very broad, and not all aspects of it will be covered here. I will be concerned, especially in Chapters 3 and 4, mainly (although not solely) with those aspects of it that have given rise to legal controversy. As we have already seen, some jurisdictions extend criminal sanctions to the dissemination of political viewpoint disinformation. In that regard, most importantly, political viewpoint information extends to statistics and other factual claims about the economy and society that commonly underpin political commitments and opinions. As we will see in Chapter 4, section 4.5, there have been examples when lying about official statistics in order to be elected has been adjudged to fall within the scope of criminal prohibitions on electoral fraud, but these cases are controversial. Statistics about complex and contentious political, social, and economic matters are inevitably open to widely differing interpretations, and the lessons one should draw from them are similarly open to debate.[56] This means that, in a free-speech culture, the way that statistics are presented and interpreted should be regarded as a political viewpoint matter. It would be helpful to focus on an example.

On 9 June 2015, the House of Commons voted by 544 to 53 in favour of holding a referendum on the UK's continued membership of the EU. The European Referendum Act 2015 received royal assent on 17 December 2015, and required a referendum to be held by the end of 2017. On 20 February 2016, the then Prime Minister, David Cameron MP announced that the referendum was to be held on 23 June 2016. So, the referendum campaign 'proper' (as one might say) lasted broadly from late February 2016 until late June 2016. As part of its campaign to persuade people to vote to leave the EU, the 'Vote Leave' group, which sought to focus on the economic case for leaving the EU, claimed that membership of the EU was costing the UK £350 million per week.[57] This claim appeared on the side of the Vote Leave campaign bus during the course of the campaign, together with a suggestion that the £350 million could be spent on the National Health Service (NHS) following the UK's departure from the EU.[58] Vote Leave's campaign was supported by, amongst others, the Rt Hon. Boris Johnson, during the final period of his tenure as Mayor of London (which ended in May 2016), while he was also MP for Uxbridge and South Ruislip. At a number of points during the campaign, Johnson—a member of Vote Leave's campaign committee—appeared to endorse the Vote Leave claim about the amount of money given to the EU each week which could instead be spent on the NHS.

56 See, in general, Law Commission (2009), Appendix D.
57 http://www.voteleavetakecontrol.org/why_vote_leave.html.
58 https://www.bbc.co.uk/news/uk-politics-48554853.

Following the result of the referendum on the UK's continued membership of the European Union, on 29 May 2019, Marcus Ball, and his crowdfunded company Brexit Justice Ltd (now know as 'Stop Lying in Politics Ltd'),[59] launched a private prosecution against Boris Johnson, alleging that his supposed endorsements of the £350-million claim involved him in the commission of the common law offence of misconduct in a public office. The prosecution was based on an allegation that the £350-million claim was false, and that Johnson knew it was false when he endorsed it publicly. After the referendum result, in a letter to Johnson on 17 September 2017, Sir David Norgrove, Chair of the UK Statistics Authority, said:

> I am surprised and disappointed that you have chosen to repeat the figure of £350 million per week, in connection with the amount that might be available for extra public spending when we leave the European Union. This confuses gross and net contributions. It also assumes that payments currently made to the UK by the EU, including for example for the support of agriculture and scientific research, will not be paid by the UK government when we leave. It is a clear misuse of official statistics.[60]

However, in a reply also dated 17 December 2017, Johnson vigorously defended the way in which he had interpreted and used the £350-million claim.[61] He accused Norgrove of confusing the way that the media had turned the claim into a simplistic headline with the substance of the claim he had in fact made. He said that his claim was not that the UK merely transferred this amount weekly to the EU, but a more subtle or nuanced claim. This was that, following Brexit, the UK would enjoy complete spending control and discretion over the equivalent of this sum each week in way that it did not as an EU member, and would no longer have to allow the EU a role in saying how some or all of such a sum was spent.[62] Irrespective of how convincing one finds such a response, the very fact that it can be made in such terms is important. The ECHR has made it clear that when controversial political words and speech are made subject to criminal prosecution, the existence of a background political context to the words or speech makes it highly likely that the court will find that the words or speech are protected by Article 10,[63] even if the

[59] Stoplyinginpolitics.org (last accessed 11/11/2021); https://www.crowdfunder.co.uk/ballvjohnson (last accessed 11/04/2021).

[60] https://uksa.statisticsauthority.gov.uk/wp-content/uploads/2017/09/Letter-from-Sir-David-Norgrove-to-Foreign-Secretary.pdf (last accessed 11/04/2021).

[61] See https://fullfact.org/europe/foreign-secretary-and-uk-statistics-authority-350-million-explained/.

[62] Johnson said that his verbatim version of the claim was that: 'once we have settled our accounts we will take back control of roughly £350m per week. It would be a fine thing, as many of us have pointed out, if a lot of that money went on the NHS.'

[63] Article 10 of the ECHR provides that, 'Everyone has the right to freedom of expression. This right shall include freedom to hold opinions and to receive and impart information and ideas without interference by public authority and regardless of frontiers . . . '.

words or speech involve insult, exaggeration, error, or possibly even some element of known falsehood.[64]

The way in which I understand political viewpoint disinformation is not purely stipulative. It is linked to the way in which partisan political narratives and identity commonly develop. For example, consider Regina Rini's defence of partisan political thinking:

> I mean to defend partisan epistemology within specific domains. Which domains? The domain of politically normative claims, certainly, such as 'equality of opportunity is more important than equality of outcome.' I include also many morally normative claims. And I include some claims that are seemingly purely descriptive when these are relevant to political decisions. Most importantly, I include characterological judgments about particular political candidates. I will call all of these *politically relevant claims*. My position, then, is that partisanship in testimony reception is reasonable with regard to politically relevant claims.[65]

Rini's notion of 'politically normative' claims, coupled with her reference to 'morally normative claims ('X's infidelities make him unfit for office'), and to 'some claims that are seemingly purely descriptive' ('most people on welfare are actually fit to work'), covers a good deal of the ground of what I am referring to as political viewpoint claims. Moreover, there is an intrinsic and probably ineradicable link between the development of highly partisan political narratives and the generation and dissemination of false claims of this nature: political viewpoint disinformation, as I have defined it. An attempt to suppress the dissemination of such information is thus necessarily an attack on the development of such narratives. Attacks of this kind are countenanced, other than in authoritarian regimes, only in militant or elitist (as opposed to tolerant) democracies, an issue considered below.

(iii) Why distinguish political viewpoint information from electoral participation information?

The spread of false political viewpoint information may diminish the value of taking part in elections, both for the individual and more generally. For the individual who wishes their political judgements to be soundly based, a vote cast on a false political viewpoint basis will not be an act of political self-realization. More generally, when many votes are cast on such a basis, there is a threat to the public good of properly informed political decision-making in elections as a whole.[66] As

[64] *Otegi Mondragon v Spain* (Application no. 2034/07) 15 March 2011.
[65] Regina Rini (2016), her emphasis.
[66] Albert Weale (2007), 80: 'When we vote we do not reason, but if we cast reasoned votes our aggregation scheme will be improved.'

Albert Weale argues, democracy is not simply a system for aggregating the widest possible range of preferences. It is also in part constituted by the debates and exchanges of information that lead to preferences themselves being formed, strengthened, or changed.[67] Can a government that gains power through the propagation of lies and misleading information about its political platform and its candidates really claim legitimate authority to govern?

In answer to that question, it might be argued, a political viewpoint-misinformed democratic polity is still a democratic polity, in which voters are fully enfranchised. By contrast, false electoral participation information threatens to undermine a basic democratic right, in a way that false political viewpoint information does not: the right to participate in the voting process on the same basis and in the same way as others. False electoral participation information threatens a breach of Article 25 of the International Covenant on Civil and Political Rights, which says that, 'Every citizen shall have the right and the opportunity . . . without unreasonable restrictions . . . to vote and to be elected at genuine periodic elections . . . [to be held] by secret ballot, guaranteeing the free expression of the will of the electors'. Further, and a point I will return to in Chapters 2 and 3, election participation disinformation aims to *silence* voters politically, denying them a key freedom of political expression through voting. In so doing, it can be placed on a par with other political silencing tactics, such as intimidation, harassment, or hate speech directed at opponents. On the other hand, the very point of publicizing political viewpoint disinformation may be to provoke 'more speech' rather than to silence: to spark a reaction from the person subject to the disinformation.[68]

To better understand the contrast between the two kinds of disinformation, let us focus on the role of political viewpoint information—including false or misleading information—in influencing, and being influenced by, the public political discourse that is an essential part of a democratic polity. In that regard, a state's legally tolerant approach to false or misleading political viewpoint information can be justified in one of two ways. First, there is what might be called the 'thin' (but nonetheless important) justification. This justification is focused on the difficulties and dangers that might arise in seeking to implement a coercive strategy designed to target false or misleading political viewpoint information. Unlike electoral participation information, political viewpoint information is commonly bound up with the expression of political opinion, on which, as I have already said, there are rarely any restrictions in liberal democratic societies. It may be hard for controversial or hard-hitting speakers to know when they may give free rein to their speech because it is purely opinion (however malevolent), and when they may face sanctions because they will be found to have made knowingly false or misleading factual

[67] Albert Weale (2007), 82.
[68] See section 1.6(ii) below, and the discussion in Chapter 2.

claims.[69] Such uncertainly impinges on speakers' political autonomy in one of its core aspects. The other side of this coin is that, being fallible and perhaps sometimes biased, officials tasked with enforcing laws prohibiting false or misleading political viewpoint information may produce spillover effects, in which sanctions are applied to political activists who are simply being outspoken or provocative.[70] Whilst it is in the nature of discretionary law enforcement that it poses a risk of spillover effects, in this instance such effects are particularly serious and troubling, precisely because they may have an undesirably chilling effect on political speech.

Second (a more substantive justification), it might be argued that a democratic state must deal with the fact that the political discourse on which the state's vitality depends may be highly fragmented. It may be comprised of a good deal of 'counter-public' speech with its own standards for the validation of argument;[71] of speech driven by prejudice, hatred, and bias; and of speech consisting of mere griping, gossiping, or unashamed cheerleading.[72] Against such a political background, to undertake the official task of identifying for prohibition what is 'genuinely' false or misleading is to identify oneself with a preference for doing politics in a certain sort of (reasoned) way. This is a kind of rationalistic politics that is uncomfortable with the political role and importance of pure emotion, unswerving faith-based commitment, rabble-rousing, personal leadership charisma, and so on. Rationalist politicians and thinkers struggle to engage with political movements within which information content (be it true or false) is not valued for its truth or falsity but for the way in which it fits and enhances a political narrative.[73] That makes aggressive or militant political rationalism itself a potential threat to a free-speech culture.

Putting aside the undoubted need to outlaw criminal incitement, intimidation, hate speech, and the like,[74] it is not the task of the criminal or regulatory law to seek to cleanse public discourse of emotive and partisan political speech, simply because it is partly or even wholly constituted by false or misleading viewpoint information. To undertake such a task would be improperly to employ the criminal or regulatory law to advantage one kind of politics (reasoned, evidence-based), by threatening adverse consequences for those who practise what are simply incommensurable kinds of politics (politically highly partisan, emotive, or even simply frivolous). A political identity or narrative forged through virulent, intemperate, and whole-hearted opposition to mainstream political nostrums is not an identity

[69] See e.g. *Otegi Mondragon v Spain* (Application no. 2034/07) 15 March 2011; *R v Zundel* [1992] 2 SCR 731.

[70] See e.g. *Otegi Mondragon v Spain* (Application no. 2034/07) 15 March 2011, and the discussion of German law in Chapter 2.

[71] See e.g. Nancy Fraser (1990).

[72] See Michael Warner (2002), 52.

[73] See Regina Rini (2016).

[74] I will say more about these criminal forms of speech at the beginning of Chapter 3. See further, Cabinet Office (2019), proposing to turn into 'electoral offences' existing criminal offences in England and Wales that outlaw intimidation.

or narrative unworthy of protection from suppression simply because its core doctrine contains what appears, from a rationalistic perspective, to be a large measure of false and misleading content. What matters about false or misleading political viewpoint information is not that its dissemination is acceptable to others, but that it is fully open to challenge, refutation, or ridicule (as appropriate).

By way of contrast, these arguments against the use of the criminal law to suppress false or misleading speech do not apply with the same force to false or misleading electoral participation information. Let us begin with the 'thin' justification for tolerance mentioned above. To prohibit the dissemination of false or misleading electoral participation information does not threaten spillover effects, or the chilling of radical political speech more generally. That is in part because there is not the same troublesome overlap with the expression of political opinion, or with the development of broader political narratives. For example, consider a false claim that voting is on Friday, when it is on Wednesday, or a fictitious claim that certain religious or racial groups will have to pay before voting. Such claims may be politically motivated, but their evaluative content is minimal and their connection to broader political narratives tangential at best (a point I return to below, in discussing the substantive justification). Consequently, there is a very low risk that peddlers of such information may be unsure where the limits of legitimate speech are, in relation to their claims, and hence an equally low risk that law officials will inevitably be drawn into political controversy and the risk of bias in enforcing or adjudicating on prohibitions. The thin justification for tolerance simply does not apply to false electoral participation information. What about the substantive justification? There is, of course, a long history in many countries of debate concerning how widely the franchise should be extended. There has also been, and in some countries continues to be, debate over the (supposed) risks to democratic legitimacy posed by frauds committed by voters themselves.[75] Moreover, even in democracies, for as long as there has been voting there has been and continues to be (notably in the USA[76]) the temptation to disseminate false or misleading information about the voting process for partisan reasons.[77]

However, putting on one side US exceptionalism in this regard, the dissemination of electoral participation disinformation has never been an important part of the formation of political identities and narratives in stable democratic countries, even identities or narratives very far removed from the mainstream. There is a very important reason for this, well-articulated by Chantal Mouffe.[78] This is

[75] https://www.pewresearch.org/politics/2021/01/15/voters-reflections-on-the-2020-election/ (last accessed 12/04/2021); https://www.electoral-reform.org.uk/latest-news-and-research/media-centre/press-releases/latest-voter-fraud-stats-show-mandatory-id-proposals-are-still-a-solution-looking-for-a-problem/ (last accessed 12/04/2021).

[76] https://thevotingnews.com/ (last accessed 12/04/2021).

[77] https://www.nationalgeographic.com/history/article/voter-suppression-haunted-united-states-since-founded (last accessed 12/04/2021).

[78] Chantal Mouffe (2005). See also the General Introduction.

that, however partisan they may be, political groupings in democracies outside the USA tend to regard themselves—to use her terminology—as adversaries, and not as enemies. In other words, they oppose each other politically *within* what she calls a common form of political association or 'symbolic space'.[79] The fairness and impartiality of the voting process forms a central part of that 'symbolic space'. As indicated in the General Introduction, what that means, in this context, is that political 'adversaries' will accept, in a way political 'enemies' will not, that the political system they share—even though it will have its faults—may hand them a systemically legitimate political defeat. The spread of false electoral participation information undermines this picture of (healthy) partisan, adversarial politics under the aegis of a non-partisan electoral system, in a way that the spread of false viewpoint information does not. The prevalence of the latter is a reflection of how partisan adversarial politics has become, but unlike the former, is not a threat to adversarial politics itself.

In that regard, it would be tempting to suppose that the kind of tolerance of false political viewpoint claims advocated here is necessarily at cross-purposes with the state's moral duty to motivate people to value and develop their political autonomy. The more lies and misleading claims traded between political parties, the more likely it is (so the argument runs), that ordinary citizens will actually be switched off by politics. In fact, the evidence for this kind of intuition is equivocal, at best.[80] In any event, it provides too insubstantial a basis for placing restrictions on the spread of false political viewpoint information. As Fredrick Schauer has remarked: '[i]nherent in the ideal of self-government is the proposition that it is for the people alone to distinguish between truth and falsity in matters relating to broad questions of government policy'.[81]

1.3 Understanding Wrongful Political Speech: A Brief Guide

A helpful starting point, in seeking to understand wrongful political speech, and what to do about it, is Twitter's 'Civic integrity' policy on false or misleading election tweets. The guidance says: 'You may not use Twitter's services for the purpose of manipulating or interfering in elections or other civic processes. This includes posting or sharing content that may suppress participation or mislead people about when, where, or how to participate in a civic process.'[82] By contrast, Twitter makes it clear that the following fall outside this ban on false or misleading electoral content: 'inaccurate statements about an elected or appointed official, candidate, or

[79] Chantal Mouffe (2005), 20; Cécile Laborde and John Maynor (2008), 14.
[80] See Jacob Rowbottom (2012).
[81] Frederick Shauer (1982), 7–8.
[82] Twitter (2021).

political party; organic content that is polarizing, biased, hyper-partisan, or contains controversial viewpoints expressed about elections or politics.'[83]

In essence, as argued in the preceding section, this is the kind of distinction that should be drawn by the law itself, in determining when it is appropriate either to tolerate, or alternatively to deter and punish, the dissemination of false political information. However, the kinds of false or misleading information that fall into each category need fuller explanation. For example, false claims about an election process are not only rightly so described in relation to the elements of the process leading up to voting; they also concern crucial elements of the process that take place thereafter, as when the claims are intended to affect the post-voting process in some way (e.g. by influencing vote-counters). By contrast, as I argued earlier, broader claims, whether false or not, about the integrity of the voting process (e.g. 'the US system is clearly wide open to fraud') should be regarded as forms of political viewpoint disinformation. That such comments might, perhaps, influence the behaviour of voters at future elections is too remote a possibility to justify suppressing them. In respect of both categories of speech, we now need to unpack some of the key terms used to identify what is liable to attract the attention of platform moderators (and also legislators or regulators): terms such as, 'manipulating', 'interfering', 'mislead', and 'inaccurate'. I will say something about all of these issues.

(i) Manipulation, interference, and foreign influences

What should we make of Twitter's highlighting of 'manipulating or interfering in elections' as a focus for censorship? Let me begin with manipulation. For X to 'manipulate' Y is for X to lead Y to be the unwitting instrument of achieving X's goals, in circumstances where Y is persuaded that they are acting in their own interests. No one doubts that manipulation aimed at interference with electoral participation should be prohibited, and Twitter's focus is clearly on this kind of manipulation. In that regard, the UK's criminal offence of exercising 'undue influence' on an elector is considered in detail in Chapter 4. What about the use of manipulation in relation to the dissemination of political viewpoint information? It is worth noting a common deficiency of legal systems, in this regard. This is that they frequently do not deal explicitly with the use of manipulation through threats or bribery designed to persuade people *not* to speak, in a way that might influence an election. A classic case would be a payment to someone (B) by a newspaper that supports Party X, to have exclusive rights to highly damaging information B possesses about the leader of Party X. Having secured B's agreement, the newspaper then suppresses the story rather than publishing it (so called 'catch-and-kill' tactics).[84]

[83] Ibid.

[84] In a US case, the Federal Election Commission found a way to capture such conduct within the scope of existing prohibitions, in the case of a payment, by deeming it to be an illegal campaign

Putting aside such cases, though, we should be sceptical, more broadly, about restrictions placed on the dissemination of political viewpoint information in the name of preventing the 'manipulation' of voters. This is for the simple reason that—whatever the moral rights and wrongs of manipulation in general—a great deal of political speech, especially at election times, takes this form. To restrict or ban it would, thus, to be impinge too greatly on the freedom to engage in a key means by which political persuasion takes place. To give a commonplace example, a politician may appeal to particular economic or social interests of mine, exploiting the fact that (as the politician knows all too well) these are intensely felt short-term interests that I tend to prioritize over my medium- to long-term interests. In that regard, the use of data gathering (even when open source) to facilitate 'micro-targeting' in election campaigns is an illustrative case in point.

Whilst noting the use of such techniques by politicians across the political spectrum, William Gorton points to the use in George W. Bush's 2004 Presidential campaign of data on 5.7 million Michigan consumers which, when combined with the campaign's own data, enabled activists to divide potential voters into 34 micro-targeting segments, including (for example) 'flag and family Republicans', and 'wage-able weak Democrats'.[85] Thus, the campaign was able to target for micro-messaging, amongst others, 'anti-porn women' with Bush's message that he intended to restrict the availability of pornographic material in public libraries.[86] Gorton regards this kind of development as harmful to democracy, because it corrodes and inhibits public dialogue, and makes it more likely that false and misleading information will be spread unchallenged. I will say more below about this kind of objection, which draws too narrowly on a rationalistic conception of political dialogue and engagement.[87] Is it correct to say, though, that any wrong is done to the prospective voters by the use of such tactics? There would be a considerable irony in such a conclusion. One aim of micro-targeting is to engage voters in the political process, by politicizing an issue they are likely to care about. Such an approach is thus one way of overcoming a majority voter view in many countries worldwide disagreeing with the statement that 'most elected officials care what people like me think'.[88] So, cynical though such tactics may appear to be, they ought to be regarded as falling within the bounds of what should be tolerated, not only by the law but by platform regulators. Unless accompanied by or embodied in some other wrong (such as an appeal to racist sentiment), when such uses of

contribution: https://www.independent.co.uk/news/world/americas/us-politics/national-enquirer-owner-fined-for-illegal-trump-campaign-aid-karen-mcdougal-michael-cohen-federal-election-commission-national-enquirer-david-pecker-b1858525.html (last accessed 04/06/2021).

[85] William Gorton (2016), 68–9.
[86] Ibid.
[87] See the General Introduction, on the rationalist fallacy.
[88] https://www.pewresearch.org/global/2020/02/27/attitudes-toward-elected-officials-voting-and-the-state/ (last accessed 12/04/2021).

manipulation are set in their context—such as encouraging political participation—they fall within the moral and legal pale.

What about 'interference' in elections, and in national politics more generally? There can be few more loaded terms currently being employed in these contexts, as a stick with which to beat political activists, than an accusation of 'interference'. The term 'interfere' very obviously carries with it an implication of wrongfulness that is not characteristic of more neutral terms, such as 'intervene' or 'participate'. Yet, attempts to influence elections (or politics more generally) are sometimes characterized as 'interference' without an explanation of exactly what is wrong with the political activity in question. If a UK politician uses Facebook to urge fellow citizens to vote for Party X at the election, this would ordinarily be described as a political 'intervention', or simply as political 'participation'. By contrast, not uncommonly, if (say) a Russian politician were to do the same thing, then that would be far more likely to be described as 'interference' in the election. Many in the West have raised and continue to raise the bogey of foreign (Chinese? Russian?) influence in shaping opinions and possibly outcomes in national elections.[89] In assessing such concerns, we should bear in mind that, when it comes to the dark arts of foreign 'interference' in elections and referendums, it is Western countries themselves who are historically the masters. The US is estimated to have interfered overtly or covertly in no less than 81 foreign elections between 1946 and 2000—far more than any other major power.[90] Even so, a number of states have gone so far as prohibit many kinds of 'foreign interference' in elections, and a good deal of legislators' time has been devoted to the (supposed) problem.[91]

In France, a 2018 amendment to earlier legislation[92] made it possible for the independent broadcasting authority, the Conseil supérieur de l'audiovisuel (CSA), to prevent, suspend, or prohibit TV or radio broadcasts controlled by a foreign state (following an initial warning), if they are judged, 'to harm the fundamental interests of the nation ... particularly by disseminating false information'.[93] Under this provision, permissible sanctions include an order to stop broadcasting, fines up to 3 per cent of the broadcaster's revenue, and in some cases withdrawal of authorization to broadcast. Section 282.4 of the Canada Elections Act 2000 (as amended in 2018–19) now prohibits for the purposes of elections 'undue influence

[89] Jens David Ohlin (2017) 1579.

[90] *New York Times*, 17 February 2018, https://www.nytimes.com/2018/02/17/sunday-review/russia-isnt-the-only-one-meddling-in-elections-we-do-it-too.html (last accessed 12/04/2021); Dov Levin (2019).

[91] See, for example, Joint Intelligence and Security Committee (2020).

[92] French Law no. 2018-1202, on the 'fight against the manipulation of information', amending the Freedom of Communication Act (No. 86-1067) 1986. For a detailed analysis, see Rachel Craufurd-Smith (2019).

[93] See, https://www.conseil-constitutionnel.fr/en/decision/2018/2018773DC.htm (last accessed 12/04/2021); https://www.loc.gov/law/help/freedom-expression/france.php#_ftn51 (last accessed 12/04/2021). There is an exceptional procedure, when the false information is distributed during an election campaign, that allows the CSA to suspend distribution of a broadcasting service during an election.

by foreigners'. Influence engaged in by a foreigner will be 'undue' if it involves influencing an elector through the commission of an offence contrary to Canadian law, such as the making of false claims about an election candidate, party leader, or official (contrary to the amended section 91 of the 2000 Act).[94]

What is it, though, about foreign intervention in elections that leads national authorities to regard it as 'interference', and hence in principle something wrongful that can be prohibited or restricted? Is it merely that the intervention comes from overseas? If true, that would be extraordinary. It could in theory mean, for example, that former Canadians who had renounced their citizenship and were residing in France would face restrictions on their ability to make claims about Canadian politics, under the 2000 Act just mentioned, that would not be faced by Francophile Canadians in Canada. It is not, in fact, necessarily unethical for one nation state (or group or party within that state) to seek to influence an election result in another nation state; far from it. An example of ethical influence might be where a foreign state acts in order to further the chances that that a government more respectful of democratic principles, or of international law and human rights, will come to power in the targeted state.[95] Indeed, it has been powerfully argued that modern failures on the part of leading democracies to champion democratic values overseas are one of the reasons for the decline in support for democratic government worldwide.[96] Further, there is a good deal of arbitrariness and indeterminacy to the notion that 'foreign' interventions amount in principle to (illegitimate) interference or meddling in elections. If, say, an institutional source of disinformation is located within a state's borders, but is sponsored from overseas, or staffed by foreign nationals, does either or both of these facts make the source sufficiently 'foreign' to make it easier to justify restrictions? Would it be different if the source was located in the jurisdiction, and staffed by nationals of the jurisdiction, but was devoted to the curating of content entirely comprised of overseas comment on politics within the jurisdiction?

A partial acknowledgement of the ethical problems that may arise is to be found in an important exception to the reformed section 282.4 of the Canada Elections Act 2000. Subsection 3 exempts from the scope of the ban:

> (a) an expression of ... opinion about the outcome or desired outcome of the election;
> (b) a statement ... that encourages the elector to vote or refrain from voting for any candidate or registered party in the election; or
> (c) the transmission to the public through broadcasting, or through electronic or print media, of an editorial, a debate, a speech, an interview, a column,

[94] See the General Introduction; also, Michael Karanicolas (2019).
[95] Cécile Fabre (2018).
[96] Susan Hyde (2020).

> a letter, a commentary or news, regardless of the expense incurred in doing so, if no contravention of subsection 330(1) or (2) is involved in the transmission.[97]

This exception is significant, in that it concedes the controversiality of trying to exercise punitive control over the substantive content of political statements intended to influence elections, even when the statements are generated in foreign jurisdictions. The exception is, thus, a nod towards the importance of protecting free political speech. It is, nonetheless, controversial in its terms, in that it makes criminal liability turn, in part, on the notoriously difficult distinction between statements of fact and statements of opinion.[98] An irony about that is that evidence indicates that, for example, Russian attempts to influence the outcome of the 2016 US Presidential election were concentrated not so much on false information as on 'opinion-making', in the form of the creation of a narrative of political identity ('Trump is with us, and against the establishment').[99]

Of course, interventions in politics from overseas may not be well-intentioned, and so may be rightly regarded as unjustifiable interference. A key difference from older examples of cold war meddling is that the modern aim of such interference—through fake online accounts, the use of net bots, and so on—is not so much the spread of the would-be influencer's ideology, as the undermining of the political and social fabric of the target jurisdiction. Accordingly, the would-be influencer may intentionally generate contradictory messages: for example, using opposing forms of content to encourage white supremacists and racial minorities to target one another.[100] Such interventions may seek to sow discord; inflame hate; drive wedges between groups of citizens; increase anxiety, political apathy, and cynicism; or to facilitate, 'espionage, terrorism, and sabotage'.[101] It is clear that such interference could have a destabilizing effect on the traditional model of liberal-democratic politics.[102] If and when that happens, though, there is no particular reason for a tolerant state to treat the intervention as more open to suppression or criminalization simply because its (ultimate) source is a foreign jurisdiction.[103] In that regard, it is worth noting that research has shown that American voters take a highly partisan approach to evidence of foreign interference. They are much more likely to condemn it, and to profess a loss of faith in the democratic process, when the

[97] See n. 94 above.

[98] See e.g. Jeffrey L. Kirchmeier (1988); *R v Zundel* [1992] 2 SCR 731.

[99] Michael Jensen (2018), 122.

[100] Jean-Baptiste Jeangène Vilmer et al. (2018), 176; see also EU High Representative of the Union for Foreign Affairs and Security Policy (2018), 77.

[101] The words, 'espionage, terrorism and sabotage' come from the Security Service Act 1989, s. 1(2), describing some of the proper targets of MI5.

[102] House of Commons, Digital, Culture, Media and Sport Committee (2019), part 6.

[103] Although—as argued in Chapter 2—a lack of authenticity when disseminating false claims within a jurisdiction may justify or require the attachment by internet platforms of unreliability warning to the claims.

interference appears helpful to their political opponents than when it helps their own party of choice.[104]

What should matter, then, is not what jurisdiction political speech comes from, but what kind of speech it is. First, is it (*ex hypothesi* prohibited) criminal incitement, hate speech, or electoral participation disinformation about, say, the date of or eligibility to vote in an election, or is it (*ex hypothesi* permissible) political viewpoint disinformation? Second, an argument addressed in Chapter 2, even if the disinformation should not be taken down or restricted as such, does its potential inauthenticity (involving the concealment of bot-generation, fake-sourcing, or anonymity) justify attaching a warning about its possible unreliability? These should be the applicable general principles, even if there may be some circumstances in which it is justified to restrict authentic viewpoint disinformation stemming from a foreign source in particular: for example, where influence is aimed at creating circumstances favourable to an invasion or takeover by a foreign state or its agencies.[105]

(ii) Lying, deceiving, and misleading

As we will see in Chapters 3 and 4, when the UK legislature has created prohibitions centred on political disinformation, it has focused mainly on the *falsity* of such information. In some instances, the offence may directly refer to the significance of falsity. An example from UK law is the offence set out in section 106 of the 1983 Act (mentioned in section 1.1(ii)), of making or publishing any, 'false statement of fact in relation to the candidate's personal character or conduct', with intent to affect the candidate's vote return. In other instances, an offence may rely implicitly on an element of falsity, as in the case of personation,[106] or of voting when one is aware of being subject to an incapacity.[107] Reliance, in law, on a requirement to prove an express or implicit element of falsity has its attractions. It might appear to provide a greater degree of certainty, in an inevitably controversial and contested arena. Either something is false, or it is not, and either someone was aware of the possibility that it might be false, or they were not (so the argument might run). If so, election disinformation offences confined to proof of falsity will simultaneously comply with requirements of fair warning and avoid prosecutors and judges being drawn into condemning people on the basis of political value judgements.

One difficulty with this line of thinking, as a guide to the justification for prohibitions on disseminating political disinformation, is that it tends to break down

[104] Michael Toms and Jessica L. P. Weeks (2019).
[105] See, for example, Kofi Annan Commission on Elections and Democracy in the Digital Age (2020).
[106] Contrary to s. 60 of the 1983 Act.
[107] Contrary to s. 61 of the 1983 Act.

or become too controversial to be of much use in the case of political viewpoint disinformation. That is one important reason for adopting a legally tolerant attitude to political viewpoint disinformation. One person's 'false' claim about (say) what is demonstrated by a set of economic forecast statistics is another person's perfectly justifiable 'interpretation' of those statistics, as we saw earlier. For some scholars, this kind of example is a clear indication that the law should steer clear of prohibiting 'misleading' political claims (whether or not they are false), because whether or not a statement is misleading clearly involves a value judgement that courts—and especially criminal courts—should not be making.[108] However, criminal courts are called on to pass judgment on misleading claims in fraud cases more generally.[109] So, it cannot be that the criminal courts are not competent to make such judgements. Further, a rigid distinction between what is known to be false and what is known to be misleading would be arbitrary.

Consider the prohibition in section 106 of the 1983 Act, outlined above. If I put it about that my opponent has committed murder, when they did not, then I make a false statement about my opponent's personal conduct, within the scope of the section 106 prohibition. But suppose, instead, that I spread the (true) information that my opponent has been convicted of murder, but I fail to mention that the conviction was overturned and my opponent completely exonerated when another person was proved to be the sole perpetrator. In this second example, in that the information I spread was strictly speaking true, it falls outside the scope of section 106.[110] However, the electoral damage and personal hurt I knowingly and wrongfully cause to my opponent may be largely the same in this example as in the last, as might the effort that would have to be expended to correct the wrong impression given to voters (even supposing my opponent has time, opportunity, and resources for that).

Moreover, electoral law does (uncontroversially) criminalize the making of some kinds of misleading statement: especially statements intended to deceive.[111] For example, section 115 of the 1983 Act prohibits the use of 'any fraudulent device or contrivance' designed to impede or prevent 'the free exercise of the franchise', or to prevail on someone (not) to vote.[112] In its reference to 'fraudulent' devices or contrivances, there can be no doubt that the legislature intended that this notion should cover deliberately misleading devices or contrivances. Suppose that,

[108] See Richard L. Hasen (2013). See also Stuart Green (2007), 78–9.

[109] The Fraud Act 2006 prohibits the dishonest making of false or misleading statements, with an intention to gain thereby.

[110] Unless, of course, a court were to hold that 'false' statements include misleading statements tantamount to false statements; but in such a politically contested area as election (mis)information, such an interpretive leap seems unlikely. Debates in the Victorian Parliament on the scope of the predecessor to section 106 indicate that Parliament intended to restrict the scope of the prohibition to false statements: see Chapter 3.

[111] On the distinction between false statements and deceptive statements, see Larry Alexander and Emily Sherwin (2003), 400–1.

[112] This provision is considered in detail in Chapter 4.

shortly before a polling station is due to close, X puts up an official-looking sign purporting to point the way to the polling station. The direction pointed out by the sign does indeed lead to the polling station, but (as X knew) it is the direction involving a long circuitous route: X intends to impede voters in their efforts to vote at the last minute. There can be no doubt that X's actions are prohibited by section 115, but not on the grounds of any false statement made. X's actions are prohibited on the grounds that the sign is a fraudulent device because it is known to be misleading (and intended to impede the free exercise of the franchise). This kind of misleading conduct is what is targeted by Twitter's ban on, 'content that may . . . mislead people about when, where, or how to participate in a civic process'. Crucially, though, the section 115 prohibition on fraudulently misleading (as well as false) devices or contrivances can be argued to be confined in scope to instances in which the offender is providing misleading electoral participation information, not political viewpoint information.

As the polling station example just given demonstrated, electoral law must inevitably venture into territory in which courts pass judgment on misleading electoral statements as well as on false ones. Further, as we have seen, what is rightly described as 'false' or 'inaccurate' may be a politically contested matter. So, how are we to prevent or reduce the extent to which courts are drawn into political controversy in the application of the criminal law, potentially making political martyrs out of intemperate, impassioned, and hyper-partisan political speakers? The answer is that, whether a statement, device, or contrivance is false *or* misleading, it should not come within the scope of any criminal prohibition if it falls within the category of political viewpoint information. So, as I will argue in Chapter 3, the criminal prohibition in section 106, outlined above, on false statements about an electoral candidate's personal conduct or character, should be abolished. In an election context, such a false statement should be tolerated by the criminal law, because it is a statement constituting political viewpoint information. That is so even if the statement involves some injury to reputation that is in principle actionable in the civil courts (not all false statements about personal conduct or character will be of that kind), and even if the influence the false statement may have had should lead, as a matter of public law, to the nullification of an election.

By parity of reasoning, as I argue in Chapter 4, the offence in section 115 of the 1983 Act legitimately extends to the use of devices or contrivances known to be misleading, as well as to ones that are known to be false; but only in so far as the offence is confined to electoral participation information (as in the polling station example just given). The section 115 offence should not be extended, as we will see in Chapter 4 that it has in some jurisdictions, to false or misleading devices or contrivances concerned with political viewpoint information. Here is an example that illustrates the way in which the distinction can be made to work, and the dangers of failing to pay attention to it.

In the 2020 US Presidential election, President Trump consistently made false claims on Twitter about the existence and prevalence of electoral fraud—fraud in the process of voting and also in the process of counting votes.[113] He made these claims before the election (principally focusing on voter fraud),[114] but also afterwards, when fraud in counting votes became another of his concerns. However, it was only in relation to his post-election claims that Twitter implemented its 'damage-limitation' policy of preventing replies or retweets (circulation of the information by other users of his remarks), and appended a note saying the content, 'is disputed and might be misleading about an election or other civic process'.[115] I come back to the issue of 'false claim shaming', and its relationship with the virtue of tolerance, in Chapter 2; but were these reactions justified? Giving a simple answer is complicated by the fact that no one was prevented from seeing the President's tweets (they were not removed from view, as such) and they received wide publicity in the media. A further complication is that his false claims of electoral fraud later came to pose, and may have been intended to pose, a clear and imminent risk (not just a theoretical or potential risk) of provoking civil disorder.[116] As J. S. Mill rightly observed, the making of a false claim that 'corn dealers are starvers of the poor' should ordinarily be allowed to circulate through the press, but the making of the same claim could be justly prohibited if it was proposed to make it to an excited mob outside the house of a corn dealer.[117] Putting these complications on one side, what we can say about Twitter's action, in relation to the early post-election claims, is that arguably too little attention was paid to the intended effect of the false claims on the integrity of the election process itself.

As far as the early post-election tweets are concerned, no one can reasonably be supposed to have been prevented or deterred from taking part in the election by these tweets, or adversely influenced in the way that they played a part in the administration of the process, after voting (e.g. by counting votes).[118] It is always possible that a disappointed election candidate may falsely say 'I was the ('real') winner of the election', or 'The election process is badly flawed, which is why I didn't win'. In the interests of protecting free speech, such generalized—'sour grapes'—claims are better viewed as (low-grade) political viewpoint disinformation, and hence tolerated. Arguably, then, whilst it may have been acceptable—indeed right—in

[113] https://www.theverge.com/2020/11/6/21552471/trump-twitter-restricted-false-election-claims-moderation (last accessed 13/04/2021).

[114] https://www.bbc.co.uk/news/blogs-trending-55009950 (last accessed 13/04/2021).

[115] See https://www.factcheck.org/2020/11/trump-tweets-flagged-by-twitter-for-misinformation/ (last accessed 01/05/2021). Facebook took similar action. https://www.theguardian.com/us-news/2020/nov/04/facebook-and-twitter-emergency-trump-false-victory-claims (last accessed 13/04/2021).

[116] https://www.theguardian.com/us-news/2021/jan/07/trump-incitement-inflammatory-rhetoric-capitol-riot (last accessed 13/04/2021).

[117] J. S. Mill (1974), 119, cited by the House of Lords (2020), para 92.

[118] I put on one side here President Trump's apparent attempt to influence the vote count in Georgia, through a false claim of fraud: see text at n. 51 above. This was clearly an illegitimate attempt to influence the bureaucratic part of an election through a false participation claim.

President Trump's case, to accompany his early post-election claims with a warning about their unreliability, preventing retweeting or replies altogether looks to have been, initially at least, a disproportionate response. The response only became proportionate once the President's later claims along such lines started to pose—or were intended to pose—imminent risks of civil disorder.[119] It should be kept in mind that, in themselves, neither retweets nor replies are necessarily in themselves intended to be endorsements of the content retweeted or replied to. Still less, thus, would it have been proportionate to make such claims subject to (in effect) total censorship by criminalizing them, before the point when it became clear that they would in all probability lead to civil disorder.

What about Trump's pre-election tweets concerning the election process? He mentioned ballot-rigging or voter fraud in some 70 tweets before the 2020 Presidential election.[120] Such messaging obviously has the potential to influence the process, by, say, leading people to consider voting not worthwhile. For someone in such a trusted, high-profile public role as the US President to make such comments is highly irresponsible. Even so, the President did not say that people should avoid voting because of the pervasiveness (as he saw it) of fraud, and his tweets took the form of fairly generalized complaints about the system—'The USA must have voter ID; the only way to get an honest count!'.[121] Hence, like his post-election tweets, his pre-election tweets also more closely resembled a kind of political viewpoint disinformation than they resembled electoral participation disinformation. Upholding the primacy of free speech in politics requires that the latter category, that of election participation disinformation, be construed strictly in doubtful cases. President Trump's false pre-election tweets might, then, have warranted an unreliability warning, but arguably no more than that. It is not for internet platforms to pass judgement on whether, given someone's position in public life, it is an especially egregious wrong—more worthy of some censoring action—for that person to seek to publicize false claims. The issue for platforms, considered further in Chapter 2, is simply what sort of false claims the claims are, and accordingly, with what should be done about them.

(iii) 'Organic content that is polarizing, biased, hyper-partisan'

As we saw above, Twitter's censorship policy is explicitly stated *not* to extend to content that is, amongst other things, 'polarizing, biased, [or] hyper-partisan', and rightly so. The language employed by Twitter to describe the policy is a nod

[119] https://www.bbc.co.uk/news/technology-55569604 (last accessed 13/04/2021).
[120] https://www.bbc.co.uk/news/blogs-trending-55009950 (last accessed 13/04/2021).
[121] @realdonaldtrump, 14 April 2020, cited at https://www.bbc.co.uk/news/blogs-trending-55009950 (last accessed 13/04/2021).

towards the internet-led explosion of anti-establishment, and 'populist' political discourse.[122] This is, of course, not purely a US phenomenon. In the UK, independent journalists researching the general election in 2017 noted an appreciable rise in hyper-partisan blogging, and in Facebook pages supporting such blogging, which they suggested was highly effective in spreading false and misleading information.[123] Something should briefly be said about that here.

As Engesser and others helpfully suggest, in anti-establishment, populist thinking:

> [t]he elite is assumed to betray the people and to deprive it of its legitimate right to exercise power. The populist actor pitches himself or herself as a challenger of the elites and as an advocate of the people.... The elite is also assumed to engage in a complicity with 'the others' and to favour them over the people.[124]

Anti-establishment populism transforms established parties and their candidates from characterization—in idealist republican terms—as essentially altruistic and dedicated (would-be) public servants, into self-interested upholders of their own 'elite' interests. I will not be concerned here with whether or not there is, in some identifiable sense, an 'elite' whose self-interested values are challenged by populism. My concern will be with the rationalistic thinking about the 'proper' (i.e. non-populist) character of political argument commonly associated with a liberal-centrist political outlook, an outlook commonly branded (whether or not accurately) as 'elitist'.

With the immense power of online distribution behind them,[125] one important populist challenge to rationalistic thinking comes from the fact that anti-establishment political narratives lead increasingly to partisan polarization and distrust.[126] Populist discourse may change the character of political debate by leading different political 'sides' to adopt more intolerant and repressive attitudes and engage in what Zachary Price aptly calls 'tit-for-tat degradation', with implications for what is regarded as 'fair comment'.[127] From a rationalist perspective, the problem then becomes that, in spite of the work of the traditional media, of regulators, and of fact-checking organizations, attempts to establish 'the truth' in political debate are likely casualties of such developments. Indeed, quests to discern the 'truth' in politics may themselves come to be seen as part of a (centrist) political agenda for the conduct of politics. Online populist politics is not only an important driver behind

[122] For an important examination of anti-establishment, populist, and 'outsider' politics, see Robert R. Barr (2009).
[123] https://firstdraftnews.org/latest/misinfo-types-uk-election/ (last accessed 13/04/2021).
[124] Sven Engesser, Nayla Fawsi, and Anders Olof Larsson (2017), 1281.
[125] Ibid.; Mark Littler and Matthew Feldman (2017).
[126] House of Commons, Digital, Culture, Media and Sport Committee (2019), part 6.
[127] Zachary Price (2018).

distrust of and contempt for politicians from established parties seeking (as well as those already 'in') office, but also behind challenges to what is to count as a 'true', a 'false', or a 'misleading' political claim. Populists typically reject orthodox liberal ways of distinguishing between political truth and fiction, and between fact and opinion or value, commonly replacing such 'timeless' values and distinctions with a preference for perceived sincerity and authenticity in political messaging.[128]

However, it is not only populist politics (considered such a threat by political rationalists) that may challenge traditional understandings about the importance of what is 'true' and 'false' in politics, giving rise to the potential for the proliferation of highly biased and hyper-partisan political narratives. Political science research shows that, very generally, ordinary people are reluctant belief-updaters, 'who admit mistakes grudgingly and defend their prior positions tenaciously'.[129] This may have implications for how seriously wrong the making of false political viewpoint statements or deceptions is understood to be, or for whether the making of such statements is even understood to be prima facie wrongful. Ordinarily, a discovery that someone has been making untrue claims, or deceiving others, would have implications for that person's reputation for trustworthiness (and consequently, in politics, for their fitness for public office).[130] However, as we will see, there is good evidence that this is not how things work, where partisan matters of political viewpoint politics are concerned. The allocation of blame, and any loss of trust, respecting wrongdoing, are often strongly affected by partisan affiliations.[131] What is unclear is whether traditional politicians and political or legal institutions have come to terms with this reality, where the expression of political viewpoint information is concerned. The European Court of Human Rights, for example, has said (in spite of the fact that their finding applied to a criminal charge) that, 'even where a statement amounts to a value judgement, there must exist a sufficient factual basis to support it, failing which it will be excessive'.[132] In criminal cases, such a restrictive approach is liable wrongly to bear down more harshly on hyper-partisan political narratives.

1.4 Partisan Political Narratives and Rationalistic Imperialism

The Twitter policy, just discussed, focused on biased and hyper-partisan political content and narrative, is at the heart of my concerns in this book. In this section, I give further consideration to the development of such content and narratives, and

128 See e.g. Martin Montgomery (2017).
129 P. Tetlock (2005), 125–6.
130 J. Sobell (1985).
131 J. Bullock (2007), 45.
132 *Otegi Mondragon v Spain* (Application no. 2034/07) 15 March 2011, para 54.

consider the approach of those who would like to see them stifled or suppressed, by the use of criminal sanctions if need be. Article 19 of the International Covenant on Civil and Political Rights (ICCPR) provides that:

> Everyone shall have the right to freedom of expression; this right shall include freedom to seek, receive and impart information and ideas of all kinds, regardless of frontiers, either orally, in writing or in print, in the form of art, or through any other media of his choice.

In principle, the right to seek, receive, and impart ideas of 'all kinds' must necessarily extend to the dissemination and reception of ideas based on false information, or forming part of hyper-partisan narratives. Nonetheless, under Article 19, the right to freedom of expression may be restricted, if this is done by law and is necessary to protect the rights and reputations of others, or to protect (amongst other things) 'morals'. Clearly, the 'rights of others' include the right to vote under Article 25 (discussed further, in due course), and 'morals' include the protection and promotion of truthfulness and honesty in public discourse. Should it be regarded as consistent with the spirit of Article 19 to use legal means—and especially, the criminal law—to prevent people spreading partisan political narratives that (often systematically) encourage and incorporate hyper-partisan and hence false or misleading political content?

(i) The defensibility of forming partisan political narratives

In the ideal republic, people would to some extent always remain open to revising their opinions, and be less susceptible to hyper-partisan messaging, through consistent exposure to alternative points of view and ways of life. This has led ideal republicans to criticize 'echo chambers', in which people listen only to political messaging that reinforces their own views. Cass Sunstein put the thesis in this way:

> People should be exposed to material that they would not have chosen in advance. Unplanned, unanticipated encounters are central to democracy itself.... They are important partly to ensure against fragmentation and extremism, which are predictable outcomes of any situation in which like-minded people speak only with themselves.[133]

Whilst the first part of this claim is relatively uncontentious, the second is more contentious. To begin with, the willingness to share and discuss cross-ideological

[133] Cass Sunstein (2007), 5–6.

material is itself a characteristically 'liberal' trait, in online political activity.[134] Evidence indicates that, in fact, it is encounters with *opposing* viewpoints that may drive hyper-partisans further into their comfort zones:[135] a phenomenon known as 'attitude polarization' or the 'repulsion effect'.[136]

One lesson that emerges from the earlier discussion of biased and hyper-partisan speech is that it is perfectly possible to enjoy an autonomous political life largely detached from a commitment to truth-finding. That is because such a life may be comprised of values such as commitment, faith, loyalty, and tribalism that are relatively impervious to ordinary processes of verification and falsification. For example, attachment to one's party—party loyalty—tends to count for a good deal, in politically engaged people's overall political viewpoint, and the thinking that accompanies the formulation and sustaining of such a viewpoint tends to involve confirmatory bias: 'obstinate partisanship'.[137] Political activists, and to some extend all people who hold political views, tend to look for and believe in evidence that supports their position (and to discount evidence that undermines it), along with evidence that challenges the viewpoint of their political rivals.[138] This political 'evidence bias' spills over into ethical evaluation of politicians' conduct more generally. For example, following the MPs' expenses scandal in the UK in 2009, research demonstrated that the extent to which people tended to think badly of MPs who had abused the scheme depended on whether the MP was from their favoured political party.[139] To give a different example (from long before the Trump era), in one experiment, information about a Republican candidate was given both to people who identified as Democrats and to people who identified as Republicans, so that they could evaluate the candidate. Then, each group was told that the information was false and asked to re-evaluate the candidate. Whilst the Democrat group to some extent revised their opinion of the candidate (downwards), the Republican group did not change their opinions at all.[140] It thus seems that how people react to political falsehood—and to biased, incomplete, or inaccurate information—depends a good deal on their political affiliations: statements by political opponents are more likely to be identified as false or misleading.[141]

Further, in relation to the development of political viewpoints, it may be perfectly defensible for someone to embrace what Regina Rini called 'partisan epistemology'.[142] As she puts it, 'given the realities of human psychology and politics, certain forms of epistemic partisanship are individually reasonable in the world as

[134] Jay J. van Bavel and Andrea Pereira (2018).
[135] See the discussion in Chapter 2; Jay D Hmielowski et al. (2020).
[136] See Alberto Ardèvol-Abreu and Homero Gil De Zúñiga (2020).
[137] Alberto Ardèvol-Abreu and Homero Gil De Zúñiga (2020).
[138] See Regina Rini (2017).
[139] Nick Vivyan, Marcus Wagner, and Jessica Tarlov (2012).
[140] J. Bullock (2007), 151.
[141] Michael Toms and Jessica L. P. Weeks (2019).
[142] Regina Rini (2016), text at n. 66 above.

we actually confront it'.[143] What is more, the sharing of such information between like-minded thinkers tends naturally to give it an appearance of confirmed truth that it might not otherwise have. As Rini puts it, 'shared partisan affiliation encourages testimony recipients to grant more credibility to testifiers than would otherwise be warranted' (on both the left and right of the political spectrum).[144]

Against that background, to judge political narratives solely by rationalist measures of truth and falsity in politics is to take too narrow (and ultimately politically partisan) a view of what may count as valuable in the development of political viewpoints. For example, identification with a hyper-partisan political narrative may provide people with a sense of political engagement and of belonging in a political community; something that they did not have before:

> An obstinate attitude ... emerges from feelings of belonging to a party-based political community in competition for power with other distinct political communities. Connected to these feelings and perceptions, obstinate partisans develop unconditional loyalty and commitment to their political party, which in turns leads to an increased tendency to support it—mainly in the form of voting—regardless of policy proposals or party performance.[145]

That may be valuable in itself, and worthy of respect, whether or not the narrative contains any element of political truth.[146] This reflects the emotional or visceral element to politics, which for some people may be the most important element. In this form of politics, identification with a party or with an individual candidate may be more important than the underlying justification for precisely what that party or person stands for, in policy terms. The emergence of a highly emotive, partisan epistemology, whether on the left or on the right, involves the adoption of a distinctive narrative, or 'ideological ordering of social and political facts', that may be relatively impervious to falsification whilst being boosted by consistently partisan and emotive messaging and support.[147] For example, in investigating emotional motivation for political engagement, Valentino and his colleagues found that 'anger, but not anxiety or enthusiasm, significantly boosts participation. Anger boosts participation by nearly one third of an act. This result confirms one of our expectations—that anger will be mobilizing but anxiety will not.'[148]

In their exposé of far-right use of internet platforms, Alice Marwick and Rebecca Lewis highlight what they regard as one of the more general consequences of this: a loss of trust in the mainstream media to provide accurate information.[149]

143 Regina Rini (2016). For a more critical view of epistemic vice, see Quassim Cassam (2019).
144 Regina Rini (2016).
145 Alberto Ardèvol-Abreu and Homero Gil De Zúñiga (2020), 325.
146 See further, Kimberley Brownlee (2019).
147 David Laycock (1996), 18.
148 Nicholas A. Valentino et al. (2011), 162 and 168.
149 Alice Marwick and Rebecca Lewis (2017).

They suggest that '[p]eople who do not trust the media are less likely to access accurate information, which has civic and political ramifications. They are more likely to vote along partisan lines rather than considering current national conditions.'[150] One issue about this suggestion is that efforts to spread distrust about the reliability and objectivity of mainstream media outlets, although often dominated by, are far from the preserve of the (far) right.[151] Allegations of right-wing bias in such outlets have for many years been a staple of left-wing politics.[152] Second, it is unclear what the authors have in mind by the distinction between voting 'along partisan lines' and voting based on an assessment of 'national conditions'. As indicated above, partisan political narratives are themselves predominantly frameworks within which 'national conditions' are understood and evaluated (both on the left and the right). The point is that the 'partisan' dimension to the understanding and evaluation is what provides the motivation for the formation of groups of like-minded thinkers, and encourages (*ex hypothesi*, valuable) political engagement and activism.

The importance of this is that it illustrates the dangers of assuming that there is a (rationalist) vantagepoint from which the political viewpoint claims of activists, bloggers, and others driven by a diverse range of ideological commitments can be assessed as making 'true' or 'false' contributions to political debate, and subjected to monitoring and control accordingly. In her study of online disinformation, Kate Jones suggests that internet platform 'neutrality' in the dissemination of content can be understood to include not only fact-checking but also 'promotion of true over false information'.[153] The latter goal (the promotion of truth) should be seen as inherently problematic when it relates to viewpoint politics. It seems to presuppose that there is a group (liberal intellectual politicians? Platform moderators?) who are uniquely placed to determine what is true and false in politics—highly controversial assumption. Many rationalist politicians and scholarsin theory, staunch defenders of free speech—have sought to argue for the construction of a *cordon sanitaire* around (evidence-based) political debate. The exclusion zone would extend—through the use of censorship and coercion, if necessary—not merely to hate speech, incitements to commit crime, and the dissemination of electoral participation disinformation, but also to the kind of political viewpoint disinformation that, spread by internet-savvy populists, has threatened to undermine the political credibility of traditional, rationalist politics.

150 Alice Marwick and Rebecca Lewis (2017), 45.

151 See Ralph Schroeder (2019)

152 See, e.g. Glasgow Media Group, *Bad News* (1976); https://www.counterfire.org/articles/opinion/20725-the-bbc-s-anti-corbyn-bias-shows-it-s-not-fit-for-purpose (last accessed 13/04/2021); https://www.culturematters.org.uk/index.php/culture/tv/item/2947-culture-punch-the-bbc-s-right-wing-bias; https://blogs.lse.ac.uk/politicsandpolicy/did-britains-right-wing-newspapers-win-the-election-for-the-tories/ (last accessed 13/04/2021).

153 Kate Jones (2019), 46.

The problem with the rationalist agenda is this. As Jennifer Hochschild puts it: 'If, for example, [liberal] elites simply hold different ... views than the mass public, then the preservation of liberalism does not necessarily require restraints on rule by the [less liberal] masses.'[154] The issue will be discussed further in Chapter 2, but in rejecting rationalist assumptions we should note that there is an important distinction between the promotion of truth (highly controversial) and simply alerting people to the possibility of unreliability or error in messaging (less controversial). Even then, when the less controversial notion of 'fact-checking' is in issue, it needs to be kept in mind that fact-checking, whilst supposedly politically neutral, is in fact more highly prized by people who are broadly liberal in outlook than by people whose thinking is more conservative or populist.[155] Speaking of attempts to ensure verification of contentious claims or supposed 'fake news', Romain Badouard has rightly observed the following in that regard: 'As fake news is the manifestation of popular distrust of the political and intellectual elite, how could verification by those same elites possibly convince those propagating it [the fake news]?'[156]

(ii) Rationalist support for the restriction of (populist) political disinformation

The public's opinion of politicians is far less favourable now that it was 30 years ago, a change that broadly maps onto the period in which there has been a rise in populist political thought in Western democracies. An online survey of 16- to 75-year-olds by scholars at King's College London showed that, whereas in 1989 36 per cent or people agreed that 'in general, politicians are good people', by 2019 this figure had more than halved, to 15 per cent.[157] It follows that politicians have an important personal incentive to discourage, deter, and (if possible) stifle the spread of political viewpoint information that fuels such negative changes of opinion. That such information is false or misleading provides a cloak of justification for steps taken towards this end. In shaping the state's response to political viewpoint disinformation that threatens their own perceived legitimacy, authoritarian steps may come to seem justified to otherwise liberal politicians, in light of their concerns about the sheer quantity of non-liberal political messaging, in many cases greatly amplified online. One could think of this development as an outworking of what I referred to earlier as 'militant' democratic thinking,[158] thinking that underlies

154 Jennifer Hochschild (1986), 399.

155 See Craig T. Robertson et al. (2020) 217.

156 Romain Badouard (2017), 48.

157 King's College Policy Institute (2019), 5, 'Conservative voters have seen the biggest changes in opinion: 45 per cent agreed with this statement 30 years ago, compared with 30 per cent today. The proportion who disagree with it has more than doubled, rising from 15 per cent to 33 per cent'.

158 See section 1.1(iii) above, and Chapter 2, section 2.2(iii) below. See also Jan-Werner Muller (2012). The following analysis is drawn from Jeremy Horder (2021b).

partisan attempts to justify restricting illiberal, typically populist political narratives that challenge mainstream rationalist political discourse.

Militant democratic politics, in a narrow sense, involves the restriction of collective rights deemed to be a direct threat to democratic values, such as the right to form political parties committed to the overthrow of democracy.[159] However, a commitment to militant democratic politics may also involve targeting individual rights, rather than just the collective rights of organizations and parties. Subject to contentious questions about proportionality, such a commitment may appear to justify authoritarian restrictions on rights such as the right to advocate non-democratic forms of government, or the right to exercise free speech in other ways that appear to challenge or undermine democracy itself.[160] Key examples are at least some instances in which freedom of speech is used for the dissemination of false political information online (discussed in Chapter 2).[161] A common militant democratic strategy, one that may mask partisan motivations for adoption of the strategy, is to elevate people's reliance on political viewpoint disinformation, as a kind of 'harm', to the level of bullying, hate speech, disinformation about health, incitements to engage in crime, or glorification of terrorism. This strategy can appear to justify the suppression or restriction of political viewpoint disinformation. However, it does so only if the contextualization of the dissemination of political viewpoint disinformation considered in this chapter is undervalued, and if one discounts the distinction (explained below) between causing harm through such disinformation, and invading rights.

An example of a militant democratic strategy turned into law is the Network Enforcement Act (Germany) 2017, discussed in detail in Chapter 2, section 2.6. The stringent obligations placed on major internet platforms by the 2017 Act to take down a range of content, including political viewpoint disinformation, were justified because (it was said) such content, 'damages ... our *culture of debate*, and ultimately freedom of expression'.[162] Another good example is the Report of the House of Lords Select Committee on Democracy and Digital Technologies.[163] In support of a rationalist narrative of decline in the quality of political culture, the House of Lords Report cites evidence that 76 per cent of the public agreed that voters were being misled by false and dishonest claims and 56 per cent stated that they tend to ignore what parties and politicians say because they know they cannot trust them.[164] However, reliance on this kind of evidence is controversial. It is based on impressionistic assessments made by individual members of the public,

[159] Jan-Werner Muller (2012), 1123–6.

[160] Heidi Tworek (2019), 2; Ian Cram (2019). For analysis of the more 'militant democratic' decisions of the Supreme Court in the immediate aftermath of the Second World War, see Zachary S. Price (2018).

[161] Jan-Werner Muller (2012), 1127; Ian Cram (2019).

[162] Heiko Maas, Minister of Foreign Affairs, Deutscher Bundestag: Plenarprotokol 18/235 at 23848 (emphasis added), http://perma.cc/WKU4-HSGJ (Germany), cited by Imara McMillan (2019), 254.

[163] House of Lords (2020).

[164] Full Fact (2019), cited by the House of Lords (2020), para 30.

who cannot reasonably hope themselves to assess how much disinformation is in the public domain, or how generally influential it is. By contrast, scholars have argued that 'the fake news audience is small and comprises a subset of the Internet's heaviest users, while the real news audience [of the major news outlets] commands a majority of the total Internet audience'.[165] Moreover, as the LSE Commission on Truth, Trust and Technology has acknowledged,[166] reputable studies have suggested that disinformation only marginally affects citizens' political knowledge, and crucially, does not tend to lead them to retreat from political engagement.[167]

Nonetheless, the House of Lords Report goes on to criticize the exemption of political advertising from the jurisdiction of the Advertising Standards Authority and its codes, as undermining confidence in the 'quality of public debate', in spite of warnings that this might lead to the effective creation of a 'Ministry of [political] Truth'.[168] Unsurprisingly, no single existing regulator wished to take on the role of regulating political advertising (a warning about the unworkability of such a solution). Even so, the House of Lords Select Committee recommended that the regulators—the Electoral Commission, Advertising Standards Authority, and Ofcom—should act together (safety in numbers?) to form a 'regulatory committee on political advertising'.[169] The task of the regulatory committee would be 'to develop a code of practice for political advertising, along with appropriate sanctions, that restricts fundamentally inaccurate advertising during a parliamentary or mayoral election, or referendum. This regulatory committee should adjudicate breaches of this code'.[170] The proposal mirrors Cass Sunstein's suggestion that, even if the government itself cannot be trusted with the task of deterring political falsehoods, there is nonetheless a strong argument that 'an independent agency, such as or akin to the Federal Election Commission', should be trusted to do so, having at its disposal the threat of monetary penalties and the power to demand retractions.[171]

However, even if political parties were willing to recognize the political legitimacy of such a body—and history is against such a possibility[172]—the criteria it would have to apply are highly contentious. What is 'fundamentally' inaccurate advertising, as opposed to (merely) 'inaccurate' advertising? The Select Committee refers, in that respect, to a phenomenon it calls, 'outright lies'.[173] Although the

[165] Jacob L. Nelson and Harsh Taneja (2018), 3732.
[166] London School of Economics Commission on Truth, Trust and Technology (2018), 12.
[167] Hansard Society (2018).
[168] House of Lords (2020), para 30.
[169] For a similar proposal, briefly discussed in Chapter 2, see the recommendations of the Coalition for the Reform of Political Advertising: https://reformpoliticaladvertising.org/blog/ (last accessed 13/04/2021).
[170] House of Lords (2020), para 36.
[171] Cass Sunstein (2021), 114.
[172] https://www.asa.org.uk/news/most-political-players-shun-ad-standards-that-big-companies-sign-up-to.html (last accessed 13/04/2021).
[173] House of Lords (2020), paras 31 and 34.

Select Committee was clearly unaware of the fact, we have been here before. In 1895, in creating the original offence (now under section 106 of the Representation of the People Act 1983) of making a 'false' statement about the personal conduct or character of an election candidate, the concern was

> to prevent the practice at election contests of making *utterly* false statements affecting the personal character and conduct of a candidate. There were many statements which were unfair, misleading, and probably dictated by a suggestion of falsehood without actual falsehood. He did not propose to deal with such cases, but only with those that could be called *absolutely* false statements of fact.[174]

To be sure, there is a difference between a statement that is misleading, and one that is false, but what is the difference between something that is false and something that is 'utterly' or 'absolutely' false? Similarly, what is the difference between an 'outright' lie and a (mere) lie? The focus, with 'outright' lies, might be on the mental state of the person responsible for disseminating the lie. So, an outright lie could be a lie *known* to be false. That would leave unclear the status of untruths which it is known *may* be false, but could (perhaps at a very considerable stretch) be true.[175] It is worth remarking, in that regard, that US law draws no distinction between the intentional and the reckless lie, in this context.[176]

Alternatively, the focus with 'outright' lies might be on the substantive content. So, an outright lie might be an unvarnished lie, a lie unaccompanied by any surrounding truthful element. Such a focus risks creating a perverse incentive for political activists knowingly to create 'half-truths', the potential influence of which on the course of a campaign may be no less significant. Arguably, it is not 'outright lies' but misleading claims, particularly about matters of central importance to a campaign, that can do more to distort political debate. The Chief Executive Officer of the Advertising Standards Authority himself indicated to the Select Committee that the vast majority of complaints would be likely to concern not outright lies but 'statements where there could be arguments for and arguments against'.[177]

More broadly, the Select Committee can be criticized for a complete failure to distinguish between kinds of disinformation, in terms of how disinformation should be treated. Disinformation about medical guidance and treatments, which might pose immediate and unjustified threats to health or life, is not distinguished from political viewpoint disinformation (about which citizens should be trusted to make up their own minds), and the latter is not distinguished from electoral

[174] (my emphasis) https://api.parliament.uk/historic-hansard/commons/1895/may/01/corrupt-and-illegal-practices-prevention, 219 Mr T. H. Bolton, St Pancras North (last accessed 13/04/2021).

[175] A number of the difficulties raised here are well explained by the Canadian Supreme Court in *R v Zundel* [1992] 2 SCR 731.

[176] *New York Times v Sullivan* 376 US 254 (1964).

[177] House of Lords (2020), para 31.

participation disinformation (which threatens political rights).[178] Further, no distinction is drawn between, on the one hand, restricting access to disinformation ('soft censorship'), and on the other hand, flagging disinformation as potentially misleading ('false claim-shaming') whilst nonetheless allowing people to continue to have access to it and make their own judgements, thus allowing freedom of communication. So, for example, the Select Committee recommends that: 'if a piece or pattern of content is identified as disinformation by an accredited fact checker then it should be flagged as disinformation on all platforms. The content should then no longer be recommended to new audiences.'[179] The second step (no recommendation to new audiences) should not necessarily be regarded as appropriately following automatically from the first step (flagging content as involving disinformation) in the way that this passage suggests. In principle, flagging content as potentially misinformative increases an audience's knowledge or critical awareness. It can, thus, be justified in a wide range of cases where disinformation, whether or not involving 'outright lies', is being disseminated. By contrast, a restriction on 'free reach' is a qualitatively different and more drastic step.[180] There is a risk of state-mandated paternalist censorship, in the form of a determination not to trust people to have access to certain kinds of substantive political content and make up their own minds in the light of it (even with the benefit of disinformation 'flags').

The latter kind of steps can only be justified in cases where to trust to people to evaluate freely available information for themselves will lead to an unacceptable risk of significant rights violations, or to physical or psychiatric (self-)harm. So, whilst such steps might be justified when we are concerned with dangerous health advice, encouragement to commit suicide, hate speech, or misinformation about the voting process, they are not justified in the case of political viewpoint disinformation (a point pursued in the next section). If that seems controversial, and citizens are indeed not to be trusted to engage in an unrestricted way with political viewpoint disinformation, a further question nonetheless arises, further pursued in a discussion of the 'principle of scepticism' in section 1.6 below. Why should we trust the judgement of those tasked with deciding what falls into the category of political viewpoint disinformation, for the purpose of targeting it for restrictions or bans? As Justice Black said in *Susan B Anthony List v Ohio Elections Commission*:[181] 'We do not want the government ... deciding what is political truth—for fear that the government might persecute those who criticize it. Instead, in a democracy, the voters should decide.'[182]

A failure to pay attention to important distinctions between different kinds of disinformation, and to advocate the use of coercion—or other formal measures of

[178] See, for example, House of Lords (2020), paras 41–55.
[179] House of Lords (2020), para 54 (recommendation).
[180] For an early criticism of restrictions on free reach, see Jennifer A. Chandler (2007).
[181] *Susan B Anthony List v Ohio Elections Commission* (2014) 45 F Supp 3d 765.
[182] Ibid. 769.

discouragement—to suppress the foundations of a populist rejection of traditional liberal-democratic politics, is the hallmark of the rationalist, militant democratic approach. Yet, as Damian Smith Pfister argues, a flourishing public sphere is open, not hostile, to counterpublic discourse: discourse that, in the way that it seeks to shape and mobilize public opinion, self-consciously sets itself up in opposition to what he calls the 'rational-critical debate of dominant publics'.[183]

1.5 A Right Not to Have One's Vote Influenced by False Claims?

(i) Political viewpoint disinformation and rights

In the USA, in the run-up to the mid-term elections in 2018, a study showed that whilst 57 per cent of people said that they had seen fake news, only 19 per cent said that it had influenced their vote.[184] This is an important testimony to the ability of the majority to sort political wheat from chaff. What, though, of the rights of the 19 per cent—as we can call them—who have been (*ex hypothesi*) duped into casting their vote on the basis of false information? Their rights are an aspect of a democratic state's guarantee of freedom in electoral participation. As we saw earlier in the chapter, Article 25 of the International Covenant on Civil and Political Rights requires, amongst other things, that an election constitute 'a free expression of the will of the electors'. It can be argued that this requirement presupposes not just a free but also an accurately informed choice, in casting a vote.[185] Putting aside the potential influence of duress or other pressures on the will, I argue in Chapter 4 that such a right was historically confined, and should continue to be confined, to accurate electoral participation information. There are a number of justifications for adopting this kind of approach.

One justification is that the risk of being duped or misled by false or distorted political viewpoint claims is a risk that all citizens must accept as part of ordinary life. In other words, it is (albeit for different reasons) like the risk of being jostled in a crowded train, of catching influenza from a colleague, or of suffering depression after watching a disturbing film. The analogy lies in the fact that these are instances in which someone suffers harm, but when their rights have not been violated in the way that the harm occurs. In these kinds of cases, we trust people to take their own precautions to avoid coming to harm, rather than relying on the threat of state sanctions against the harm-doers to reduce the incidence of harm. We do this, in

183 Damian Smith Pfister (2019), 1129.

184 https://www.brookings.edu/blog/techtank/2018/10/23/brookings-survey-finds-57-percent-say-they-have-seen-fake-news-during-2018-elections-and-19-percent-believe-it-has-influenced-their-vote/ (last accessed 13/04/2021).

185 See generally Kate Jones (2019).

order to preserve the freedoms (for both harm-doers and harm-sufferers alike) that may flourish when that threat from the state is absent.[186] This is a version of the explanation I gave in the General Introduction for tolerating political viewpoint misinformation. We should trust people to evaluate (false or misleading) political viewpoint information for themselves, in part to respect them as 'citizens', as people capable of forming and acting on a conception of the political good.[187] In part, though, we should also trust people in this respect in order to avoid the threat of coercion hanging over speech that is merely opinionated, intemperate, or provocative. That is so, even if people are induced by false political viewpoint information to 'waste' their vote and thus suffer a form of political harm. Of course, it is sadly true both that race hate forms part of a conception of the political 'good' for some people, and also that there can be borderline cases in which it may be a disputed matter whether speech is genuinely 'hate speech' or merely controversial viewpoint politics. However, as I will argue in Chapter 2, there is an important difference with hate speech, that means it should be prohibited in spite of these difficulties. Hate speech is, whether intended in this way or not, a path to political 'silencing' of the individual or group subjected to hate, something that should not be tolerated in a democracy. To continue with the offences-against-the-person analogy, hate speech should be treated not like jostling in a crowded train, but like street fighting or affray.[188] Whilst there may be some risk that (say) vigorous and passionate—but legitimate—street protest will occasionally be mistaken for an affray, that risk does not undermine the case for prohibiting affrays, in the light of the degradation of public space they consistently tend to involve.[189]

Alternatively, though, a lie that persuades someone to vote for a particular candidate, or for a ballot proposition, might seem more like a claim known by the seller to be false or misleading, which persuades people to buy the seller's product. In such circumstances, not only is the buyer likely to have an individual remedy for breach of their rights, but the state will have its own remedies, perhaps in the form of criminal sanctions against fraudulent sellers under consumer protection legislation. We should note, in that regard, that some citizens have themselves recently taken an actively consumerist approach to what they perceived to be false promises made to secure election results or ballot outcomes, pursuing (albeit unsuccessfully) criminal law actions against the alleged disseminators of political falsehoods.[190]

A problem with this approach, favouring the view that political viewpoint lying should lead to some kind of remedy for breach of rights, is that it takes a

[186] See the discussion in Jeremy Horder (2001); *Collins v Willcock* [1984] 3 All ER 374.
[187] See the discussion of the 'autonomy principle' below.
[188] Public Order Act 1986, s. 3.
[189] *Attorney-General's Reference (No. 6 of 1980)* [1981] 2 All ER 1057.
[190] See *Boris Johnson v Brexit Justice Ltd* (2019) EWHC 1709; https://democracywatch.ca/democracy-watch-calls-on-commissioner-of-canada-elections-to-rule-prime-minister-trudeau-violated-federal-elections-law/ (last accessed 13/04/2021).

disintegrated, consumerist view of politics, and of party-political activity in particular. It treats these phenomena as no more than the assembling of a constellation of issues packaged in such a way that they will tempt the 'buyer' (the voter) into parting with their vote. This view oversimplifies how people understand and evaluate political programmes, and the truthfulness or otherwise of their content. These need to be understood in terms of reflexivity within electoral cycles. Politicians and their parties certainly make claims, assertions, and promises that help to secure election, not least through the publication of party manifestos. However, political success within the electoral cycle is not necessarily or even commonly linked narrowly to delivery on those promises, as stated in their original form: perhaps they were either too modest, too vague, or too grandiose ever to form a stable basis for governance.[191] Success in governance within the cycle may turn, instead, on extraneous matters—for example, successfully weathering an unexpected national crisis. Crucially, that success in turn may then change how voters perceive the claims, assertions, and promises originally made by the successful party: the reflexive element to political evaluation. For example, the (now politically successful) governing party's original election campaign assertion that the leader of the main opposition party was 'temperamentally unfit to govern' may—however controversial or unsupported at the time—come to seem more plausible simply in virtue of the election-winning party's success in government.

To give a different kind of example, suppose that the UK had instantly flourished spectacularly well, economically, after leaving the EU. Then, the (allegedly) false claim made during the referendum campaign that leaving the EU would generate hundreds of millions of pounds weekly to spend on public health[192] might come to be understood by voters as—at worst—merely a 'white lie' or advertising 'puff', rather than the grave deception it was alleged to be by opponents of leaving the EU. On this 'electoral cycle' view of how political claims are evaluated, as Weale puts it: 'the electorate does not mandate a prospective political programme, but rather makes a retrospective judgement about the tolerability of past performance.'[193] What Weale says here should be applied not only to the party in government (in a first-past-the-post system) but also to the opposition. For example, claims by the opposition to be the trustworthy party that will deliver on its manifesto promises, having initially been disbelieved by the majority, may come to be seen very widely as in fact having merit, if the party in power fails badly in office. These points have implications for how we should view challenges to, and possible remedies for, false and misleading political viewpoint information.

[191] For insights on the difficulty of delivery on a manifesto, see Emma Norris (2019). There is some evidence that governments do, generally, deliver on their election manifestos: see https://www.theguardian.com/commentisfree/2015/apr/14/politicians-keep-manifesto-promises (last accessed 13/04/2021).

[192] http://www.voteleavetakecontrol.org/why_vote_leave.html (last accessed 13/04/2021). See also section 1.2(ii) above.

[193] Albert Weale (2007), 131.

Article 25 of the International Covenant on Civil and Political rights (cited above) protects the right to vote, but the gist of my argument is that this right does not extend to an enforceable demand for accurate political viewpoint information. Adversarial legal action, focused on the falsity of political viewpoint claims, and their consequent effects on voters, inevitably takes a misleadingly consumerist approach to politics, of the kind described above. A consumerist legal focus must inevitably be on the status of the claims at the time that they were made, and their impact on voters in casting their votes. If, by contrast, the nature and extent of falsity or distortion in political claims can only properly be understood reflexively, as part of an electoral cycle in which the overall performance and trustworthiness of those making the claims (and their opponents) are evaluated by the electorate, that makes adversarial litigation over such claims inherently problematic. This suggests that the problem of lying or misleading in viewpoint politics requires a collective, political solution, and is not best addressed through an approach based on individual (legal) rights not to be lied to or misled on political viewpoint matters. That is so, whether or not proof that one cast a vote in response to a false or misleading political viewpoint statement is proof that one's political interests were set back, and hence that one was in that sense led to suffer a political harm stemming from the making of the statement.

None of these points applies to false or misleading claims about electoral participation information. The normative significance attributed to an 'electoral cycle', in which political viewpoint claims come to be evaluated, rests on an assumption that elections are conducted fairly and with integrity. That assumption will be put in question if malign activists are free to use fraud, duress, or other kinds of improper means, to prevent or manipulate electoral participation. Moreover, in democratic countries it is not enough simply to ensure that, by and large, attempts to use such improper means are not effective. Each person entitled to vote in a democratic country is not simply harmed, politically, when they are denied their vote, or when it is interfered with, through fraud or other improper means. In such circumstances, they have suffered a violation of the *right* not to have their (non-)participation in voting procedures subjected to manipulation by such means. The respect for that right is an intrinsic part of what it means for a state to be a (flourishing) 'democracy', a matter considered further in the next section.

There is an additional reason not to treat electoral participation fraud aimed at influencing voters in the same way as political viewpoint fraud, namely as something the voters should be trusted to take their own steps to avoid. Elections are relatively infrequent events. Accordingly, the nature of what is a highly rule-governed process will not be all that familiar to many—perhaps most—ordinary people (including some candidates for election), even though in practice relatively little knowledge is needed by voters to make use of the process. Consequently, the opportunities to exploit such ignorance for politically partisan ends are very great, especially in countries (most fall into this category) where there is no prominent and sustained public discussion of electoral participation issues, of a kind likely to ensure that familiarity with electoral rights is widespread. All the more reason, then, to deter and punish attempts to exploit such opportunities. I now turn to a more detailed examination of electoral participation.

(ii) Electoral participation: public goods, freedom, and rights

Electoral participation is an unusual phenomenon, in at least one important respect. This is that such participation relies on the support of the political (including the legal) system for its existence and integrity, whilst also providing—in democratic countries—an important plank of the legitimacy of that system. I will be mainly concerned here with certain aspects of the former dimension, the support provided by the political system, and in particular electoral law, for electoral participation. However, we need to keep in mind from the start the importance of the link between the two dimensions, what can be called the 'due process' dimension, and the 'legitimacy' dimension.

Support for the due process dimension to electoral participation is legally systematic, in that taking part in elections is, by its nature, a bureaucratic exercise; even if only a single person in a whole country was entitled to vote, there would still have to be *some* process to be followed to indicate that their vote had been cast, to check its validity, and so on. However, in a large democracy, even considered simply as a 'box-ticking' exercise, the voting process requires sophisticated and organized state support (considered below), backed by the force of law. By contrast, as argued earlier, support for the legitimacy dimension to electoral participation is largely non-systematic. Most certainly, in a thriving democracy, people can and should be encouraged to exercise their political autonomy, whether by engaging in activism, educating themselves politically, or simply by voting. The legitimacy of a democracy depends in part on how widespread such conduct is. For example, a lack of willingness on the part of state officials to encourage voting has been given as an explanation for the fact that 40 per cent of those entitled to vote in the 1968 US Presidential election did not do so.[194] However, it may be counterproductive, or simply illiberal, to provide a system to coerce people into behaving in one or more such ways.[195] So, encouragement for positive input into the legitimacy dimension is probably best achieved through voluntary, including state-sponsored, efforts.

Nonetheless, there is an important link between the (legally systematic) due process, and the non-systematic legitimacy dimensions to electoral participation. As far as the due process dimension is concerned, (a) more people are likely to take

194 Faye H. Williams (1972), 164.

195 Obviously, in some countries, voting is compulsory. See House of Commons Select Committee on Home Affairs (1997–8), paras 26–29.

part if the costs—in terms of effort required, time spent, and so on—of participation are low; (b) a wider range of people may be encouraged to vote if their special needs are met and their vulnerabilities addressed, in relation to the act of voting; and (c) a guarantee that the 'box-ticking' exercise is both confidential and secure from abuse, whether at the hands of officials, candidates, or voters themselves, will avoid what might otherwise be a significant discouragement to engage in the process, and consequently the development of politically troublesome voter cynicism. This issue is worth exploring in more detail.

The freedom to vote is clearly a kind of 'positive' freedom in the form of a claim right, the freedom or right 'to do' something, rather than a negative freedom (freedom 'from' something). In that regard, as a claim right, it is a freedom that requires significant state support for its meaningful exercise, particularly in countries where there is a universal franchise. In the UK, for example, the state provides over 1,200 polling stations where votes may be cast, in over 300 constituencies;[196] but the mere provision of such facilities for voting, even on such a scale, is obviously not in itself enough to support the freedom or claim right to vote. The state, preferably through the work of one or more arms-length agencies (such as an Election Commission) acting on its behalf, must provide the means by which a number of key issues are determined. These include the settling of constituency boundaries, the establishment and maintenance of the voter register, the registration of parties and candidates, the appointment of registration or returning officers and vote counters (to manage the process at local level), communication with actual and potential voters, the determination of good practice to be followed in the administration of the process (such as the maintenance of political neutrality and voting secrecy at polling stations), and the investigation—and perhaps prosecution—of bad practice, including fraudulent and misleading practices.[197] In the UK, these (and other) issues are addressed in law through no less than 17 major statutes and 30 sets of regulations.[198]

An important theme of these statutes and regulations is the UK's commitment to substantive freedom, and not just to formal freedom to vote. The exercise of the political freedom to vote is an important form of political expression, something akin to the religious freedom to light a candle in a church. Accordingly, the freedom to express oneself politically through voting is not treated in the same way as less politically significant freedoms, important though they may be in other ways, such as the freedom to buy an expensive car or house. What matters, in the case of voting, is not simply the legal entitlement to engage in that activity, but being provided by the state with a reasonable opportunity in practice to engage

[196] House of Commons Select Committee on Home Affairs (1997–8), para 87. See Representation of the People Act 1983, ss. 18A–E and schedule A1.
[197] A quasi-independent body may also have a role in relation to wider issues, such political party funding, party political broadcasting, and citizenship education.
[198] Roger Morris and Mark Heath (2020), 208.

in it. For example, sections 18A to 18E of the 1983 Act require that the division of areas into polling districts must be made so that voters have, so far as is practicable, similarly convenient facilities or districts for going to vote, bearing in the mind local topography and other local circumstances.[199] To the same end, regulations require, for example, election information to be published in minority languages, and recognize the need to set up tactile voting facilities for those with impaired sight, and voting booths appropriate for wheelchair access.[200] A commitment to substantive freedom also requires that there be no artificial (and in practice, biased) barriers to voting, such as disproportionately onerous identification requirements.[201] A commitment to substantive freedom to vote, and not just to formal freedom to vote, is thus an indication that a state recognizes the important role that the due process element in electoral participation may have in supplying an elected government with legitimacy.

State provision of facilities and processes for electoral participation is, in a broad sense of the term, a significant public good. In that regard, theorists have long recognized that the need to protect state provision of public goods may justify the creation of criminal offences, albeit not necessarily serious criminal offences. As Antony Duff puts it:

> Such rules protect or assist the efficient working of [the] regulatory system, which serves as an important aspect of the common good.... [T]he criminal law need not deal only with serious wrongs—it can also provide modest punishments for offences that are, whilst still genuine wrongs, relatively minor.[202]

The claim-right to vote, protected by state provision of public goods in the form of voting processes and facilities, can obviously be threatened by the use or threat of force, intimidation, or fraud. As argued earlier, by way of contrast with the position where political viewpoint disinformation is in issue, there are no significant issues (considered in the next section) militating against straightforward prohibitions on fraudulent participation information that compromises this right. Indeed—and here is a link between the due process and legitimacy dimensions to electoral participation—the toleration of lies and misleading claims about electoral participation is a sign of a corrupted or indifferent political environment. Authoritarian regimes or leaders will, of course, by their nature be likely to tolerate (or even to promote) such false or misleading claims—claims, for example, about eligibility to vote, or the time and place to vote—in so far as they are claims liable to frustrate the

[199] Roger Morris and Mark Heath (2020), 76.
[200] Ibid. 81.
[201] William D. Hicks et al. (2015); https://www.electoral-reform.org.uk/latest-news-and-research/media-centre/press-releases/latest-voter-fraud-stats-show-mandatory-id-proposals-are-still-a-solution-looking-for-a-problem/ (last accessed 14/04/2021).
[202] Antony Duff (2007), 173.

aims of opposition parties. Such a partisan attitude to electoral participation may also creep into the running of democratic regimes, especially those where elections are closely contested between parties with little or no mutual respect.[203] In that regard, the governing party within a democratic state may become politically partisan in its approach to electoral participation, because (for example) the party fears either or both of the erosion of the voting influence wielded by its own supporters, and political activism amongst voter groups unlikely to support the governing party. Such a development may lead the governing party into, for example, gerrymandering.[204] It may also lead to a more or less orchestrated campaign of lies and misleading claims designed either to deter voter groups supposedly hostile to the party from exercising their vote at all, or to frustrate their efforts to do so. Such conduct should be condemned as an illegitimate perversion of vigorous adversarial politics rather than being regarded as—like political viewpoint disinformation—one of its manifestations.[205]

1.6 Viewpoint Disinformation: The Politics of Litigation and Counter-Speech

An irony of the litigation over Brexit is that those who voted to leave the EU were not those complaining about the possibility that reliance might have been placed by voters on one or more false claims or on Russian influence.[206] Instead, this possibility was weaponized by political *opponents* of Brexit, who hoped, through legal challenges including criminal prosecution, if not to achieve legally what they had failed to achieve politically,[207] then to take some measure of revenge against leading supporters of Brexit.[208] This provides an illustration of the unsuitability of the legal process—and of criminal prosecution in particular—for resolving highly politicized disputes about viewpoint politics.[209] In that regard, even if a call for an investigation into political viewpoint disinformation is *bona fide*, when it is made during an election period, then if the police say that the investigation must be delayed until after the election, that decision will inevitably appear as much open to political motivation as a decision to launch an investigation straight away would be.[210] In this section I foreshadow the discussion in Chapter 4, by considering

[203] The US Presidential election of 2020 springs to mind. For discussion of the link between electoral systems and the threat of electoral corruption, see Sarah Birch (2007).

[204] For discussion of a notorious UK example, see https://api.parliament.uk/historic-hansard/commons/1998/jan/21/westminster-city-council (last accessed 14/04/2021); Birch (2007).

[205] See Chantal Mouffe (2005), and the discussion in the General Introduction.

[206] Rachel Ellehuus and Donatienne Ruy (2020).

[207] See e.g. Ewan McGaughey (2018).

[208] See *Boris Johnson v Brexit Justice Ltd* (2019) EWHC 1709.

[209] See further, Jeremy Horder (2021a).

[210] See e.g. *Oberschlick v. Austria No.1* (Application no. 11662/85), of 23 May 1991.

some reasons to regard the criminal legal process as inappropriate for deterring and suppressing false or misleading political viewpoint information. I then go on to consider alternative means of countering false or misleading political viewpoint claims.

(i) The fallibility of the criminal sanction.

When considering what powers to grant to governments, courts, or regulators to suppress and deter political disinformation, one important principle of restraint is what might be called the principle of scepticism.[211] Frederick Shauer defends the principles thus:

> Freedom of speech is based in large part on a distrust of the ability of government to make the necessary distinctions, a distrust of governmental determinations of truth and falsity, an appreciation of the fallibility of political leaders, and a somewhat deeper distrust of government power in a more general sense.[212]

Thus described, the 'principle' of scepticism is not so much a principle as a (healthy) public attitude, an attitude diametrically opposed to blind faith—encouraged by authoritarian regimes—in the judgement of public officials when exercising existing or creating new powers. However, it is convenient to speak in terms of the 'principle' of scepticism, a principle which may have a number of manifestations.

An important aspect of Shauer's account of the principle's application is his claim that it involves 'distrust of governmental determinations of truth and falsity'. If political viewpoint disinformation is to be prohibited or restricted, *someone* must be obliged to pick and choose—in a fair and unbiased way—who is to be prosecuted for spreading alleged disinformation, or who is to have their freedom to speak or access to their speech restricted in some way.[213] In that respect, the scepticism principle is to be found at work, for example, in a refusal—or least, a deep reluctance—to give government agencies, or private bodies (such as social media platforms) when directly coerced by such agencies, the responsibility for determining the (in)appropriateness of false political viewpoint content for dissemination. In declaring unconstitutional a prohibition on the malicious publication of a false statement of material fact about a candidate for public office, the Washington Supreme Court said the statute was unconstitutional because it caused 'the government, rather than the people, [to] be the final arbiter of truth in political

[211] This subsection draws on Jeremy Horder (2021b).
[212] Frederick Shauer (1982), 86. For more recent reliance on the principle, in this context, see Cass Sunstein (2021).
[213] Media Legal Defence Initiative (2015), 20.

debate'.[214] Knowing that distrust and suspicion may arise in such circumstances, it can be tempting to turn the responsibility for policing political discourse over to courts (usually, more highly trusted by ordinary people[215]). The acceptability of doing this will depend on the legal culture in which such move is made, but there are significant risks associated with it. These risks are linked to the principle of scepticism, in that judges called on to make the relevant judgments will lay themselves open to accusations of politically motivated censorship. As we will see in Chapter 4, this point was raised by the Lord Chief Justice for England and Wales as long ago as 1868, in a letter criticizing the proposal to transfer jurisdiction to hear complaints about corruption in elections from Parliament to the courts.[216]

Scepticism, potentially corrosive of judicial authority, is likely to be fuelled by what was referred to earlier as the possibility that legal remedies for political viewpoint disinformation will be weaponized by embittered losers or vindictive winners. An illustrative example of the latter is provided by *Rickert v State Public Disclosure Commission*, a decision of the Washington Supreme Court.[217] In this case, Green Party candidate Marilou Rickert stood against incumbent Senator Tim Sheldon, in the election for state senator form Washington's 35th Legislative District. Sheldon was returned as Senator with 79 per cent of the vote. Nonetheless, Sheldon complained to the Public Disclosure Commission that, during the campaign, Rickert had sponsored a mailing that included a brochure claiming that whereas Rickert 'supports social services for the most vulnerable of the state's citizens', Senator Sheldon, 'voted to close a facility for the developmentally challenged in his district'. Hardly, one might think, an allegation of the utmost gravity, not to mention an allegation made by a fringe candidate against the overwhelming favourite to win. Even so, Sheldon alleged that the latter claim was known by Rickert to be false, and that it hence violated the relevant statutory provision, which read, 'it is a violation of this chapter for a person to sponsor with actual malice ... (p) olitical advertising or an electioneering communication that contains a false statement of material fact about a candidate for public office'.[218] Rickert was initially fined $1,000 for knowingly making the false claim, but this was overturned when the law itself was found on appeal to fail a strict scrutiny test in relation to the First Amendment.[219]

In this kind of case, investigating and decision-making bodies are likely to find themselves caught between, on the one hand, allegations that they are colluding in the oppression of political opponents by the victor, and—even if they can avoid

[214] *Rickert v Public Disclosure Commission* (2007) 168 P 3d 826, 827.

[215] https://www.ipsos.com/ipsos-mori/en-uk/politicians-remain-least-trusted-profession-britain (last accessed 04/06/2021).

[216] See Chapter 4, section 4.4 for fuller discussion. For further discussion of this point, see e.g. Alan Renwick and Michela Palese (2019), ch. 2.

[217] 168 P.3d 826 (2007).

[218] Revised Code of Washington 42.17.530(1).

[219] *Rickert v State, Public Disclosure Commission* 168 P 3d 826 (2007).

charges of bias—on the other hand, allegations that they are improperly assuming what the court in *Washington ex Public Disclosure Commission v. 119 Vote No! Committee*,[220] referred to dismissively as a 'guardianship of the public mind'.[221] These tensions would be resolved, were it to be made clear that neither false personal claims about candidates, nor false political viewpoint claims more generally, are legitimately subjected to criminalization. Candidates who are libelled in the course of elections should be left to civil law remedies (which may be crowdfunded by their supporters),[222] perhaps under a cheaper and quicker procedure that acknowledges the enhanced risk of defamation during election periods. As we saw in the General Introduction, it is also open to electors who believe that they were duped into voting for a candidate to challenge the result of the election if illegal or corrupt practices—including, but not confined to, fraud—have so extensively prevailed that they may reasonably be supposed to have affected the result.[223]

Threats, posed by criminalization of false or misleading political viewpoint information to the (perceived) impartiality and integrity of the enforcement authorities, and of the judiciary, must also be considered alongside the effects on individual speakers. In that regard, for would-be provocative or controversial speakers, criminalization will pose a number of what can be called 'political falsehood dilemmas' concerning the making of false or misleading statements. To begin with, legal prohibitions on false statements require officials to grapple with the problem (raised earlier[224]) of 'half-truths': content that contains an element of truth, but which is packaged in accompanying mistruths, or selective reporting of factual information that creates a skewed view.[225] Is a statement comprised of an untrue and a true element a 'false' statement, or perhaps merely a 'misleading' statement? When it is known that legal uncertainties of this kind may arise, people may find themselves facing a political dilemma over whether to speak, and could be deterred from making political claims that are simply provocative or controversial, to the detriment of a free-speech polity.

Political falsehood dilemmas may arise in other instances. One example is when at least some—and perhaps all—of what the speaker intends to say is known by them to be untrue or misleading, but they nonetheless believe that there is sufficient reason to make the statement: in other words, when they may not be acting 'dishonestly' in a broad sense of that term.[226] An example might involve the publication of falsely exaggerated figures for a particular MP's Parliamentary expenses,

[220] 135 Wash 2nd 618 (Washington 1998).

[221] Ibid. 625.

[222] 'Civil law remedies' should be understood to include procedures provided by internet platforms to complain about defamatory content and have it removed. See further Chapter 2, section 2.7.

[223] Representation of the People Act 1983, s. 164. See the discussion in Jeremy Horder (2021a).

[224] See text at n. 177.

[225] https://www.theguardian.com/technology/2019/nov/12/far-right-use-russian-style-propaganda-to-spread-misinformation (last accessed 12/11/2021); Kate Jones (2019).

[226] John Gardner (2005), 67–70.

for the purpose of spurring the MP into complying with a legal obligation to account for their actual expenses. In this instance, the political falsehood dilemma arises even though the would-be speaker may share a conception of political truth with those who will stand in judgment over their utterances.[227] However, it is obvious that such a dilemma also arises when someone disseminates or shares political information they believe to be true or defensible, but which they appreciate is regarded by those who will stand in judgment as false or indefensible ('President Obama was not born in the United States'[228]). Even if 'honest believers' in false claims should in theory not find themselves subject to sanctions, someone may appreciate that if they make a political statement that turns out to be false, their claim that they honestly believed in its veracity when the statement was made is—perhaps because they are widely disliked or distrusted—unlikely to be believed.

In all these instances, the existence of the political falsehood dilemma raises the worry that would-be contributors to political debate may be wrongly deterred by the prospect of sanctions from engaging in what is simply combative or attention-grabbing political speech, by the prospect of sanctions imposed by those (including the courts) they regard as political enemies. If that happens, any criminal-law cure for lying in politics may—as suggested at the outset—turn out to be worse than the disease. For these reasons, in *R v Zundel*, the Supreme Court of Canada struck down as unconstitutional a criminal prohibition on 'wilful publication of false statement or news that a person knows is false and that is likely to cause injury or mischief to a public interest'.[229] It is also for such reasons that the principle of scepticism should be connected to another principle: the principle of political autonomy.[230]

One aspect of the autonomy principle is that, in Eric Barendt's words (drawing on Thomas Scanlon[231]), 'a person is only autonomous if he is free to weigh for himself the arguments for various courses of action that others wish to put before him'.[232] In itself, this statement of the principle does not take us far. That is because it is focused primarily on the autonomy of the potential audience members and not on the autonomy of speakers. The freedom to weigh arguments for oneself will be worthless without access to those arguments. So, an important—perhaps more important—moral dimension to the principle of autonomy is that speakers must be free to put forward (and undeterred in putting forward) political arguments, so that they may be weighed.[233] The moral dimension to autonomy is buttressed

[227] A number of other illustrative examples where spreading false information can be justified may be found in *R v Zundel* [1992] 2 SCR 731 (judgment of McLachlin J).

[228] https://www.bbc.co.uk/news/election-us-2016-37391652 (last accessed 14/04/2021).

[229] *R v Zundel* [1992] 2 SCR 731.

[230] Thomas Scanlon (1972).

[231] Ibid.

[232] Eric Barendt (2007), 16.

[233] Bernard Williams (2005), 131, discussed further in Chapter 2.

by a political dimension concerned with, in Ronald Dworkin's terms,[234] how the state ought to treat political speakers, and their audiences, whatever it may think of them morally. Does the freedom to propagate political argument include the freedom to put forward claims that are (intended to be) false or misleading? In striking down a statute creating an offence of knowingly or recklessly making a false statement about political candidates or ballot initiatives, the Massachusetts Supreme Court answered 'yes' to this question. The court suggested that such an offence was likely to chill 'the very exchange of ideas that gives meaning to our electoral system'.[235]

It is important not to misunderstand the point being made by the Massachusetts Supreme Court. The point is not that the propagation of false or misleading information has something positive to contribute to a flourishing political culture, or that (in itself) it enhances the political autonomy of speakers. It does neither of these things. The point is that the risks to such a culture, and to the autonomy of speakers generally, of (say) biased or over-zealous prosecution, and of legal uncertainty in relation to the scope of prohibitions, indicate that it is better—in law, at least—to tolerate the spread of political viewpoint disinformation, even if such disinformation should be vigorously countered through counter-speech activism.[236] Neither the principle of scepticism nor the autonomy principle should, though, be regarded as inconsistent with any kind of government activity in the area of free speech and free expression, even in relation to elections and political participation. For example, just because (as Shauer rightly remarks) political leaders are fallible, that does not mean government should avoid striving to provide access to political information for citizens, and to promote as public goods widespread political debate and participation.[237]

(ii) The remedy of counter-speech and its limits

The principle of scepticism holds that the taking by the state of coercive steps to deter and punish the dissemination of false political viewpoint information is illegitimate, because officials are fallible and potentially biased. Even if they manage to avoid breaching the trust placed in them by error, they may breach that trust for self-interested reasons. Under the autonomy principle the taking of such steps is

[234] Ronald Dworkin (1977), 181: 'Equal respect means that government must respect the dignity of each individual by allowing each individual to determine for himself or herself what would count as a good life.'
[235] *Commonwealth v Lucas* (2015) 34 NE 3d 1242.
[236] See Frederick Shauer and Richard H. Pildes (1999), 1812 and 1814, and the discussion of toleration in Chapter 2.
[237] See, generally, Eric Barendt (2007), 30–8.

equally to be ruled out, but primarily for speaker-focused reasons.[238] Consequently, more important to the autonomy principle are the rights of speakers, the disseminators of (false) political viewpoint information, to be free from the threat of coercion in creating their own political narrative and disseminating it—taking advantage of available technology—in a manner of their own choosing. For adherents of the autonomy principle, the use of coercion to deter disseminators of false political viewpoint information is regarded as unnecessary, because a flourishing political culture can adequately address falsehood through the republican remedy of 'more-speech' solutions. As Justice Brandeis famously put it in *Whitney v California*:[239]

> To courageous, self-reliant men [sic], with confidence in the power of free and fearless reasoning applied through the processes of popular government ... [i]f there be time to expose through discussion the falsehood and fallacies, to avert the evil by the processes of education, the remedy to be applied is more speech, not enforced silence.[240]

Notwithstanding the moral attraction of Justice Brandeis's fine-sounding sentiments, it is clear that there is no simple correlation between the 'offensive' power of false political information to convince and the 'defensive' power of counter-speech to negate that offensive power. A number of studies have illustrated the limited power of simple contradiction or counter-speech to shift political thinking based on false information.[241] Even so, that may indicate simply that non-coercive, counter-speech tactics and strategies for the internet age are, as yet, in their infancy and can be dramatically improved and scaled up. As far as political viewpoint disinformation is concerned, the resort to censorship and coercion should be regarded as a misguided pre-modern solution to a twenty-first-century problem. In Chapter 2, I will advocate particular 'more-speech' solutions as central to the task of countering online political disinformation: the attachment of unreliability warnings to suspect claims in some instances, along with links to counter-speech, and requirements on occasion to disclose one's identity.

Nonetheless, it is worth considering an attempt to give expression through criminal law to one key aspect of (the stated exception to) the Brandeis 'more-speech' principle, as set out above. This is Justice Brandeis's own qualification to his endorsement of a 'more-speech' solution, in cases where there is no 'time to expose through discussion the falsehood and fallacies, to avert the evil by the processes of

238 Worries about paternalism dog the audience-focused argument that what matters is how one addresses the risk that voters will encounter false political speech and hence take a 'wrong' turning in terms of their political beliefs and intentions.

239 *Whitney v California* (No. 3) 74 U.S. 357 (1927).

240 Ibid., at 377 (Brandeis J).

241 See e.g. Jacob L. Nelson and Harsh Taneja (2018), 3733.

education'.[242] We can call this the 'Brandeis gap' in the more-speech principle. The focus of an election-related offence may be the 'Brandeis gap', a gap which is at its most glaring when a false statement is made just before the closure of the polls. An example of such an offence is to be found in section 81 of New Zealand's Electoral Amendment Act 2002:

> Every person is guilty of a corrupt practice who, with the intention of influencing the vote of any elector, at any time on polling day before the close of the poll, or at any time on any of the 2 days immediately preceding polling day, publishes, distributes, broadcasts, or exhibits, or causes to be published, distributed, broadcast, or exhibited, in or in view of any public place a statement of fact that the person knows is false in a material particular.[243]

By making criminalization dependent on a false statement falling within (an interpretation of) the 'Brandeis gap', section 81 is meant to target instances in which it may prove difficult or impossible adequately to rebut false claims in the time available. However, Jacob Rowbottom has rightly observed that such time limits are not only necessarily somewhat arbitrary, but perhaps over-generous, given the instantaneous nature of claim and counter-claim in the internet age.[244] More significantly, it is notable that New Zealand has not seen a single prosecution under section 81 of the 2002 Act.[245] That suggests, even if it does not prove, that the criminal law—however carefully crafted—is not especially well suited to the regulation of substantive political debate.

The EU defines disinformation as 'verifiably false or misleading information that is created, presented and disseminated for economic gain or to intentionally deceive the public, and may cause public harm',[246] and has called for urgent and immediate action to protect the Union, its institutions, and its citizens against such disinformation. However, its proposed 'four-pillars' response involves not the threat of coercion, but a 'more-speech' solution, focused on quickly identifying and calling out disinformation. The four pillars are:

(i) improving the capabilities of Union institutions to detect, analyse, and expose disinformation;

[242] See text at n. 239 above.

[243] Renwick and Palese (2019), ch. 2. As Jacob Rowbottom points out, until 1999, the UK's Advertising Standards Authority was prepared to apply its provisions on taste and decency to political advertisements, but political advertisements are now excluded from the Authority's remit: Jacob Rowbottom (2012), 533. The Authority's Chair, Lord Rodgers, justified this move by saying, 'The free flow of argument in the cut and thrust of open debate is the best antidote to political advertising that misleads or offends': Advertising Standards Authority, Annual Report (1999), 2.

[244] See Jacob Rowbottom (2012), 523–4.

[245] Alan Renwick and Michela Palese (2019), 36.

[246] European Union High Representative of the Union for Foreign Affairs and Security Policy (2018), 1.

(ii) strengthening coordinated and joint responses to disinformation;
(iii) mobilizing the private sector to tackle disinformation;
(iv) raising awareness and improving societal resilience.

In relation to (ii) for example, what is proposed is, 'prompt reaction via fact-based and effective communication ... to counter and deter disinformation, including in cases of disinformation concerning Union matters and policies'.[247]

Similarly, in France, a Report from the Policy Planning Staff (Ministry for Europe and Foreign Affairs) and Institute for Strategic Research (Ministry for the Armed Forces) defines political disinformation as 'the intentional and massive dissemination of false or biased news for hostile political purposes',[248] and says that: 'Governments can and should come to the aid of civil society ... [because they] cannot afford to ignore a threat that undermines the foundations of democracy and national security.'[249] Yet, once again, the primary response proposed is not the use of coercion but a 'more-speech' solution. In preference to a top-down method, the Report recommends 'horizontal, collaborative approaches, relying on the participation of civil society', albeit that these approaches are to be accompanied by the establishment of a national entity responsible for the detection and countering of information manipulation.[250]

In that respect, a state can non-coercively encourage political engagement and the fostering of a culture of truthfulness and honesty in politics by, for example, introducing and promoting codes of electoral conduct, or by providing tax breaks for independent fact-checking organizations. The UK government is also to create an Advisory Committee on Disinformation and Misinformation in England and Wales,[251] whose task will be to provide guidance for the communication regulator on the right approach for platforms towards these issues. As far as the EU's 'fourth pillar' above is concerned ('improving societal resilience'), a state can also embark on a strategy to popularize and embed media literacy in society at large. To its credit, the UK government has placed considerable emphasis on 'more speech' and critical engagement by citizens, as opposed to take-down and restriction:

> [T]he government has continued to build audience resilience to disinformation and misinformation, enabling people to critically assess, appraise and challenge information online. Through the 'Don't Feed the Beast' campaign and SHARE checklist, UK users have been given five easy steps to identify false content, encouraging them to consider information they share online.[252]

247 Ibid. 8.
248 J.-B. Jeangène Vilmer (2018), 12.
249 JIbid. 13.
250 Ibid. 167. See also, NATO STRATCOM (2016), https://www.stratcomcoe.org.
251 Online Safety Bill 2021, clause 98.
252 Department for Digital, Culture, Media and Sport, and Home Office (2020), para 2.79.

In relation to material generated and spread through electronic media, there has long been an obligation in England and Wales on the communication regulator (Ofcom), amongst other things, 'to bring about, or to encourage others to bring about, a better public awareness and understanding of the processes by which such material is selected, or made available, for publication'.[253] The UK government is to replace and extend this duty, in part, to cover:

technologies and systems which—
(i) indicate the nature of the material (for example, show where it is an advertisement),
(ii) indicate the *reliability and accuracy* of the material.[254]

As Damian Tambini has suggested, the proportionate (regulatory) response is generally not the threat of take-down or restriction, but 'monitoring, advice and transparency', with a focus on, 'consumer information, competition and switching'.[255] A citizenry educated to engage critically with (allegedly) false or misleading information is a citizenry that needs to rely far less—if at all—on official coercion in order to deter the propagation and spread of such information: a point that goes well beyond political viewpoint disinformation and misinformation.

Of course, it is possible to dismiss such approaches as based on wishful thinking. For example, a number of studies have shown that hyper-partisan political narratives tend to be relatively impervious to counter-speech tactics, tactics the narratives condemn as part of a discredited elite, liberal-centrist way of doing politics.[256] What, though, is the alternative? Whilst we explore various means by which jurisdictions have pursued deterrence and suppression strategies in Chapter 2, it is as well to be clear now that such strategies are just as likely to play into the hands of those at whom they are targeted, as they are to exercise any of the deterrent effect they are intended to have.[257] As the French Institute for Strategic Research (Ministry for the Armed Forces) and Policy Planning Staff (Ministry for Europe and Foreign Affairs) puts it:

> Overregulation is a real danger, and even a trap set by our adversaries: far from being bothered with overzealous regulations, they will actually benefit from the controversy and divisions that it will create. We must be mindful of the risk of our actions having such unintended effects.[258]

253 Communications Act 2003, s. 11(b).
254 Online Safety Bill 2021, clause 103 (my emphasis).
255 Damian Tambini (2019), 29.
256 See Alice Marwick and Rebecca Lewis (2017).
257 Even if one puts on one side the possibility of unintended deterrent effect on speakers who are merely provocative or controversial.
258 Jean-Baptiste Jeangène Vilmer et al. (2018), 176.

2

Online Disinformation: Between Free Speech and the Pursuit of Truth

2.1 Introduction

In this chapter, my focus is on state regulation of social media platforms, along with these platforms' policies for self-regulation, in relation to false or misleading political information spread online.[1] In general terms, I argue—as have many others—that government policies and legislation worldwide, when making attempts to require platforms to commercialize content responsibly, tend to risk (or even actively to promote) unnecessary and inappropriate blocking or restriction of false or misleading political viewpoint content. In different ways, even well-intentioned governments commonly strike the balance wrongly between the duty to respect freedom of speech and the duty to honour the pursuit of truth.

Although, in Chapter 1, I was almost exclusively concerned with the values and attitudes appropriate for a free-speech culture, it seems obvious that freedom of speech and the pursuit of truth are both universally important. A commitment to both must be reconciled. After all, as Grisez, Boyle, and Finnis remark, 'in the moral domain truth is the whole, and falsity is apart, abstracted from the whole and thereby made to rationally guide action in a misguided way'.[2]

The way to respect the freedom to lie or mislead in making political viewpoint claims, whilst honouring the pursuit of truth, is through the promotion of critical engagement with (allegedly) false or misleading political viewpoint content, even if this provides no guarantee that people will become immune to the charms of consistently repeated lies.[3] This policy is to be preferred to a policy of either restricting or blocking such content or, alternatively, actively promoting an alternative (supposed) truth.[4] For internet platforms, that means prioritizing certain kinds of 'more-speech' solutions[5] to political viewpoint lies and distortions. Examples are the highlighting of evidence-based content, and the use of unreliability warnings

[1] This chapter is based in part on the arguments in Jeremy Horder (2021b).
[2] Germain Grisez, Joseph Boyle, and John Finnis (1987), 126.
[3] G. Pennycook, T. D. Cannon, and D. G. Rand (2018).
[4] For a recognition of the importance of critical engagement, see Department for Digital, Culture, Media and Sport, and Home Office (2020), para 2.79. See also the government's webpage, https://sharechecklist.gov.uk/ (last accessed 15/04/2021).
[5] See Chapter 1, section 1.6(ii).

Criminal Fraud and Election Disinformation. Jeremy Horder, Oxford University Press.
DOI: 10.1093/oso/9780192844545.003.0003

attached to suspect content. Such solutions should be preferred to both deterrent strategies (threats of bans) and to the denial or restriction of benefits, such as the benefit on online content-sharing. Banning and denial of benefits are approaches appropriate for preventing the dissemination and spread of electoral participation disinformation.

I will go on to develop a less familiar point. This is that whilst, in their regulatory policies and legislation, governments have—sometimes wilfully—failed to draw any distinction between false political viewpoint and electoral participation disinformation, the internet platforms these governments regulate have been appropriately sensitive to this distinction (in their stated policies, at any rate). The platforms have, for example, drawn convincing analogies between hate speech and electoral participation disinformation, and rightly treated them both in the same highly restrictive way. One can only speculate on the reasons for this difference of approach. Politicians have, perhaps, become too fond of criminal laws, and regulatory strategies, that serve to protect them from all manner of false accusations and misleading claims.[6] Hence, relying on the oft-repeated mantra that 'what is illegal offline is illegal online',[7] they expect platforms to stem the tide of such content in a relatively indiscriminate way, even though the mantra gives carte blanche to authoritarian regimes to stifle legitimate political debate online by reference to their own repressive laws. However, emerging from a First Amendment culture, the platforms themselves have (rightly) shown little tendency to conform with this catch-all expectation. That is significant, not least because more people worldwide support the idea that journalists (75 per cent) and online platforms (71 per cent) should take the lead in removing (online) disinformation, than support the idea that this is a government responsibility (61 per cent).[8]

In 1985, UK voters gave as their most important source of political information: television (63 per cent), newspapers (29 per cent), and radio (4 per cent).[9] Only a tiny fraction claimed that their political and world news more broadly came from contact with other people, a position radically changed—when one includes virtual contact—since the advent of the internet age.[10] Correspondingly, for much of second half of the twentieth century, the perceived need for reform of the law governing false or misleading political statements was perhaps kept adequately at bay (i) informally, by reliance on the perceived need to maintain tolerable working relations between politicians and journalists,[11] and (ii) more formally, by some regulation[12]—albeit typically 'light touch'—and journalists' codes of conduct,

[6] See the discussion of militant democracy in Chapter 1.
[7] See the discussion in Thomas Wischmeyer (2018).
[8] Reuters Institute (2019) 19.
[9] Ralph Negrine (1994), 2.
[10] See London School of Economics Commission on Truth, Trust and Technology (2018), ch. 2.
[11] Aeron Davis (2009), 204.
[12] See e.g. https://www.ofcom.org.uk/tv-radio-and-on-demand/broadcast-codes/broadcast-code/section-six-elections-referendums (last accessed 15/04/2021).

applicable to the traditional press.[13] However, these restraints have become less significant, as those governed by them have been rivalled in terms of influence by social media users whose conduct falls outside their scope.[14] In the USA, for example, the Federal Election Commission noted in 2006 that only 18 per cent of all Americans cited the internet as their leading source of news about the 2004 Presidential election. By contrast, the Pew Research Centre found that 65 per cent of Americans identified an internet-based source as their leading source of information for the 2016 election.[15] Some important reasons for this shift are clear. The New Zealand Law Commission noted the following special features of online or digital communication, distinguishing it from offline communication:

(1) The viral nature of cyberspace and the potential for information to be disseminated instantly to worldwide audiences;
(2) The ubiquity of the technology which means communications are no longer constrained by time and place but can be accessed anywhere, anytime by anyone;
(3) The persistence of information disseminated electronically;
(4) The ease with which digital information can be accessed and searched;
(5) The facility for anonymous communication and the adoption of multiple online personae.[16]

The US Supreme Court has gone so far as to call the main social media platforms 'perhaps the most powerful mechanisms available to a private citizen to make his or her voice heard'.[17] As far as making one's voice heard in elections is concerned, taking Twitter as just one example, in the 2018 US mid-term elections more than 99 million tweets involving political content were sent from the first primaries in March through to election day.[18] Accordingly, the focus of political speech gatekeeping is now at least as much on content moderation by internet platforms as it is on the attitudes and policies of publishers or broadcasters.[19]

In that regard, a recent study of 126,000 news stories distributed on Twitter between 2006 and 2017 revealed that falsehoods (as established by fact-checking

[13] https://www.nuj.org.uk/about-us/rules-and-guidance/code-of-conduct.html (last accessed 08/06/2021).

[14] House of Commons, Digital, Culture, Media and Sport Committee (2019), para 202. This has become a particular problem for centre-left political narratives, which rely more on traditional media outlets than (far-) right-of centre political activists: Robert Faris et al. (2017).

[15] https://www.congress.gov/bill/116th-congress/senate-bill/1356/text (last accessed 15/04/2021), para 12; Michael Erbschloe (2019), 2.5.

[16] New Zealand Law Commission (2012), 38, cited by the Law Commission for England and Wales (2020), para 5.31.

[17] *Packingham v North Carolina* (2017) 137 S Ct 1730, 1737 (Justice Roberts).

[18] https://blog.twitter.com/en_us/topics/company/2019/18_midterm_review.html (last accessed 09/06/2021).

[19] See, generally, Kate Klonick (2018), 1603–4.

organizations) were 70 per cent more likely to be retweeted than true stories.[20] Partly instrumental, in this respect, have been the use of (semi-)automated bots—fake Twitter or Facebook accounts that enable the spread of false claims though retweets and 'likes'—and non-state agencies organizing internet 'trolling' on a wide scale.[21] An example of the significance of this development is the finding that, from 2014 onwards, the St Petersburg-based Internet Research Agency at one point is reported to have controlled 3,814 human accounts and 50,258 bots on Twitter (with which nearly 1.5 million US citizens had some interaction), and 470 Facebook accounts that reached at least 126 million Americans.[22] Similarly, in the lead-up to the UK referendum on leaving the European Union, it was widely reported that over 150,000 Twitter accounts sourced in Russia posted content on Brexit.[23]

How do, and how should, legislatures respond to these developments? Consistent with the theme set out in Chapter 1, as far as political disinformation is concerned, my case will be that legislatures should only require internet platforms to ban or restrict access to electoral participation disinformation. This kind of speech should be classified alongside other banned or highly restricted forms of communication, such as hate speech, intimidation, and harassment. The dangers of going further, by requiring platforms to restrict or ban political viewpoint disinformation, will be made clear, in so far as they have not already been addressed in Chapter 1. The importance of making the case for tolerance in the latter case is a troubling persistence on the part of legislators and other officials, in equating political viewpoint disinformation with rights-invading harms of a much more serious nature.[24] For example, reflecting on the contribution of online conspiracy theory to the 2020 invasion of the Capitol building in Washington, Thierry Breton, then European Commissioner for the internal market, said:

> Our European laws and courts will continue to define what is illegal, both offline and online—from child pornography to terrorist content, from hate speech to counterfeiting, from incitement to violence to defamation—through democratic processes and with appropriate checks and balances. But currently, online platforms lack legal clarity about how they should treat illegal content on their

[20] Soroush Vosoughi, Deb Roy, and Sinan Aral (2018), 1148.

[21] David Murray (2018).

[22] Jean-Baptiste Jeangène Vilmer (2018), 85. America is yet to adopt measures to require transparency in relation to internet political advertising by overseas entities: see https://www.brennancenter.org/our-work/research-reports/honest-ads-act-explained (last accessed 15/04/2021).

[23] David Wolchover and Amanda Robinson (2020). See e.g. House of Commons, Digital, Culture, Media and Sport Committee (2019), part 6; *The Guardian*, 4 November 2017, https://www.theguardian.com/politics/2017/nov/04/brexit-ministers-spy-russia-uk-brexit (last accessed 15/04/2021); Ewan McGaughey, 'The extent of Russian-backed fraud means the referendum is invalid' (2018), https://blogs.lse.ac.uk/brexit/2018/11/14/the-extent-of-russian-backed-fraud-means-the-referendum-is-invalid/ (last accessed 15.04.2021); Ewan McGaughey (2018), 334–6.

[24] See the discussion of 'militant' democracy, and of the distinction between harm and rights-invasion, in Chapter 1.

networks. This leaves our societies with too many questions about when content should or shouldn't be blocked.[25]

Whilst Breton is right to say that there is a lack of clarity about how platforms should deal with online content (and not only illegal content), is it right seemingly to equate, as he does, incitement to violence and *defamation*? The case for immediately and urgently restricting or banning the former could scarcely be clearer. How to deal with the latter is far more problematic, especially when it takes the form of political viewpoint disinformation about serving politicians, as the European Court of Human Rights has recognized.[26]

Defamation law is a classic 'go-to' remedy for political officials seeking to intimidate their rivals into silence.[27] Indeed, as former New Zealand Prime Minister Sir Geoffrey Palmer has argued, 'in a free and democratic society, *defaming the government is the right of every citizen*. In times beset with threats of terrorism we should not close the open society. To do so would only encourage its enemies.'[28] Having said that, in a broad sense, all political disinformation is a bad thing. So, I will go on to explain how tolerance of some of its manifestations is consistent with requiring platforms to adopt measures to counteract the possible influence of such information. In particular, as I indicated above, false political viewpoint information should be countered with certain kinds of 'more-speech' measures, such as promoting reliable sources of information, and insisting on the attachment to false or misleading posts of unreliability warnings.[29]

2.2 Hate, Harassment, and Harm: Political Disinformation in Context

I will not be concerned here with the broad range of complex and detailed questions about how properly to constitute the relationship between the state, citizens, and internet platforms.[30] Nonetheless, we should start by noting that the political sensitivity of internet platform freedom has long been recognized by legislators. In passing a 1996 amendment to the Communications Act of 1934 dealing with 'common carriers',[31] the US Congress sought to secure the immunity of internet

[25] Thierry Breton, 'Capitol Hill: The 9/11 Moment of Social Media' (10 January 2021), https://www.politico.eu/article/thierry-breton-social-media-capitol-hill-riot/ (last accessed 15/04/2021).

[26] *Otegi Mondragon v Spain* (Application no. 2034/07) 15 March 2011, para 50.

[27] See e.g. Article 19 (2000), 7–8.

[28] Cited at https://publications.parliament.uk/pa/ld200809/ldhansrd/text/90709-0013.htm (last accessed 15/04/2021), my emphasis.

[29] On 'more speech' remedies, see Chapter 1, section 1.6(ii).

[30] For a comprehensive discussion, see London School of Economics Commission on Trust, Truth and Technology (2018).

[31] Added by Communications Decency Act 1996, 47 U.S.C. § 230, s. 9; Telecommunications Act 1996, s. 509.

platforms from liability (civil liability, in particular) in relation to content posted by users, and in relation to platforms' attempts to moderate such content.[32] The amendment—section 230—has proved controversial ever since,[33] in virtue of the broad scope of the immunity that it provides: a matter considered in detail, in relation to other jurisdictions, below. More important for present purposes, though, is the motivation that lay behind it. Congress wished to confer immunity from suit because, as it declared:

> The Internet and other interactive computer services offer a forum for a true diversity of political discourse, unique opportunities for cultural development, and myriad avenues for intellectual activity.... Americans are relying on interactive media for a variety of political, educational, cultural, and entertainment services.[34]

Taking this point seriously has implications not just for the way in which limits are set for private law actions, but also for state regulation, and enforced self-regulation by platforms.

The flourishing of a 'true diversity of political discourse' within a society, and not just the proliferation of more speech, depends on a number of factors. For example, suppose that this diversity does not manifest itself in some Habermas-style ideal of conflicting opinion brought together in the dominant public sphere to forge new political directions agreed—or grudgingly accepted—in common.[35] Suppose that, instead, what happens is the proliferation of counter-public spheres, each with its own political standards for the evaluation of true and false, acceptable and unacceptable, and each in part constructed through the demonization of other (counter-)public spheres.[36] In the latter case, those responsible for maintaining a vibrant, tolerant public sphere ought to be encouraging, and if necessary enforcing, self-restraint in the conduct of political discourse, so far as counter-public speech is (say) violent, hateful, or intimidatory.[37]

An important reason for adopting such a policy in a free-speech context is the worry, not just about harm done in individual cases, but about the development of a significant 'public negative': too much (or the wrong kind of) self-censorship.[38] Self-censorship can take an insidious and powerful form, when it enables the state

[32] The EU equivalent is European Union E-Commerce Directive (2000/31/EC).

[33] See e.g. https://www.theguardian.com/technology/2021/mar/24/mark-zuckerberg-congress-facebook-google-twitter-capitol-attack (last accessed 24/03/2021).

[34] https://www.law.cornell.edu/uscode/text/47/230 (last accessed 15/04/2021).

[35] Jurgen Habermas (1998).

[36] See, generally, Damian Smith Pfister (2019).

[37] See Crown Prosecution Service (2017), https://www.cps.gov.uk/south-east/news/cps-publishes-new-public-statements-hate-crime: 'The Crown Prosecution Service actively pursues online hate crimes in this category with over fifteen thousand prosecutions in 2015/16 and announced its reinforced willingness to pursue online hate crime in August 2017' (last accessed 15/04/2021).

[38] On public negatives, in a criminal law context, see Jeremy Horder (2019).

to disassociate itself from the suppression of free speech whilst benefitting from that suppression at the hands of others. Self-censorship may also have a tragic dimension, reflecting the fear of would-be political speakers that to speak (in certain ways, or about certain topics) will lead to threats, hate, harassment, discrimination, or all of these and more, undermining the would-be speakers' political autonomy.[39] For such reasons, those who are prone to or might be tempted to use a public platform to engage in intimidatory or hateful impulses—whether or not against people in authority—are quite reasonably expected to hold their tongues, even in the face of provocation. An expectation of self-restraint, in relation to threats, intimidation, harassment, and hate, is not in itself an undesirable form of (self-)censorship, in a society committed to democratic equality.[40] Instead, such an expectation contributes to, rather than detracting from, a flourishing free-speech culture within such a society.[41] Such a culture is not one that simply gives licence to untrammelled self-assertion, but is one in which, amongst other things, freedom from fear gives citizens the confidence that they, in common with everyone else, can add value to their (and others') lives through active political engagement.

No doubt, in part for that reason, internet platforms commonly have a broad-ranging commitment (at least in theory) to prevent social media becoming a vehicle for hate. Google, for example, says that it will not allow content that 'incites hatred against, promotes discrimination of, or disparages an individual or group on the basis of their race or ethnic origin, religion, disability, age, nationality, veteran status, sexual orientation, gender, gender identity, or other characteristic that is associated with systemic discrimination or marginalization'.[42] In pursuit of its own policy of preventing the platform from becoming a vehicle for hate speech, Facebook removes between 3 and 4 million posts adjudged to involve hate speech each quarter.[43] In so far as platforms are true to such commitments, these are examples of commitments to responsible commercialization of content in a democracy.

How does online dissemination of false political information fit into this context? In Chapter 1, I made the general argument for tolerance of political viewpoint disinformation, by way of contrast with electoral participation information. The main focus in this chapter is what should be required of internet platforms (and what action platforms should take themselves), in terms of restraints, prohibitions,

[39] See Lynne Tirell (2018–19); G. S. Hans (2021).

[40] See Robin Edgar (2010).

[41] For a discussion of the law of the European Convention on Human Rights on this issue, see Dominika Bychawska-Siniarska (2017), ch. 3.

[42] https://support.google.com/adsense/answer/9335564?hl=en&visit_id=637491849670431104-1481837764&rd=1 (last accessed 15/04/2021). See also https://transparency.facebook.com/community-standards-enforcement#hate-speech (last accessed 15/04/2021).

[43] https://ec.europa.eu/digital-single-market/en/news/annual-self-assessment-reports-signatories-code-practice-disinformation-2019 (last accessed 15/04/2021). About a quarter of these decisions were appealed, leading to the content being restored in roughly 10 per cent of cases.

or other measures to prevent, restrict, or discredit the spread of false or misleading political information, the main focus being political viewpoint disinformation. In relation to online content that must be taken down, the EU works with what is called a 'notice-and-take-down' model, in relation to illegal content.[44] This model is located somewhere between on the one hand complete platform immunity for content posted by others, and on the other hand a duty of care to ensure that illegal content is either not posted at all, or is tracked and disabled (or otherwise dealt with) by the platform.[45] Under a 'notice-and-take-down' model, a platform is meant to be immune from liability if it does not have knowledge of the illegal activity or information, and removes or disables access to it 'expeditiously', upon becoming aware of it.[46] A platform is not required to go looking for needles in haystacks, but must act promptly if it finds one. One controversial feature of 'notice and take-down' is that it removes any element of judgement on the part of a platform concerning the public interest in taking content down. We will return to this issue later, when considering proposed changes to English law. However, whilst the adoption by a platform of a 'notice-and-take-down' policy is necessary, EU member states may find that it is not sufficient. It has been held that merely having a notice-and-take-down procedure in place will not necessarily protect a platform from (civil) liability, if the procedure is not adequate to deal with certain kinds of prohibited speech, such as hate speech.[47] It follows that civil liability may be imposed by an EU member state in respect of a failure to remove (certain kinds of) illegal content, even if the platform did not have notice of the content, if a platform's procedure for take-down is found to have been inadequate regarding the kind of content in issue. That is, in effect, to impose a duty of care to take adequate steps to prevent the spread of some kinds of content, such as hate speech—an issue to which I will return.

The notice-and-take-down approach was designed in part to guard against the possibility of overreach. Faced with a stringent duty to take down all prohibited material of which they should have been aware, as well as that which has in fact come to their attention, platforms might respond by censoring large volumes of unoffending material in order to ensure that offending material is not disseminated. We will return to the problem posed by this risk; but for the state to encourage or permit overreach to occur—either in the absence of or facilitated by regulatory intervention—would be, inappropriately, to allow collateral censorship

[44] Article 14 of the Electronic Commerce Directive 2000. European Commission Staff Working Document (2012), 39.

[45] For discussion of the duty of care model, see section 2.3(iii) below, and Victoria Nash (2019). The issue of the right approach to take arises because platforms aim to facilitate the display of content created by others rather than making judgements about what content to post, or not to post, for themselves.

[46] Committee on Standards in Public Life (2017), 35.

[47] *Delfi AS v Estonia* (2015) ECtHR 64669/09. This effectively leaves platforms at the mercy of different understanding of adequacy in different courts in different member states. For discussion see Robert Spano (2017).

to flourish.[48] The danger of collateral censorship emerging through the policy responses from platforms comes, in part, from the sheer scale of uploading to the major platforms. For example, some 500 hours of content is being uploaded by YouTube users every single minute.[49] Against that background, speaking of potential for liability in tort to encourage collateral censorship, a US court has aptly remarked: 'Congress recognized the threat that tort-based lawsuits pose to freedom of speech in the new and burgeoning Internet medium. The imposition of tort liability on service providers for the communications of others represented, for Congress, simply another form of intrusive government regulation of speech.'[50]

However, a simplistic quantitative argument in favour of platform immunity from liability, or from 'hard' regulation, may not do justice to important qualitative arguments about the severity of harm that different kinds of content have the potential to do. The quantitative argument does not fully address the need for preventative steps to be tailored to judgements of the severity (and, say, immediacy) of harm that may be done by allowing certain kinds of content to be posted and to spread. Should we be taking the same permissive approach (or placing online platforms under the same regulatory obligations) with respect to, say, offensive language or images involving adult nudity, as we should with respect to beheading videos, imminent terrorist attacks, and child pornography?[51] This was the question that led the EU Grand Chamber in the *Delfi AS* case to impose what amounted to duty of care on platforms to have adequate, proportionate procedures for removing hate material, whether or not the platform had notice of the material in an individual case.[52] A similar approach to electoral participation information would be fully justified and proportionate, given the threat to civil rights (discussed in Chapter 1) involved. However, bearing in mind the difficult free-speech issues involved in tackling political viewpoint disinformation, it is far from clear that it would be right to apply either a 'notice-and-take-down' or a duty-of-care model to such information.[53]

In that regard, the special importance of discrediting (or ridiculing) political viewpoint disinformation, as a form of counter-measure, should be noted. The great advantage of discrediting and ridiculing—what I referred to in Chapter 1 as 'false claim-shaming'—is that it has a power, in relation to false political information, to take the political sting out of such information (however widely it is spread) that it may lack in relation to other kinds of free-speech abuses. As an example of

[48] See Chapter 1, section 1.1.

[49] https://www.statista.com/statistics/259477/hours-of-video-uploaded-to-youtube-every-minute/ (last accessed 08/06/2021); European Commission (2018a).

[50] *Zeran v America Online Inc* 129 F 3d 327 (4th Circuit 1997).

[51] Victoria Nash (2019).

[52] See text at n. 47 above.

[53] In broad terms, thus, I agree with Irina Katsirea on the need to prioritize the protection of free speech, in the face of the threat posed by 'fake (political) news': see Irina Katsirea (2019). See also Ian Cram (2019).

good practice, in that respect, when asked what plans he had to counter baseless and defamatory allegations that he was a paedophile, President Biden indicated that he has no such plans, and that 'I don't want to get down in the mud with these guys'.[54] It is in that context that one should examine measures less draconian than take-down or the prevention of fresh circulation (reposting or retweeting), such as the attachment to allegedly false information of unreliability warnings.[55] By contrast, it is hard to see how the likely negative effects of race-hate speech, or incitements to engage in terrorism or violence, could ever be adequately countered simply by a mere discrediting or ridiculing of the speech in question. That is why the priority in such cases is take-down or (severe) restriction. As the ECtHR Grand Chamber has indicated:

> in cases where third-party user comments take the form of hate speech and direct threats to the physical integrity of individuals, the rights and interests of others and of the society as a whole might entitle Contracting States to impose liability on Internet news portals if they failed to take measures to remove clearly unlawful comments without delay, even without notice from the alleged victim or from third parties.[56]

However, as we will see in section 2.7 below, at the highest level the UK government has signally failed to draw such distinctions. For example, the House of Lord Select Committee on Democracy and Digital Technologies has said:

> Disinformation, abuse and bullying ... were also identified in our evidence as posing a threat to representative democracy. Disinformation undermines the ability of citizens to have a meaningful conversation about the future shape of society.... Abuse and hate speech can deter people from taking part in public life.[57]

What is contentious about these claims? To begin with, political viewpoint disinformation will only 'undermine' the ability of citizens to have meaningful political conversations if it is very highly pervasive: effectively walling off citizens from access to reliable sources of information. Simply encountering such information, even regularly, cannot be assumed necessarily to have such effects. Even putting that point on one side, the Select Committee fails to provide criteria for what is to count as a 'meaningful' conversation about the future shape of society.

[54] https://www.forbes.com/sites/jackbrewster/2020/05/20/biden-responds-to-obamagate-trump-jr-pedophilia-attacks-i-dont-want-to-get-down-in-the-mud-with-these-guys/?sh=76e62c9753e1 (last accessed 15/04/2021). Of course, President Biden would have had every right to take action for defamation in such a case, but the fact that serving politicians in established democracies tend not to do this is significant.

[55] See the brief discussion of the use of these measures in the case of President Trump, in Chapter 1.

[56] *Magyar TE and Index.hu Zrt v Hungary Application No 22947/13*, Merits, 2 February 2016, para 91.

[57] House of Lords (2020), paras 94–95.

The Select Committee appears to take for granted an elite, rationalistic, or 'high-table-debate' view of what such a conversation must involve, but that is wrong. As argued in Chapter 1, hyper-partisan narratives are perfectly legitimate forms of counterpublic political engagement.

Further, the Select Committee fails to take on board that the contentious issues raised by proposals to censor political viewpoint disinformation are raised in far less stark a form, if at all, when 'abuse and hate speech' (the Select Committee's other examples) are in issue. Disinformation may be used—sometimes justifiably—to provoke more speech. It may, for example, be designed to provoke a statement from a politician about some important matter in relation to which they have remained (culpably or suspiciously) silent.[58] By contrast, intimidation, hatred, and harassment of those engaged in politics, as forms of abuse, involve attacks on an important negative political freedom,[59] the freedom from fear of coming to some physical or psychological harm by remaining politically engaged. This is a freedom far less commonly, if ever, threatened by mere political viewpoint disinformation.[60]

Intimidation, hate, and harassment are 'silencing' techniques. Hate speech, in particular, involves speech supporting someone's (or a group's) inferiority, in virtue of their race, religion, gender, sexual orientation, or a similar protected quality.[61] Like a good deal of partisan political viewpoint disinformation, when used in political contexts hate speech may act as a discrediting technique (as much as a silencing one), but it is nonetheless to be distinguished from political viewpoint disinformation. Hate speech violates an important equality value, in liberal societies, as well as having an impact on the value of (negative) freedom.[62] Political viewpoint disinformation does not *per se* do either of these things, even when it concerns a group rather than an individual. As indicated in the General Introduction, it may very well be that most viewpoint disinformation about (say) particular ethnic or religious groups is motivated by—or liable to cause—hate. In itself, though, that is not a reason to regard the distinction between viewpoint disinformation and hate speech as unimportant, particularly when what is at stake is the legitimacy of criminalizing speech. For example, knowingly spreading a false claim that people from a particular ethnic group have difficulty gaining entry to university is likely to be an example of hate speech.[63] By contrast, knowingly spreading the false claim that religious people are more intelligent than atheists is simply viewpoint

[58] See the discussion in Chapter. Further examples of justified dissemination of disinformation may be found in the judgment in *Zundel v R* [1992] 2 SCR 731.

[59] On freedom from fear and negative liberty, see the discussion in George Crowder (1988). See also Jeremy Horder (2021a).

[60] See the critique of the Law Commission's proposals for reform of communication offences, in Article 19 (2020).

[61] See, for example, Kathleen Mahoney (2009).

[62] Robin Edgar (2010), 127.

[63] For some background figures on this issue, see https://fullfact.org/education/bme-students-oxford/ (last accessed 16/04/2021).

disinformation.[64] Electoral participation disinformation, though, *is* a kind of 'silencing' technique, designed to deny or impede people's right to have their say through voting. For that reason, alongside other speech-based silencing techniques (such as intimidation, harassment, and hate speech) it should be categorized as a harm the threat of which justifies a ban or severe restriction.

Major internet platforms, unlike government bodies across Europe, have long appreciated the importance of such distinctions. So, for example, Facebook's policy on the removal of content includes the view that 'there are some extreme forms of disinformation that we remove from our platform, including disinformation that leads to offline violence and disinformation that leads to voter suppression'.[65] It is absolutely correct to make this equation between speech (including hate speech) that may lead to offline violence and electoral participation disinformation, and it is proportionate to regard take-down (or at the very least, severe restriction) as the appropriate remedy.[66]

2.3 Platform Toleration, Free Speech, and Critical Engagement

(i) Platform speech policies: the case for 'more-speech' solutions

In Chapter 1, I suggested that it was wrong to place restrictions on Donald Trump's false claims on Twitter that the 2020 Presidential election was subjected to fraud on a wide scale. It was wrong, because those claims—baseless though they were—were political viewpoint claims and not electoral participation claims, as those notions were defined in Chapter 1. Of course, for someone in so high a public office to make such claims, without clear and compelling justification, is an abject failure of responsibility to the voting public. However, the question of whether someone in high office betrays that office by disseminating false political viewpoint information is a separate question from the question of whether they should be legally free to engage in such conduct, or be subject to censorship. The issue is whether, and in what circumstances, people (and not just presidents of the USA) should be entitled to post such material and see it spread to and by others.

In that regard, as indicated in the General Introduction, I will be concerned exclusively with 'top-down' initiatives (by government or platforms) to restrict or prevent access to content, or in some other way impact on its spread. In what follows, I am not concerned with 'bottom-up' initiatives, in which, typically, someone

[64] https://neurosciencenews.com/religion-atheism-intelligence-8391/ (last accessed 16/04/2021).

[65] https://about.fb.com/news/2018/10/voter-suppression-policies/; https://ec.europa.eu/digital-single-market/en/news/annual-self-assessment-reports-signatories-code-practice-disinformation-2019.

[66] Indeed, as Facebook itself points out (ibid.), some hate speech is directed at voter suppression, such as a claim that someone of a particular race or religion is unfit to vote or hold office.

with a private law claim to stop the spread of false information seeks to use that claim as a basis for influencing or controlling platform policy in relation to that information. My focus is what platform policies should be developed for general application, whether or not they impact on private law rights and duties. As far as top-down initiatives are concerned, there are a number of possible approaches to false information that it would be helpful to set out, before embarking on further discussion:

(a) False claims are allowed to be made and viewed, and then allowed to spread through user-sharing, and also in accordance with whatever algorithms the platform in question has, for its commercial purposes, set to determine how that occurs.
(b) As in (a), but false claims (or, at least, some such claims) are accompanied by (i) a warning about the unreliability of the claims that is attached to instances of viewing and sharing ('claim-shaming'), and perhaps also (ii) a link to alternative sources of information challenging the claims.
(c) False claims are allowed to be made and viewed, with or without an unreliability warning, but there is a restriction or prohibition on algorithmic spreading, such that sharing can be done only by those who find the material for themselves (whether through search or through others' sharing).
(d) False claims are allowed to be made and viewed, with or without a warning as to their unreliability, but no sharing of any kind is permitted.
(e) The false claims, if made, are taken down and sharing is prevented.

Some initial points should be made. First, the mere fact that algorithmic spreading is likely to work most actively when shocking or outrageous claims and content are the subject matter[67] is not, in itself, a ground for intervention to prevent such spreading. Many mainstream media outlets rely on such claims and content to maintain their own sustainability, perfectly consistently with broadcasting standards.[68] One difference with algorithmic spreading is its inherent intrusiveness, given users' relative lack of choice over platforms to engage with. There is simply not much of a range of platforms (as compared with the range of mainstream media outlets), and so there is limited ability to avoid the impact of algorithmic spreading.[69] Algorithmic spreading poses significant ethical challenges, when what is at issue is dangerous content, such as fake health advice, incitements to

[67] https://www.vox.com/science-and-health/2018/3/8/17085928/fake-news-study-mit-science (last accessed 15/04/2021).

[68] House of Lords (2020), paras 175–178.

[69] One plausible answer to this problem is to insist on a requirement that users actively consent—without adverse penalty—to receiving such content. See, further, on proposals for consent to tracking, in that regard: https://www.theguardian.com/world/2021/jan/28/apple-and-facebook-at-odds-over-privacy-move-that-will-hit-online-ads (last accessed 15/04/2021).

crime or terrorism, hate speech, extremely offensive or degrading content (such as, for example, filming of suicide victims[70]), or when what is at issue is electoral participation disinformation. However, it is suggested that there is no justification for preventing its use in cases of political viewpoint information, because other ('more-speech') measures are more appropriate and less controversial.

What about restrictions on user-sharing? Again, such measures can be justified and proportionate when speech falls within the categories just mentioned (cases of incitement to commit crime or terrorism, dangerous health advice, hate speech, electoral participation disinformation, and so on).[71] However, such measures cannot be justified, I suggest, in cases of political viewpoint disinformation, unless such information is inauthentic as a form of political expression, such as when it is spread for reasons *solely* of economic gain. Even when false political viewpoint information is spread in order to make a commercial gain of some kind, if the user's motives for doing this are mixed (they are partly commercial and partly political) it may be right to do no more than insist in such cases that the commercial interest is clearly and unambiguously declared and visible.[72] Other than in cases where the sole purpose of a communication is to make money, using 'made for gain' as a basis for restricting the creation or spread of political content—whether true, false, or misleading—gives too much scope for discretionary impingement on free political speech.

To share is not necessarily to agree with or endorse. So, if we think that people's engagement in political discussion and viewpoint-sharing has value for its own sake (and the internet provides hitherto unrivalled prospects for the flourishing of this value), then we should be extremely wary about placing restrictions on user-sharing of political viewpoint disinformation. The imposition of restrictions is also a relatively blunt instrument with which to address a false (political viewpoint) information problem, because it is unlikely pay attention to the reasons for user-sharing. Perhaps I want to share false content in order to highlight its falsity and ridicule it, to indicate which well-known individuals appear to have supported it, or (more prosaically) to use it as an example to my students of grammatically poor sentence construction. Such perfectly justified sharing of false information may not count for much in the face of a need to restrict access to, say, false information about how it is best to avoid medical treatment for cancer; but it is another matter

[70] https://www.theguardian.com/technology/2018/feb/02/how-youtubes-algorithm-distorts-truth (last accessed 15/04/2021).

[71] For the proportionality argument, in the case of electoral participation disinformation, see Chapter 1.

[72] Facebook reserves the right to disrupt the spread of (allegedly) false information made for gain: https://www.facebook.com/communitystandards/false_news (last accessed 15/04/2021). In itself, this commitment is too ambiguous to evaluate in any detail. However, Facebook does require paid-for political advertising to be labelled as such. Similarly, Google makes it clear that paid-for political content must make clear the commercial element to the content: 'When an advertisement appears in a medium containing news or editorial matter, it should be presented in such a way as to be readily recognizable as a paid-for communication or labelled as such': Google (2019), 11.

where false or misleading political viewpoint information is concerned. That leaves us, in the latter cases, with solution (b): 'claim-shaming', by the attachment of warnings that a claim being made may be false or misleading, coupled with links to (supposedly) more reliable sources of information. This is the solution that best exemplifies Justice Brandeis's famous claim that the best remedy to counter false speech is 'more speech'.[73] That makes it the most important remedy in these cases, from a free-speech perspective.

Clearly, some of the objections to monitoring and control of political viewpoint disinformation inspired by rationalistic thinking, discussed in Chapter 1, may apply just as much to decisions made by platform moderators about claim-shaming as they do to decisions about take-down or restriction on viewing and sharing. Who is to decide which claims are to be subject to unreliability warnings, and on what grounds? It is easy to imagine, in that regard, the political leanings of those on oversight or moderating panels and boards, and the bodies they listen to, becoming a focus for activist struggle.[74] Google's YouTube, for example, relies in part on the BBC in deciding whether or not to flag up the potential unreliability of election and health content.[75] Whilst that might satisfy many as to the objectivity of the decision-making involved, it would only deepen the suspicions of others (albeit a minority).[76] What standards of evidence and what kind of procedures—including procedures subsequently to detach warnings, in appropriate cases—should be adopted in such cases? A 'soft' regulation approach to these kinds of issues requires platforms to draw up robust sets of community guidelines—ideally, following a standard code of practice—to deal fairly and effectively with user complaints, take-down policies and the like.[77] The questions relating to claim-shaming, just asked, ought to be answered in such guidelines.

Internet platforms have sought to increase the sophistication with which they try to verify sources and hence justify claim-shaming. For example, Facebook has claimed that, in dealing with false information of various kinds:

> Today we have 56 (fact-checking) partners in 45 languages ... Our program works by identifying content to be reviewed by our fact-checkers through a combination of technology and human review. Our machine learning models identify links to

[73] See Chapter 1, section 1.6(i).

[74] https://www.telegraph.co.uk/technology/2020/05/06/facebook-will-rue-left-wing-oversight-board-appointments/ (last accessed 08/06/2021).

[75] https://www.cnbc.com/2020/09/24/youtube-expands-fact-checking-feature-for-video-searches-to-europe.html (last accessed 28/06/2021). On Facebook's Oversight Board, see Kate Klonick, (2020) 129 Yale Law Journal 2232.

[76] See https://reutersinstitute.politics.ox.ac.uk/risj-review/bbc-under-scrutiny-heres-what-research-tells-about-its-role-uk (last accessed 08/06/2021).

[77] See further Kate Klonick (2018).

articles which might be false and we can use the model predictions to prioritize the links we show third-party fact-checkers.[78]

In that regard, though, the need for rethinking of guidelines became plain, in the way that platforms handled the false information being circulated by Donald Trump during the 2020 Presidential election. As we saw in Chapter 1, having wrongly done little or nothing to provide an adequate and consistent 'more-speech' counterbalance to his false election claims in the crucial period before the election, the major platforms then together rounded on him only after the election.[79]

In the present context, more important than the detail of such guidelines—for example, ought an unreliability warning to be attached before the posting user has had a chance to object?—is an issue of principle lying behind such detail. There is an obvious distinction between preventing or restricting access to allegedly false or misleading political viewpoint information—the issue addressed in Chapter 1—and allowing such access whilst seeking to spark or influence critical judgement on it. Steps taken to prevent or restrict access, in the case of political viewpoint disinformation, trigger the objections to censorship and denial of free speech set out in Chapter 1, not least a lack of concern and respect for the speaker *qua* speaker and their (potential) audience. By contrast, claim-shaming leaves intact respect for the speaker's right to speak unhindered, and the unrestricted right of the (potential) audience to hear. Instead, a different issue arises. Claim-shaming involves demeaning the speaker, by denying him or her what might otherwise be a prima facie moral right to have a claim considered on its unadorned merits.[80] There is or may be an implicit element of belittling in having an unreliability warning attached to one's posts (although for some, no doubt, it could become a much sought-after badge of honour).

However, it seems right to suggest that the prima facie moral right just mentioned can be lost, when someone persistently makes a variety of false claims, or constantly repeats such a claim without responding to evidence contradicting it. In such cases, no wrong is done when an unreliability warning is attached to the claim(s). It follows, first, that in cases where a particular individual (or organization) persistently makes false claims, an internet platform is entitled to reverse—and may be required to consider reversing—the prima facie position, by automatically attaching unreliability warnings to material uploaded by the user (in various guises, including 'sock puppets') until such time as the user ceases to engage

[78] https://transparency.fb.com/en-gb/features/how-fact-checking-works/ (last accessed 16/11/2021).

[79] https://www.bbc.co.uk/news/technology-55571291 (last accessed 15/04/2021);https://www.theverge.com/2020/11/6/21552471/trump-twitter-restricted-false-election-claims-moderation (last accessed 15/04/2021).

[80] This prima facie right is reminiscent of the old notion of 'natural' honour which is, as described by sixteenth-century Italian writer Romei, 'grounded upon a secret supposition, that man is good, if there appear nothing to the contrary': Annibale Romei (1598), part III.

in the practice. Second, even when it is not the user's own efforts but algorithmic spreading, or third-party sharing, that repeats a false claim, this can in some circumstances count as 'constant repetition' of the claim: if, for example, the user has failed to make reasonable efforts to take down their own post. Accordingly, one may lose the prima facie moral right to have one's (false) claims taken at face value, if—as every user is aware—their claims may be subject, over time, to automated or third-party sharing if they make them public.[81]

More generally, it is important to bear in mind that there is a crucial difference between the belittling involved in attaching warnings to false claims, and the belittling involved in, say, hate speech. The former is a side-effect of an intrinsically valuable attempt to reconcile a commitment to freedom of speech with a commitment to honour the pursuit of truth. The aim is to encourage audiences to engage in evaluation of claims they encounter, rather than just accept or endorse (allegedly) false assertion. By contrast, the latter is a directly intended attempt to make someone seem and feel small, to make them seem and feel something less than their fellow citizens. Nonetheless, we should acknowledge the shadow of disrespect that inevitably falls on someone whose political viewpoint assertion is subject to claim-shaming. Side-effects still matter, morally, even though it is for some purposes important to distinguish them from intended effects.[82] For that reason, I will briefly say something about how the practice of claim-shaming, through the attachment of unreliability warnings and links to material contradicting the claims, can be understood within the framework of a theory of toleration.

(ii) The case for moral and legal toleration of political viewpoint disinformation

What is toleration? Suppose politicians and activists do little or nothing to deter lying, because they have become indifferent to it, or would like to lie and mislead themselves when it suits them. So, they avoid condemning lying or misleading for fear of being accused—surely, far worse!—of hypocrisy. If so, then we have what might be called 'toleration in practice' of lying, but there is no *attitude* of toleration towards it.[83] In a broad sense (refined below), an attitude of toleration exists, in relation to some activity, when someone (a) with the power to constrain, deter, or to in some other way detrimentally affect that activity (by damaging criticism, for example), (b) believes that they ought to permit the activity to continue without the

[81] Obviously, it follows that if one is permitted to, and does, opt out of automated or user-sharing, then these remarks do not apply, and there is no basis for attaching an unreliability warning to one's claims.

[82] See the discussion in, for example, A. P. Simester (1996), ch. 4.

[83] See Bernard Williams (2005), 128. In what follows, I rely substantially on Williams' account of toleration.

exercise of one or more such powers on their part, even though the person (c) disapproves of the activity or otherwise thinks that it is wrong.[84] In Chapter 1, I made what was in effect a general case for an attitude of toleration towards lies and misleading statements coming under the description of political viewpoint disinformation. I will not repeat those arguments. More important to the present context is the relationship between toleration as a (broad) moral outlook and toleration as a (narrow) political doctrine.[85]

In modern Western liberal democracies, a version of the moral outlook is the outlook typically associated with the public relationship between different mainstream religions. In public fora, whilst each religion obviously regards the others as in some crucial respects wrong, each will generally prefer to concentrate on the defence and practice of its own faith narrative, rather than seeking openly to disparage or *a fortiori* limit the scope for the development of, the counter-narratives of other religions and their adherents. Indeed, mainstream religions tend to go out of their way publicly to respect the development of other faiths. That is to adopt the moral outlook on toleration. By contrast, in their private dealings, individual members of particular religions may adopt an attitude shaped more narrowly by tolerance as a political doctrine, rather than by tolerance as a moral outlook. What does that involve? As Bernard Williams puts it, speaking of toleration as a political doctrine:

> [W]e should do everything we decently can to persuade [someone] to change his ways and to discourage other people from living like him. We may ... discourage as many people as we can from thinking well of him so long as he lives in this way. However, it is not appropriate that the power of the state be used in this way.[86]

Unlike toleration as a moral outlook, toleration as a political doctrine is a theory of state action that does not bind and need not guide private individuals and groups respecting their personal attitudes. So, the pursuit of tolerance as a political doctrine is consistent with the moral isolation and shaming of those living the disapproved form of life. Accordingly, whilst publicly endorsing both the political doctrine and the moral outlook of toleration, in their private conduct—for example, when guiding children and family members—some members of a particular religion may in practice adhere only to the narrow political doctrine. They may acknowledge the appropriateness of the legal freedoms of those who do not share their faith, but nonetheless actively discourage those close to them from

[84] This understanding of toleration is a refinement of Bernard Williams' claim that, 'T]he sphere of toleration has to be one in which the agent has some very strong view on a certain matter; thinks that people with conflicting views are wrong, and thinks at the same time that, in some sense, those others should be allowed to have and express those views: Bernard Williams (2005), 130.

[85] Bernard Williams (2005), 131.

[86] Bernard Williams (2005), 131.

association with the latter (whose belief and practices they may disparage or cast doubt on). Naturally, other members of the same religion may take a different private attitude, one that manifests not just respect for the legal doctrine of tolerance but also a tolerant moral outlook. They may respond to, say, a family member's interest in or association with another religion by seeking simply to encourage the family member to take a reflective (as well as heartfelt) approach to the matter, and to make choices that are fully informed. I will now seek to show how these considerations are relevant to the present context, and how the final approach just discussed (the moral outlook) is the best way to deal with political viewpoint disinformation.

(iii) Platform responsibilities, toleration, and the pursuit of truth

The argument of Chapter 1 was that liars or truth-distorters about viewpoint politics should be left free from state coercion to make their false or misleading claims, and their gullible audiences should likewise be left to listen to (and spread) those claims. That approach is perfectly compatible with the vigorous construction—including by state agencies—of truth-reliant narratives, and the rejection of narratives based on false content.[87] What, though, is the right approach for private individuals, groups, and bodies with politics-related responsibilities, such as the responsibility platforms have for moderating online political content?

To begin with, there is the question of harm prevention. There is little or no scope for political toleration of harms such as hate, intimidation, harassment, and the like.[88] Indeed, at a political level, the state is under a duty to take steps to prevent such harms rather than tolerate them, and internet platforms may also be under a similar duty (in relation to speech content that may lead to these harms). To provide an analogy, suppose a lawful visitor comes onto my land and leaves behind a dangerous structure, which I discover but do nothing (or very little) to inspect, to render safe, or to remove. Other lawful visitors to my land then access the structure, and suffer harm when, say, poison leaks from the structure. In English law, as owner of the land, I am regarded as under a duty to take steps to make the structure safe for visitors, or to remove it, even if I was responsible neither for the presence of the structure on my land nor for the presence of the visitors.[89] Platform responsibility for dealing with dangerous content posted by others may be justified in a similar way.[90]

[87] See the discussion in Chapter 1.

[88] Bernard Williams (2005), 129: 'Towards murder and child abuse, one is not supposed to hold back one's disapproval, or one's disposition to deploy the law, in the name of toleration.'

[89] *Jolley v Sutton London Borough Council* (2000) 2 Lloyds Rep 65 (HL). The facts given in the text here are very loosely based on the facts of this case.

[90] See, further, the discussion of proposed changes to English law in section 2.7 below.

Further, there is no reason for platforms to adhere to the doctrine of moral toleration either, respecting such harms. Platforms should feel at liberty to call out hate, harassment, and the like, and to make clear the unacceptability of such speech; and they do. Twitter, for example, unequivocally states: 'We are committed to combating abuse motivated by hatred, prejudice or intolerance, particularly abuse that seeks to silence the voices of those who have been historically marginalized. For this reason, we prohibit behaviour that targets individuals with abuse based on protected category.'[91]

Beyond harm prevention, though, what other duties are owed by platforms? There is no doubt that some significant private organizations or individuals—such as charities, landowners operating quasi-public spaces,[92] or internet platforms—can have public responsibilities beyond harm-prevention attached to the way they conduct themselves. For example, even though Facebook is a private body, a German court has argued that the platform is under a duty to honour the value of freedom of expression because it is 'a public marketplace for information and exchange of views'.[93] This analysis links the nature of duties owed by a publicly significant private body to the nature of the function it performs. That is not wrong, but as a way of explaining the source of duties on such bodies it may unduly narrow their range. For example, a privately owned shopping mall that is open to the public does not hold itself out as a 'public marketplace for information and exchange of views', but it might nonetheless be found to be under a duty to respect freedom of expression, in the rules that it devises to govern the conduct of shop owners or visitors.[94] A publicly significant private body—one that has a genuinely public dimension to its operation—may be, simply in virtue of having that dimension, under a duty to respect a range of (civil) rights, including freedom of expression.

To establish that a platform must respect freedom of expression takes us only so far. It establishes that a platform must adopt the political doctrine of toleration with respect to speech: avoiding (the coercive threat of) bans that impinge on political speech so long as harm or outrage to decency and so on, are not in issue. However, it seems likely that platforms must also adopt the moral outlook on toleration, when political viewpoint disinformation is in issue. It would not, for example, be appropriate for a platform itself to criticize a speaker for the (false) political views expressed in posts, or to suggest that other platform users avoid reading particular posts because the speaker espouses certain views or peddles certain theories. Equally, no one suggests that internet platforms' public responsibilities extend,

[91] https://help.twitter.com/en/rules-and-policies/hateful-conduct-policy (last accessed 16/04/2021).

[92] See e.g. the decision of the German Federal Constitutional Court, applying the doctrine of horizontal effect to airports and shopping malls: BFG Case 1 BvR 699/06 Fraport [2011].

[93] Von Constantin Van Lijnden, 'Facebook, Geben Sie Redefreiheit', *Frankfurter Allgemeine Zeitung* (6 September 6 2018), http://www.faz.net/aktuell/feuilleton/medien/facebook-darf-nicht-eigenhaendigbeitraege-loeschen-15773244.html (last accessed 16/04/2021), cited by Imara McMillan (2019), 283.

[94] See e.g. *Pruneyard Shopping Center v Robins* 447 U.S. 74 (1980).

simply in virtue of the position that they occupy, to becoming active campaigners on behalf of evidence-based politics, and against conspiracy and false-narrative politics. That kind of campaigning is for groups who use the platforms. There appears to be, in other words, a duty of political viewpoint impartiality on platforms (political 'net neutrality'), associated with the moral outlook on toleration.[95]

Platforms have never, of course, been entirely neutral with regard to the spread of political content. As indicated earlier, they may try, for example, to benefit from algorithm design that favours sensational or attention-grabbing content—including political content—likely to be viewed more frequently.[96] However, this kind of activity is consistent with political viewpoint impartiality.[97] It reflects the market decision-making of a commercially minded private body, just like headline selection in the mainstream media, rather than politically partisan motives. Let us assume that there is a duty of political viewpoint impartiality or neutrality on platforms, in accordance with the moral outlook on toleration. That is important, because it would be inconsistent with a morally tolerant outlook to place restrictions on the posting—or on the spread through sharing—of political viewpoint disinformation, which rules out policies (a), (c), (d), and (e) above in respect of such disinformation. Does an embrace of moral toleration mean that platforms, private bodies creating and maintaining a quasi-public sphere, should play no role in relation to political viewpoint speech on their platforms?

As indicated at the outset, it is not politically partisan to show commitment to universal values, including not only freedom of speech but also the pursuit of truth. Adherence to the political doctrine of toleration may rule out a platform's use of take-down or restriction threats, to deter the spread of political viewpoint disinformation. Adoption of the moral outlook on toleration may rule out active campaigning by platforms for evidence-based politics, along with any engagement by them in criticizing individual peddlers of false or misleading political viewpoint content. However, that still leaves option (b) above, as a way of showing commitment to the value of truth. Option (b) involves the attachment of unreliability warnings to allegedly false political viewpoint content (together with links to alternative sources of content), whilst leaving users free to post and share the content. Option (b) honours the value of truth by inviting users to engage critically with content they encounter online, and to explore alternative viewpoints. The same goes for a

[95] A difficult question, not further addressed here, is whether platforms should remain neutral with regard to the voting process more generally. Twitter, for example, has become involved with the promotion of voter registration in the USA: https://blog.twitter.com/en_us/topics/company/2018/be-a-voter-2018.html (last accessed 09/06/2021).

[96] See section 2.1 above; https://www.theverge.com/interface/2019/4/11/18305407/social-network-conservative-bias-twitter-facebook-ted-cruz (last accessed 16/04/2021).

[97] There is, in any event, some evidence that right-leaning pages on Facebook received about the same number of interactions as left-leaning pages, indicating that sensationalization may not favour the political right, at least in terms of engagement: https://www.theverge.com/interface/2019/4/11/18305407/social-network-conservative-bias-twitter-facebook-ted-cruz (last accessed 16/04/2021).

policy of making allegedly more reliable and trustworthy sources of information easier to find.[98] In that regard, lest there be doubt about the effectiveness of unreliability warnings, in the official response to the consultation on the Online Harms White Paper,[99] the UK government noted that, in March 2020, Facebook displayed warnings on roughly 40 million posts related to COVID-19, based on 4,000 articles reviewed by independent fact checkers; and when users saw the warnings, in 95 per cent of cases they did not go on to visit the original content.[100]

Having said that, it is probably neither possible nor desirable (it smacks of zealotry) for platforms actively to pursue all false or misleading political viewpoint content across their domain, with a view to attaching unreliability warnings to it. Is it, then, possible to devise principles for prioritizing this task? Here are two possibilities. First, where a source or viewpoint information ought by its nature to be highly trustworthy (such as a government source), but that trust has been betrayed, then there is a case for an assertive policy of claim-shaming. Donald Trump's use of his Twitter account is a case in point. With 88 million followers, he tweeted 16,000 times whilst in office, and of his 100 most popular posts 36 contained election-related falsehoods.[101] Second, there is a case for saying that a policy of claim-shaming should be actively pursued in cases where false viewpoint claims are reasonably believed to be 'inauthentic'. For example, false viewpoint claims are inauthentic if (i) it is not made plain they are computer-generated viewpoints, perhaps created through the use of an intelligent chat-bot or hijacked Facebook page to form a manufactured or fake viewpoint; (ii) they are given the false appearance of popularity and influence through the use of bot-generated 'likes' and shares; (iii) their source is misrepresented; or (iv) they are posted for reasons solely of financial gain. In relation to (i) and (ii), one report has claimed that, in the 2016 Presidential election, around 20 per cent of political debate and discussion on social media was generated by about 400,000 social media bots.[102]

A concluding remark on foreign sources is apposite here. Even though, as argued in Chapter 1, there is normally no greater case for restricting overseas sources of political viewpoint disinformation than there is for domestic sources of such disinformation,[103] it is perhaps particularly a risk, in relation to sources emanating from 'hostile' states, that their claims may involve inauthenticity.[104] Inauthenticity

[98] A requirement of the EU's Code of Practice on Disinformation: https://ec.europa.eu/digital-single-market/en/code-practice-disinformation (last accessed 16/04/2021).

[99] Department for Digital, Culture, Media and Sport, and Home Office, Online Harms White Paper: Full government response to the White Paper (2020).

[100] Department for Digital, Culture, Media and Sport, and Home Office (2020), para 5.32.

[101] https://www.cnbc.com/2021/01/13/trump-tweets-legacy-of-lies-misinformation-distrust.html (last accessed 16/04/2021). Some of these falsehoods were examined in Chapter 1.

[102] https://www.cloudflare.com/en-gb/learning/bots/what-is-a-social-media-bot/ (last accessed 16/04/2021).

[103] See the discussion in Chapter 1, section 1.3(i).

[104] See also the discussion in Chapter 1, section 1.3(i).

is, of course, an issue addressed by internet platforms. For example, in its community guidelines Facebook says:

Do not:

- Use multiple Facebook accounts or share accounts between multiple people.

...

- Conceal a Page's purpose by misleading users about the ownership or control of that Page.
- Engage in, or claim to engage in, inauthentic behaviour, which is defined as the use of Facebook or Instagram assets (accounts, pages, groups, or events), to mislead people or Facebook:
  - about the identity, purpose, or origin of the entity that they represent,
  - about the popularity of Facebook or Instagram content or assets,
  - about the purpose of an audience or community,
  - about the source or origin of content.[105]

However, the mere fact that a source of political viewpoint disinformation is anonymous is not necessarily an indication that its content is inauthentic, and that it is hence a candidate for an unreliability warning. That issue is addressed further in the next section.

2.4 Inauthenticity and the Issue of Anonymity

It is obviously perfectly possible for printed sources and broadcasts to involve manufactured content (a newspaper column could be created by artificial intelligence), and to disseminate discourse anonymously. Even so, as indicated in section 2.1 above, the lack of binding standards governing the posting of such content on internet platforms has made the issues ones of particular concern in that context. In this section, I briefly consider the problem of the potential inauthenticity of content, and the issue of anonymous posting. I will hence be discussing a version of a First Amendment distinction between what the US Supreme Court calls 'content-neutral' (but I will call 'source-based') and content-based grounds for intervention.[106] A ban or restriction on a post which fails a transparency test, as when it is anonymous or when it is not revealed that it was generated by a bot,[107] is a source-based measure. The same is true of the imposition of a requirement on

[105] https://www.facebook.com/communitystandards/inauthentic_behavior (last accessed 16/04/2021).

[106] https://www.mtsu.edu/first-amendment/article/937/content-neutral (last accessed 16/04/2021).

[107] See Protection from Online Falsehoods and Manipulation Act 2019 (Singapore), s. 8, discussed in section 2.5 below.

social media platforms to maintain a register of those who disseminate election-related 'partisan' or advertising messages.[108] Likewise, a ban on the publication of political messaging coming from outside a jurisdiction, or on anonymous posting, is a source-based measure.[109] By contrast, as the term makes clear, a content-based legal measure is focused on the substance of what someone has said. We find such measures in law when their target is defamatory statements; holocaust denial; threatening, insulting, and hate-filled speech; or incitements to engage in violence or terrorism; as well as false political statements.[110]

In some cases, a legal measure aimed at false political statements is in part source-based, and in part content-based. Frequently—an issue discussed in Chapter 1—measures that are partly source-based and partly content-based are aimed at false claims considered to be part of an attempt by one jurisdiction to influence political developments in another.[111] Closer to the concerns of this chapter, recent legislation in Singapore, discussed further in section 2.5 below, makes it an offence to generate a false claim (the content-based element), if the claim is disseminated by a bot (the source-based element).[112] More generally, in policing political statements, it is in one sense easier to justify source-based control and regulation than it is to justify content-based measures of that kind. The basis of a purely source-based ban is usually a relatively straightforward factual finding: for example, that someone putting up, further distributing, or sponsoring a post is based outside the jurisdiction; that 'they' are in fact a bot; or that they have failed to reveal their identity or location.[113] So, the intervention of courts or regulators to impose or police source-based restrictions may seem less politically charged and controversial than when such bodies must police content-based restrictions.[114] Going beyond this point about process, Kate Jones has argued that 'the right to freedom of expression does not entail that techniques for the manipulation of attention, such as use of bots and trolls, must be free of restriction'.[115] 'Trolling', of course, may involve threats, hate speech, or other harms justifiably made subject to criminal sanctions

108 Canada Elections Act 2000 (as amended), s. 325(2) and (3). In English law, the name and address of the printer and promoter must be included on printed election material: Representation of the People Act 1983, s. 110; Political Parties, Elections and Referendums Act 2000, s. 143.

109 See e.g. Electoral Commission (2018), para 26. See also the ban proposed on foreign political advertising via the internet, in the Honest Ads Act (USA) 2019: https://www.congress.gov/bill/116th-congress/senate-bill/1356 (last accessed 16/04/2021). See further, Representation of the People Act 1983, s. 92.

110 See e.g. Liberty, https://www.libertyhumanrights.org.uk/human-rights/free-speech-and-protest/speech-offences (last accessed 16/04/2021).

111 See the discussion in Chapter 1. For a defence of such banning measures, see Joshua S. Sellers (2018).

112 In Singapore law, the significance of the false claim having been generated by a bot is that, to justify insisting on its suppression, it will not be necessary—as it would in other cases—to show any likelihood of harm resulting therefrom: see section 2.5, below.

113 As in the case of English law governing requirements for printed election material: see Electoral Commission (2021).

114 For more detailed discussion of this point, see Chapter 4.

115 Kate Jones (2019), 45 and 53.

on content-based grounds.[116] In the case of online abuse of politicians, in a sample of 4.2 million tweets collected during the 2019 UK General Election campaign, abusive messages sent to candidates were found in nearly 4.5 per cent of all replies, compared to just under 3.3 per cent in the 2017 General Election.[117] If compelling online platforms to reveal the identity of 'trolls' (a source-based measure) serves to deter the dissemination of material that is harmful in terms of its content, then so much the better.[118]

What, though, about the use of bots to generate or disseminate false political information? The Singaporean approach, criminalizing this kind of activity, is clearly acceptable in the case of electoral participation information, but more controversial in the case of political viewpoint information. If one accepts the case made in Chapter 1 for tolerating the generation and spread of false political viewpoint information, then what is the objection to its generation or spread through novel means, such as bots? The root of the problem is not the false nature of the content, but a potential lack of 'authenticity' accompanying its generation and spread. To discover that a celebrated 'novel' was in fact miraculously generated by the random hammering on computer keys of a monkey is to find reasons for a profound change in the nature of one's critical appreciation of the work.[119] Similarly, to discover that provocative and perhaps persuasive (false) political viewpoint content was in fact generated by editing software creating a 'deepfake', or by a chat-bot mashing together opinions and related facts through the use of keyword search, is to have reason to think very differently about that viewpoint content. Even if it were practical to restrict or ban artificial (false) content generation of this kind, legislatures and platforms should not seek to do so. Experimenting, through the use of artificial intelligence, with the auto-generation of political viewpoint content is (subject to concerns about defamatory, criminal, or hate content, and so forth) a legitimate use of a free speech right. Seeking to amplify one's message—whether through the use of bots or otherwise—in a manner consistent with the right of others to do likewise, is legitimate for the same reason.[120] However, we have no reason to tolerate the *concealment* of such practices, even if we should not be prohibiting them. As the EU Code of Practice on Disinformation rightly insists, platforms should 'establish clear marking systems and rules for bots to ensure their activities cannot be confused with human interactions'.[121] Political organizations, in particular, should be forced to be more honest about their use of bots to amplify their messages, or to

[116] See Maeve Duggan, 'Online Harassment' (2014), https://www.pewresearch.org/internet/2014/10/22/online-harassment/ (last accessed 16/04/2021).

[117] Genevieve Gorell et al. (2019).

[118] See e.g. the Harmful Digital Communications Act 2015 (New Zealand), s. 22.

[119] For this example, see Arthur Eddington (1928), 72.

[120] For a defence of the use of bots, under the First Amendment, see Madeline Lamo and Ryan Calo (2019). For further discussion, focusing on deepfakes, see Cass Sunstein (2021), 115–19.

[121] European Commission Code of Practice on Disinformation (2018b), 1.v, considered further in section 2.8 below.

generate the appearance of influence through fake likes and shares.[122] Here is one important example of how to legislate on the basis of this principle.

In California, it is now a form of unlawful competitive behaviour to use a bot via a major online platform to communicate or interact, with a view to influencing an election vote, without disclosing (in a manner that is 'clear, conspicuous, and reasonably designed') that the communication or interaction is through a bot:[123]

> 17941. (a) It shall be unlawful for any person to use a bot to communicate or interact with another person in California online, with the intent to mislead the other person about its artificial identity for the purpose of knowingly deceiving the person about the content of the communication in order to incentivize a purchase or sale of goods or services in a commercial transaction or to influence a vote in an election. A person using a bot shall not be liable under this section if the person discloses that it is a bot.

As Senator Robert Hertzberg said, in introducing the legislation, 'as long as bots are properly identified to let users know that they are a computer-generated or automated account, users can at least be aware of [what] they are interacting with and judge the content accordingly'.[124]

What about the vexed question of anonymous posting? An initial issue to address concerns cases in which an author is not known because they are masquerading as someone else, in order to gain the trust of an audience, or to further their reach in that regard. In simple cases of identity theft or deception, there is no reason for any jurisdiction or platform to tolerate such behaviour. The UK government initially suggested in 2019 that any code of conduct governing the taking down of content by social media companies must include steps to deter 'users who deliberately misrepresent their identity to spread and strengthen disinformation'.[125] However, when later responding to consultation in 2020, it drew back from making any specific recommendation on the issue. That seems unduly pusillanimous.[126] There is a difference between inventing a persona, for the purposes of online (political) engagement—which is simply a form of anonymity, discussed below—and pretending to be another person. One can be honest—or compelled by a platform to be honest—about the anonymous adoption of a fictitious persona, which will put one's audience on notice that they should not necessarily take statements at face value. By contrast, it seems obvious that intentionally to pretend to be another

[122] Kate Jones (2019), 53.

[123] See the Bolstering Online Transparency Act 2018, SB 1001. For criticism, see https://www.wired.com/story/law-makes-bots-identify-themselves/ (last accessed 18/04/2021).

[124] Cited at: https://www.jdsupra.com/legalnews/not-even-bots-are-safe-from-california-31858/ (last accessed 18/04/2021).

[125] HM Government (2019), para 7.28.

[126] Department for Digital, Culture, Media and Sport, and Home Office (2020), para 2.35 (box 8).

person, in order to gain an audience, or to gain credibility with an audience, should not be regarded as the exercise of any kind of free speech right on the platform in question. In that regard, it is worth noting that, in a political election context, in August 2018, Twitter removed approximately 50 accounts misrepresenting themselves as members of various state Republican parties.[127]

Turning to the broader question of anonymity, it is obvious that individuals and political organizations—whether domestic or based overseas—may perfectly understandably wish to conceal their identity when articulating political claims.[128] They may have well-justified fears of government censorship and prohibition, or of retaliation from violent groups and individuals. As the UN Special Rapporteur has argued, anonymity provides individuals with

> a means to protect their privacy, empowering them to browse, read, develop and share opinions and information without interference and enabling journalists, civil society organizations, members of ethnic or religious groups, those persecuted because of their sexual orientation or gender identity, activists, scholars, artists and others to exercise the rights to freedom of opinion and expression.[129]

Compelling would-be speakers to reveal their identity, in such circumstances, may thus unacceptably confront them with a free-speech dilemma (further considered).

As against this, of course, there is the risk that the protection of anonymity will remove any moral deterrent from posting defamatory and inflammatory content. Further, anonymity could provide cover for official (government, or party) sources to denigrate their political opponents whilst maintaining a public façade of political decency and restraint. The House of Lords Communications Committee has suggested a 'middle way', for the purposes of criminal liability, according to which someone would have to identify themselves in order to register with an internet platform, but would be permitted to post anonymously thereafter.[130] The Communications Committee recognized, though, that this was controversial, and that seems particularly true when we are concerned with false political viewpoint information. If, for example, someone fakes statistics to bring to the world's attention the extent of human rights abuses in their country (because, say, no official statistics are kept), should they not be able to maintain anonymity in order to protect themselves and their family? If, as the Communications Committee suggested,

[127] https://blog.twitter.com/en_us/topics/company/2018/an-update-on-our-elections-integrity-work.html (last accessed 18/04/2021).

[128] For discussion, see Carissa Véliz (2019).

[129] UN Special Rapporteur (2015); Privacy International (2019), para 43. See also Article 19 (2015).

[130] House of Lords Select Committee on Communications, *Social Media and Criminal Offences* (2014–15), para 54. This approach facilitates a model of liability for defamation, in respect of anonymous posting, under which the complainant must first pursue the person making the alleged defamatory statement, and only if they are unreachable because a platform has permitted them to post anonymously would the platform itself face possible liability: see Ronen Perry and Tal Zarsky (2015) 162.

platforms insist—or if they are compelled to insist—that someone reveals their true identity to the platform before being permitted to post anonymously, this must be accompanied by an explicit power for the platform to refuse to reveal the name of the person, if there is a clear public interest in their remaining anonymous.

In that respect, giving priority to freedom of political speech means accepting that there is only a public interest in securing the identification of online agents posting political viewpoint disinformation in a limited range of cases. An example might be where political viewpoint information involves an invasion of private rights, as long as the law that makes the offending statement an instance of rights-violation is itself consistent with human rights jurisprudence.[131] Other examples might be where there is a threat of harm inextricably linked to the spread of the viewpoint disinformation (including election participation disinformation), or where a post has links to official state or political party sources. That might seem to amount to an unduly tolerant attitude to the irresponsible spread of false or misleading political viewpoint information. However, it should be kept in mind that protecting such a freedom is consistent with a platform policy of insisting that some kind of 'potentially unreliable information' warning is displayed prominently in all anonymous posts. As indicated earlier, in seeking to promote a flourishing free-speech culture, solutions encouraging critical engagement on the part of the audience are generally to be preferred to solutions inhibiting the freedom of speakers to engage with an audience.

2.5 The Authoritarian Approach to Political Disinformation: Singapore

As Bradshaw and Howard rightly observe,[132] authoritarian jurisdictions use the internet and social-media technologies to enhance their control over information, and their use of legislation to counter 'disinformation' may be an important dimension to that.[133] What differentiates, in that regard, authoritarian disinformation strategies from the strategies at work in democracies? In democracies, as far as the spread of disinformation is concerned, concerted disinformation campaigns tend to arise mainly at election times,[134] and will not involve official state action to propagate such disinformation. By contrast, in authoritarian regimes, political viewpoint disinformation (and sometimes participation disinformation) is likely to be employed by state officials themselves on an ongoing basis: often, to target individuals such as dissidents or journalists as well as citizens at large. In

131 See, further, the discussion in Eric Barendt (2009) 141.
132 Samantha Bradshaw and Phillip Howard (2018), 25.
133 The discussion in this section is based on Jeremy Horder (2021b).
134 Samantha Bradshaw and Philip Howard (2018), 28–9.

democracies, targeting of this latter kind may be (routinely) engaged in by political parties, and regime-friendly media outlets, bloggers, and so on, but will nonetheless be outside the scope of morally permissible state action, either directly or through agents.

Turning to strategies to counter political disinformation, we will see in due course that there will be overlap in important respects, in terms of what is legally proscribed or permissible, between authoritarian regimes, and militant democratic regimes which employ coercion in the service of rationalistic thinking (which tends to favour traditional or established political individuals and groups).[135] In that regard, two key points of overlap are the extension of the criminal law to cover defamation of public officials or election candidates, and the grant of powers—backed by the threat of coercion—to require the suppression of false political viewpoint information on the grounds of the alleged harmfulness of its false content. By contrast, democratic states which reject militant forms of democracy will generally not use the criminal law—or other forms of coercion—to protect officials or candidates from political viewpoint disinformation, whilst vigorously countering (through coercion if need be) electoral participation disinformation and other equivalent harmful wrongdoing, such as engagement in intimidation and hate speech.

An authoritarian response to viewpoint disinformation, whether or not confined to election periods, will typically be characterized by a number of features, including one or more of the following:

(a) The strengthening and broadening of coercive powers to deter and punish the dissemination of disinformation, including powers over social media platforms on which such information appears, without any attempt to prefer source-based measures to content-based measures.
(b) Giving power to the executive to invoke procedures or to determine what information has false or misleading content, perhaps even confining such powers to the executive,[136] both in and beyond election times.
(c) Making a focus (in some instances, an exclusive focus), in law or in enforcement policy, alleged disinformation concerning government actions or the actions of other state officials, whether or not in relation to elections.
(d) Making high, often disproportionate levels of punishment available.
(e) The use of state-sponsored 'trolling', targeting dissidents and journalists.[137]

It is important to note that at least the first of these features, and to some extent the next two, will also be found in some liberal legal systems influenced by militant

[135] On 'militant' democracy, see Chapter 1, section 1.1(iii), and section 2.6 of this chapter.
[136] Samantha Bradshaw and Philip Howard (2018), 26–7.
[137] Ibid. 28, speaking of Bahrain, Turkey, Azerbaijan, and Russia.

democratic thinking (this is discussed later), even though liberal regimes will generally eschew the fourth and fifth features.

I will take as exemplar of an authoritarian approach a controversial recent set of legal changes in Singapore. I focus on Singapore because in 2019 it introduced measures to counter disinformation that have a number of authoritarian characteristics. This is in spite of Singapore's status as a constitutional republic with a Westminster style of representative, democratic government based on the separation of powers, with a constitutional guarantee of freedom of speech (Article 14).[138] Under section 7 of Singapore's Protection from Online Falsehoods and Manipulation Act 2019, 'a person must not do any act in or outside Singapore in order to communicate in Singapore a statement knowing or having reason to believe that ... it is a false statement of fact', when that communication of the statement, amongst other effects, is considered likely to:

(i) be prejudicial to the security of Singapore or any part of Singapore;
(ii) be prejudicial to public health, public safety, public tranquility, or public finances;
(iii) influence the outcome of an election to the office of President, a general election of Members of Parliament, a by-election of a Member of Parliament, or a referendum;
(iv) incite feelings of enmity, hatred, or ill-will between different groups of persons; or
(v) diminish public confidence in the performance of any duty or function of, or in the exercise of any power by, the Government, an Organ of State, a statutory board, or a part of the Government, an Organ of State or a statutory board.

There are a number of important points to note about this provision, which in essence contains all the first four features (a) to (d) of authoritarian responses listed above.[139]

The first point is that the provision applies not only to content known to contain a false statement of fact, but to cases in which the maker has 'reason to believe' that their communication involves a statement that is false. Clearly, this greatly extends the scope of the provision, giving both individuals and media outlets far less control over and knowledge of the extent of their potential liability. Second, the communication of a false statement is not, as such, prohibited,[140] unless it is likely

[138] Asean Law Association (2018), ch. 2. On a constitutional-theoretical map, Singapore could perhaps be located between a genuine Westminster-style democracy, and a fully authoritarian regime that has only a 'facade constitution': Gábor Attila Tóth (2017), para 19.

[139] For example, an individual found guilty under section 7 can be imprisoned for up to five years: section 7(2).

[140] Unless, by virtue of section 8, it stems from a 'bot', in which case communication of the false information—or enabling another person to communicate it—is itself sufficient to amount to an offence.

to have one of the effects mentioned in the criteria listed in (i) to (v) above; but these criteria are both broad and vague. In truth, the criteria should be seen less as a restraint on the scope of the prohibition, and more as an encouragement to the prosecution to target certain kinds of conduct. Third, the prohibition draws no distinction between cases in which (say) one person communicates—perhaps relatively informally—to only one other person or to a small number of other people, and cases in which a more wide-ranging and systematic attempt is made to spread disinformation widely or to a identified target audience. The need to satisfy one of conditions (i) to (v) might appear to rule out low-level informal communications, but that is far from clear. More liberal jurisdictions have sought to confine draconian online disinformation laws—such as Germany's Network Enforcement Act 2017 (considered below)—to platforms with millions of registered users. Fourth, Part 3 the 2019 Act provides for an alternative to prosecution, namely the issuing of a 'correction direction' or a 'stop communication direction', measures extending even further than section 7. As the names imply, such directions require the person subject to them either to stop communicating the allegedly false information, or to declare a given communication by that person to be false and to publish a 'correction' in a form specified.[141] As well as applying to persons outside as well as within Singapore (as long as the communication is in Singapore), the 'stop communication' and 'correction' directions can be issued to and will bind the person who communicates the false statement of fact *irrespective* of whether they knew or had reason to know that the information was false.[142] In that regard, we should note the broad-ranging definition of 'false statement of fact' given in the definition section of the 2019 Act:

(a) a statement of fact is a statement which a reasonable person seeing, hearing or otherwise perceiving it would consider to be a representation of fact; and
(b) a statement is false if it is false or misleading, whether wholly or in part, and whether on its own or in the context in which it appears.

There is little or no scope here for the courts to rein in the operation of the 2019 Act by interpreting 'statement of fact' in a restrictive way.

Particularly notable, in this respect, are the evaluative elements to the determination of whether a statement is false, namely whether it is 'misleading' and whether it is false or misleading 'in context'. This definition deprives the determination of whether a statement of fact is indeed 'false' of what would otherwise be an important element of objectivity, making it hard for speakers to determine whether they have 'reason to know' that a statement is false. By this means, the section 7 offence is turned into one of, in effect, strict liability and (what is more) liability dependent as

[141] The full extent of what may be required is set out in sections 11 and 12.
[142] Ss.11(4) and 12(4).

much on how a minister evaluates a statement as on anything done by the speaker. Finally, it is a government minister—not an independent body—who, by virtue of section 10(1) may require that a competent authority[143] issues a stop-communication or a correction direction, politicizing the process in an authoritarian way.[144] For example, in November 2019, the Singapore Ministry of Finance issued a correction direction to a member of the opposition Progress Singapore Party (Brad Bowyer), on the grounds that one of his Facebook posts contained 'false statements of fact, and undermines public trust in the Government'.[145] Bowyer had alleged that the government effectively controlled investment decisions taken by commercial companies. Bowyer complied with the correction direction. Almost needless to say, breach of a stop-communication or correction direction, without reasonable excuse, is a criminal offence, punishable by up to 12 months' imprisonment.

These developments must be set alongside three already well-known features of Singaporean law that make it more authoritarian than democratic, in this area of law. First, defamation is a criminal offence under section 499 of the Singapore Criminal Code, if D makes or publishes any imputation concerning any person, intending to harm, or knowing or having reason to believe that such imputation will harm, the reputation of such person.[146] Second, there is the fact that the right to free speech under Article 14 of the Singaporean Constitution may be overridden not only when it is 'necessary' but also when it is 'expedient' to do so, in the interests of security, public order, friendly relations with other countries, or morality (Article 14(2)).[147] Liberal-democratic countries do not regard expediency as a legitimate ground for restricting freedom of speech in pursuit of such ends. Third, there is the fact that no greater licence is given to criticize public figures at elections times, either in criminal law or in the civil law of defamation. Section 14 of Singapore's Defamation Act 2014 expressly rules out the application of qualified privilege to allegedly defamatory statements made by or one behalf of election or presidential candidates. Further, the courts have held that there is no defence of qualified privilege in defamation law applicable to criticism of public figures

143 A statutory board appointed by the minister under section 6, and required to give effect to minister's instructions.

144 Although s. 17 permits an appeal to the High Court against the issuing of a direction, this may occur if and only if the person affected has first asked the minister to withdraw the direction and been refused. No time scale is given for the minister to respond, making the issuing of a direction a particularly powerful weapon at election times. In section 2.7, we will see how, albeit in a more moderate way, the proposals for change to UK law are similarly politicized through the involvement of ministers.

145 https://www.channelnewsasia.com/news/singapore/brad-bowyer-facebook-post-falsehood-pofma-fake-news-12122952 (last accessed 08/06/2021).

146 Although there is an exception for good-faith expression of opinions respecting the conduct and character of another touching a 'public question'. See, further, https://www.theguardian.com/world/2021/mar/25/singapore-blogger-ordered-to-pay-nearly-us100000-damages-to-pm-for-facebook-post (last accessed 25/03/2021).

147 For criticism, see Michael Hor (1992), 547–8.

respecting the performance of their duties, even when the offending statements are made at a political rally.[148]

By way of contrast, in countries governed by Article 10 of the ECHR, although (controversially) offences involving defamation of public officials have been held to be consistent in general terms with rights to freedom of expression, the European Court of Human Rights has found such consistency hard to establish when political speech is involved. In *Lingens v Austria*,[149] in considering false claims made about politicians, the European Court of Human Rights observed that, 'freedom of political debate is at the very core of the concept of a democratic society which prevails throughout the Convention'.[150] Authoritarian regimes will typically reject such an approach, because it threatens the element of political domination at the heart of such regimes—regimes in which citizens are in law and practice subject to the will of those in authority, and both legally and politically insecure in so far as they seek to challenge that subjection.[151] For authoritarian regimes, control over 'disinformation' is a dimension to their control over the power narratives for that jurisdiction, such as control of what political issues are on the agenda,[152] which are not to be determined through free citizen engagement.[153]

2.6 Authoritarian Liberalism? Germany

The spread of false political content on the internet, and its impact on—as well the participation in it of—the public at large, has reawakened militant democratic ('establishment') fears that, as some American sociologists sought to demonstrate in the 1980s, 'political elites are more tolerant than the masses and ... the mass public is dangerously intolerant in at least some areas'.[154] In Germany, the *Netzwerkdurchsetzungsgesetz* (NetzDG) 2017, the Network Enforcement Act 2017, has sought to establish an uneasy compromise between a commitment to free speech and an authoritarian drive to suppress disinformation, in the (militant democratic) interests of preserving a rationalist culture of debate.[155]

Freedom of expression in Germany is protected by Article 5(1) of the Basic Law: 'Everyone shall have the right freely to express and disseminate his opinion by speech, writing, and pictures and freely to inform himself from generally accessible

[148] *Jeyaratnam Joshua Benjamin v Lee Kuan Yew* (1992) 1SLR(R) 791 (CA).
[149] *Lingens v Austria* (1986) 8 EHRR 407.
[150] Ibid., para 42.
[151] See further, European Audiovisual Observatory (2019).
[152] See Steven Lukes (1974).
[153] See Gábor Attila Tóth (2017).
[154] Jennifer Hochschild (1986), 386–7, summarizing the main claim of Herbert McClosky and Alida Brill (1983), 1.
[155] See Chapter 1, and e.g. Matthias Kettermann (2019). For the political background to the introduction of the 2017 Act, and a more sympathetic view of its provisions, see Thomas Wischmeyer (2018).

sources. Freedom of the press and freedom of reporting by means of broadcasts and films are guaranteed. There shall be no censorship.' However, in interpreting Article 5(1), it has been held that the propagation of 'incorrect information' is not an interest that merits protection,[156] although the threat of sanctions must not be used in such a way as to chill freedom of expression.[157] In that regard, the 2017 Act builds on an implied permission to make network platforms responsible for controlling content, in certain circumstances (where there is knowledge of the content, and an absence of diligence in responding appropriately to that knowledge), first created by section 10 of the Telemedia Act (Germany) 2007:

> Service providers shall not be responsible for the information of third parties which they store for a recipient of a service, as long as
> 1. they have no knowledge of the illegal activity or the information and, as regards claims for damages, are not aware of any facts or circumstances from which the illegal activity or the information is apparent, or
> 2. upon obtaining such knowledge, have acted expeditiously to remove the information or to disable access to it.[158]

The 2017 Act imposes on major social networks (those with over 2 million registered users in Germany)—other than those providing essentially 'journalistic or editorial' content[159]—an obligation to remove (i.e. delete or block) a range of prohibited content. Knowledge of such content (triggering the applicability of the provisions) is liable to come from users' complaints, respecting which section 3 of the 2017 Act requires that networks provide 'effective and transparent procedures for handling complaints about unlawful content.' In the case of 'clearly violating' content, it must be removed within 24 hours, and in the case of 'violating' content, within seven days; but there is no indication of how the line between these categories is to be drawn, and no defence that the network platform was acting in good faith in drawing it in a particular place subsequently found to be inappropriate. A failure to comply in an individual case will not lead to a fine, but systematic and persistent management failures that have permitted violating content to appear may lead to an administrative penalty of up to 50 million euros (in the case of corporate bodies and legal persons).[160] Under section 3(3) of the 2017 Act, a network platform can itself avoid the seven-day deadline to act, if (i) there needs

[156] BVerfGE 85, 1 (1991) ('Critical shareholders' case'), discussed in Irina Katsirea (2019), 179.
[157] BVerfGE 54, 208 ('Böll case'), discussed in Irina Katsirea (2019), 179.
[158] See the discussion in Article 19 (2017), and in Stefan Theil (2019), 46. On the inspiration of militant democratic thinking behind the Act, see Heidi Tworek (2019).
[159] These terms are not defined in the 2017 Act. For criticism, see Article 19 (2017), 12–13.
[160] See Network Enforcement Act: Regulatory Fining Guidelines (2018); Stefan Theil (2019), 48. See further, the discussion of the approach in England and Wales in section 2.7 below.

to be an investigation into the truth or falsity of a claim, or (ii) a procedure has been put in place whereby an independent self-regulatory body, accredited by the Ministry of Justice, has been established by a platform to make a binding decision on whether to delete or block content.[161] Facebook, which had not at that point set up an independent body to meet the regulatory challenge, was fined 2 million euros under the 2017 Act for providing incomplete transparency reports.[162]

How effective might such a self-regulatory body (or a platform acting on its own behalf) be in drawing up a clear and robust human rights jurisprudence relating to content removal? The difficulty here is the controversial nature of the content covered. 'Violating' content includes content amounting to or involving the incitement of offences under some 22 statutes in the German Criminal Code. Included are such offences as hate crime, child pornography, and other content harmful in analogous ways;[163] but 'violating' content under the 2017 Act goes further. It covers content amounting to such offences under the German Criminal Code as criminal insult (Article 185), malicious gossip (Article 186), criminal defamation (Article 187), and treasonous forgery (Article 100a).[164] These are controversial extensions, liable to draw platforms directly into major free-speech controversies better suited to resolution in the courts. For example, as Stefan Theil observes, platform policy on 'pro-life' advocacy will be engaged because 'one might attract criminal liability for defamation when describing a specific abortion doctor's work as 'babycaust' even though this does not fall under most definitions of hate speech: it is not based on attributes such as race, religion, ethnic origin, sexual orientation, disability, or gender.'[165] The 2017 Act expects network platforms to implement political censorship policies in relation to such content, and more broadly in relation to supposedly false political claims falling under the headings of criminal insult, gossip, or defamation.[166]

In spite of the inherently controversial character of such censorship, there is to be no prior *official* determination of whether the content in question in fact contravenes one of the 22 statutes to which the 2017 Act applies. So, for example, network platforms will themselves be required to give consideration, in appropriate cases,

[161] An example of such a body is the Voluntary Self-Regulation of Digital Media Service Providers: https://www.fsm.de/en/netzdg#N1_2 (last accessed 09/06/2021).

[162] Stefan Theil (2019), 48; Ben Wagner et al. (2020). Facebook has an independent Oversight Board, to which complaints about content can be taken, if the matter is not resolved satisfactorily internally. Facebook will regard itself as bound by the Board's decisions. The Oversight Board can request that its decisions in individual cases are applied to similar cases, and may also issue policy recommendations to Facebook: https://oversightboard.com/ (last accessed 19/04/2021).

[163] Studies show that platforms remove 70 per cent of all hate speech notified to them within 24 hours: Matthias Ketterman (2019), 2.

[164] Although criminal defamation of the President of the Federation (Section 90); and criminal defamation of the state and its symbols (Section 90a) were excluded.

[165] Stefan Theil (2019), 44. See *Hoffer and Annen v Germany* (Application nos. 397/07 and 2322/07), 20 June 2011.

[166] The European Court of Human Rights regards the development of such measures as consistent with Article 10: *Delfi AS v Estonia* (Application No. 64669/09), 16 June 16 2015.

to whether the person posting allegedly violating content possessed the relevant fault element for the offence, and—in a case where the complaint is about content containing an allegedly false claim—to whether there is an appropriate factual basis to the content.[167] There is, then, plenty of scope for activists to launch contrived or blatantly false allegations of contraventions by their opponents, in the hope that the content will then (wrongly) be taken down.[168] Faced with the prospect of sanctions for under-blocking, the rational network platform must inevitably incline towards over-blocking, impinging on Article 10 rights.[169] What makes that especially serious is that platforms are obliged to remove content that might be viewed anywhere in the world where a German citizen might view it; not only when viewing of the content is likely to be confined within German borders.[170] In the light of such concerns, a law adopted by the French National Assembly and designed to replicate the 2017 Act was struck down by the French Constitutional Court as inconsistent with the right to free speech: '[The legislation] undermines freedom of expression and communication in a way that is not necessary … and proportionate'.[171]

Internet platforms are now to be the modern equivalent of the 'political police' envisaged in the late 1930s by Karl Loewenstein (who coined the term, and defended, 'militant democracy') whose task it was to be to defend democratic ideals in Germany, 'even at the risk and cost of violating fundamental principles'.[172] Inevitably, this kind of indirectly enforced self-censorship will lead to the taking down of what is merely challenging or provocative political content,[173] even though section 3(1) provides that social networks with over 2 million registered users must provide a complaints procedure for those whose content is taken down (as well as for those who wish to complain about content).[174] Under the 2017 Act, not only is there no prior determination by a court of what counts as 'violating' content, but it is also left to network platforms to decide how to balance the right to free speech against the risk that content will be found to be violating.[175] As Ian

[167] Article 19 (2017), 16 and 20. In the case of an allegedly false claim, section 3(2)(3)(a) of the 2017 Act requires the person who posted the content to respond to the complaint before the network platform takes its decision.

[168] Thomas Kasakowskij et al. (2020).

[169] For this argument, see Wolfgang Schultz (2018); Imara McMillan (2019).

[170] Imara McMillan (2019), 257.

[171] https://www.conseil-constitutionnel.fr/decision/2020/2020801DC.htm (last accessed 19/04/2021).

[172] Karl Loewenstein, 'Militant Democracy and Fundamental Rights II' (1937) 31 American Political Science Review 638, 656–7, cited by Jan-Werner Muller (2012), 1120.

[173] Heidi Tworek (2019), 3. However, for a contrary view, see Stefan Theil (2019), 49.

[174] See Heidi Tworek (2019). A social network receiving more than 100 complaints in a year must publish its internal moderation practices. For Facebook's development of its complaints procedure, see https://about.fb.com/news/2019/09/oversight-board-structure/ (last accessed 19/04/2021).

[175] Heidi Tworek (2019), 3: 'The NetzDG process does not require a court order prior to content takedowns nor does it provide a clear appeals mechanism for victims to seek independent redress.' See also Article 19 (2017), 15.

Cram observes, for commercial platforms, the priority for shareholders will inevitably be the avoidance of legal penalties.[176] Consequently, as Imara McMillan argues: 'Because of the punitive nature of the fines, social media companies are incentivized to err on the side of caution and remove any content that is reported. This includes unlawful content, but also clearly satirical tweets parodying actual illegal content and heated, but ultimately harmless, comments.'[177]

Almost needless to say, under the 2017 Act there is no penalty for taking down too much inoffensive content. That creates a significant tension between the policy pursued by the 2017 Act and the principle famously set down by the German Federal Constitutional Court in *Lüth*, that there must be 'a presumption in favour of freedom of speech in all areas, and especially in public life'.[178] It can certainly be argued that these downsides must be set against the importance of ensuring that, to give a graphic example, live streaming of murder, rape, torture, or child abuse is taken down immediately, and any complaints about that action dealt with after the fact. What, though, is the justification for including alongside such a possibility the requirement to take the same action, in the same way, against insults hurled at politicians?[179] If states insist on criminalizing such activity—which they ought not to—they should at least require that censorship, restriction, and sanctions are dealt with through court processes.

In 2018, Twitter received 264,818 complaints in Germany regarding content, blocking 10 per cent of content in consequence, and YouTube received around 215,000 complaints, blocking 27 per cent of content in consequence.[180] A troubling feature of these statistics is that, taking the actions of Twitter, Facebook, and Youtube together, 19.65 per cent of reports by official bodies led to content being removed or restricted, whereas only 17.87 per cent of all reports submitted by private persons resulted in such action being taken.[181] This raises questions about the criteria used in each instance as a justification for taking the decision to remove content.[182] In its disaggregation of take-down statistics, Google indicated that 8,695 complaints involving defamation or insult led to content being taken down because of breach of Google's community guidelines, and 3,206 complaints led to defamatory or insulting content being taken down because the content was adjudged to breach the 2017 Act (but not the guidelines).[183] Theil's research

176 Ian Cram (2019), 125.

177 Imara McMillan (2019), 255.

178 Bundesverfassungsgericht, Case 1 BvR 400/51 ('Lüth case').

179 Imara McMillan (2019), 280.

180 Matthias Kettermann (2019), 3. However, most of these complaints involved a breach of the platforms' community guidelines rather than the 2017 Act: Heidi Tworek (2019), 5. Imara McMillan has different figures for YouTube, recording 58,300 complaints rather than 215,000: Imara McMillan (2019), 260.

181 Thomas Kasakowskij et al. (2020), part 3.

182 Heidi Tworek (2019), 5.

183 Tworek describes the 2017 Act, in consequence, as a 'community guidelines enforcement law': Heidi Tworek (2019), 7. Insult-related offences under the 2017 Act were the most common kind

reveals that in 2018–19, Facebook logged 500 NetzDG reports, with deletion of content following in 159 cases (roughly 33.8 per cent of cases), and Twitter logged 256,462 reports of which 23,165 led to the deletion of content (roughly 9 per cent of cases).[184] Hate speech and 'political extremism' are the most common reason given by platforms for content restriction or removal (41.2 per cent of cases), with defamation and insult being the reason in 19.8 per cent of cases.[185] These categories are comfortably ahead of any others, in percentage terms. Google (incorporating YouTube) received 45,190 complaints about defamation and insult in all compared to, for example, 27,308 complaints about sexual content.[186] Some 57 per cent of Google's removed content fell into the category of defamation.

Nonetheless, Theil argues that 'the vast majority of reports do not result in deletion of content. This is problematic for critics of online regulation as a cornerstone of their argument relies on demonstrating that overblocking is more than a theoretical possibility.'[187] In his view, sophisticated systems of online regulation can not only address online harms, but may also, 'have a civilizing influence on online expression instead of foreshadowing the end of a free and open discourse'.[188] If so, then achieving that influence comes at a considerable cost. A comparative analysis conducted by Kasakowskij and his colleagues in 2020 showed that Germany is restricting more content than even Russia or Turkey.[189] Moreover, 80 per cent of content complained about led to no action being taken by the platforms, suggesting that the 2017 Act is posing a risk of creating a culture of denunciation, and providing a means illegitimately to put one's (political) opponents on the defensive.[190] Against that background, it is hard to see the justification for the German Parliament's recent decision to require platforms to send details about users who post allegedly illegal content directly to the police.[191]

I suggest that Theil's pious hope does not do full justice to the arguments against militant democratic justifications for employing coercive pressure, in cases involving false political viewpoint content.[192] In that regard, as I will argue below when analysing the proposals for the UK, there is a need for a 'tiered' approach that tailors legal-regulatory steps to the nature of the harms or risks in issue. As

offence complained about to Facebook (460 complaints), with Twitter reporting 75,925 insult-related complaints. By 2019, complaints had dropped in overall numbers by around 15 per cent.

[184] Stefan Theil (2019), 50.
[185] Thomas Kasakowskij et al. (2020), part 3.
[186] Heidi Tworek (2019), 5–6.
[187] Stefan Theil (2019), 50.
[188] Ibid.
[189] Thomas Kasakowskij et al. (2020), part 3.
[190] Ibid.
[191] https://www.bundestag.de/dokumente/textarchiv/2020/kw25-de-rechtsextremismus-701104 (last accessed 19/04/2021)
[192] See also Ian Cram (2019), 138, discussing the potential for suppression of controversial political speech in online platforms' in-house or 'community' guidelines themselves.

I suggested above, there is no justification for subjecting network platforms to the same governance structures, and risks of sanctions, in respect of the toleration of false or misleading political viewpoint speech, as in the case of toleration of child pornography or incitements to engage in terrorist violence. The problem is that the figures show that the threat of sanctions is playing a role in Germany, albeit a minor one, in influencing major social media platforms in the way they seek to disassociate themselves from the dissemination of false political information.[193] So, the concern remains that, along with genuinely harmful content, provocative and challenging political content is also being unwittingly suppressed. As Ian Cram eloquently puts it: 'by excluding all but the rational, consensus-seeking, civilized speaker, deliberative accounts of political pluralism impede the creative power of the demos. In consequence, very little contestatory discourse is let in.'[194] It is significant, in that regard, that there have been several high-profile deletions of content posted by German politicians, as we will see.

Moreover, making public the use of the relevant provisions to suppress speech in controversial cases may have the opposite effect to that intended: usage may highlight the content to a wider audience ('to refute is also to reiterate'[195]) and, ironically, enhance its credibility amongst those disposed to support the speaker. In cases of hate speech (or other justifiably prohibited kinds of speech), this may be a sideeffect of suppression with which we ought to live. For example, in the case of prominent AfD politician, Beatrix von Storch, her Twitter account was temporarily suspended when she responded to a police department decision to post a New Year greeting in Arabic by accusing the department of, 'appeas[ing] the barbaric, Muslim, rapist hordes of men.'[196] This is hate speech and restrictive action against von Storch was clearly justifiable. However, widespread media coverage of this incident, including the post's content and its potential illegality, seemed to confirm fears that taking action might more widely publicize and legitimize von Storch's hate speech, in a way simply ridiculing or criticizing it would not have done.[197] Whatever one's views on that difficult issue, though, it is quite wrong to allow the same dilemma to arise in the case of insults and false political viewpoint disinformation. In such cases, there is no justification for taking censoring or restrictive action in the first place. For example, when Alice Weidel, leader of the AfD party in Germany, was referred to in a Huffington Post article as a 'filthy Nazi swine', Facebook immediately blocked the comment from German IP addresses.[198] Further, a court ordered Facebook to ensure that the comment could also not be

[193] Although, as Heidi Tworek points out, it is unclear to what extent a take-down leads to suppression of the false information, insult, or other offending content, or simply brings greater attention to it through its publication elsewhere: Heidi Tworek (2019), 7.

[194] Ian Cram (2019), 140. See also Article 19 (2017).

[195] J.-B. Jeangène Vilmer (2018), 169.

[196] Imara McMillan (2019), 263.

[197] See Heidi Tworek (2019), 4.

[198] Imara McMillan (2019), 265.

viewed by people in Germany using a VPN, threatening a fine of up to 250,000 euros or imprisonment for two years.[199] Yet, given the context in which it appeared, this was simply a highly provocative political insult (inclusive of false viewpoint information). Even allowing for special sensitivity in Germany in relation to insults of this nature, it is simply mistaken to treat such cases in the same way as hate speech, incitements to commit offences, electoral participation disinformation, and so on. With this problem in mind, France's Institute for Strategic Research (Ministry for the Armed Forces) and Policy Planning Staff (Ministry for Europe and Foreign Affairs) counselled against Government heavy-handedness, on the grounds that: 'As one of the roots of the problem is distrust of elites, any 'top down' approach is inherently limited. It is preferable to champion horizontal, collaborative approaches, relying on the participation of civil society.'[200] Accordingly, only one of their 50 recommendations (recommendation 12) is concerned with the creation of prohibitions on the dissemination of false information.[201]

One danger in an authoritarian-liberal response to digitally propagated political viewpoint disinformation is that it becomes, in effect, almost indistinguishable in form (even if intended to operate differently in practice) from the response of the more fully authoritarian regimes whose 'fake news' practices liberal regimes are, ironically, seeking to counter.[202] There is another danger. By giving government agencies, or even courts, the power to prohibit and punish the dissemination of political viewpoint disinformation, states will diminish what ought to be a 'republican' commitment to nurture citizens who, rather than being cowed by or automatically deferential to authority, 'can speak their minds, walk tall among their fellows, and look others squarely in the eye. They can command respect from those with whom they deal, not being subject to their arbitrary interference.'[203]

2.7 'Your Safety is Our Priority'? The UK Approach

(i) 'Duty is what one expects from others': the Online Safety Bill

In its 2019 White Paper on online harms,[204] the UK government made clear its intention to carve out a middle way between, on the one hand, a libertarian guarantee of free speech, and on the other, an authoritarian system permitting the suppression (*ex post facto*) of substantive content deemed by a government regulator

[199] Ibid.
[200] J.-B. Jeangène Vilmer (2018) 172.
[201] J.-B. Jeangène Vilmer (2018), 173.
[202] See European Audiovisual Observatory (2019).
[203] José Luis Martí and Philip Pettit (2010), 38.
[204] HM Government (2019).

or court to be false or misleading.[205] However, the result has been a draft law which, first, probably does too little to prioritize the (urgent) removal of content liable to lead to the most serious types of harm. Second, left unclear is the importance to be attached to freedom of speech more generally, in devising policies for content restriction and removal. Moreover, the approach to disinformation, and in particular to the dissemination and spread of such information at elections times, remains opaque at key points. Ironically, under the government's approach, the only instance in which the provision of false information may clearly and unequivocally lead to the commission of a criminal offence has nothing to do with instances in which users post disinformation on an internet platform. It is, instead, an offence committed against the communications regulator, when a 'user-to-user service' itself provides false information in response to a request made by the regulator in the discharge of its duties.[206]

Under the UK approach, internet providers of user-to-user services , large and small, will be bound by statutory duties of care, in relation to a range of harms.[207] All such providers will be under five universal duties. These are an 'illegal content risk-assessment duty', an 'illegal content duty', a 'duty about rights to freedom of expression and privacy', a 'reporting and redress' duty, and a 'record-keeping and review' duty.[208] Beyond these universal duties, all providers whose services are likely to be accessed by children will come under additional care duties (not further considered here) similar to those just described but focused specifically on children. Additionally, the biggest providers of the broadest range of services (providers of 'Category 1 services') will do so under an extended range of duties, concerned with conduct that is legal but potentially harmful. These are (i) the duty to conduct adult risk-assessments, (ii) the duty to protect adults' safety online, and corresponding to these duties not only (iii) the duties about rights to freedom of expression and privacy (see above), but also (iv) the duty 'to protect content of democratic importance', and (v) the duty 'to protect journalistic content'.[209] The regulator (Ofcom) is obliged to provide codes of practice in relation to the discharge of all of these duties,[210] the broad overarching aim of which is to ensure that providers' systems and processes in relation to the discharge of their duties are 'effective and proportionate' and that their controls over access and use are 'adequate'.[211]

[205] For a penetrating critique, see Victoria Nash (2019). The quotation in this section's heading—'Duty is what one expects from others'—is from Oscar Wilde, *A Woman of No Importance* (1893).

[206] Online Safety Bill, clause 72(4).

[207] HM Government (2019), para 35; Online Safety Bill, clauses 5–13. Relevant harms include hate speech, encouragement to engage in terrorism, harassment, offences against children, children accessing inappropriate content, and encouragement to commit suicide or self-harm.

[208] Online Safety Bill, clauses 7, 9, 12, and 15 respectively.

[209] Additionally, there are reporting and redress duties, in relation to these additional obligations. See Online Safety Bill, clauses 7 and 11–15.

[210] Online Safety Bill, clause 29.

[211] Online Safety Bill, clause 30.

As Victoria Nash has suggested, the UK government's approach can be understood as a 'manifesto for government-led platform governance':[212] soft regulation,[213] in which 'states design a choice architecture without enforcing a particular choice'.[214] A provider will be regarded as having complied with a code of practice bearing on its duties to provide effective and proportionate systems and processes, etc, if it takes the steps recommended by the regulator to that end;[215] however, the provider is free to take other steps to comply with any code of practice, as long as those steps meet the objectives of the code of practice and ensure that the provider fulfils its relevant duties.[216] The provider's duties are enforceable by Ofcom, which in appropriate cases of breach may impose a fine of up to the greater of £18 million or 10 per cent of the provider's qualifying worldwide revenue,[217] even though—most importantly—individual breaches of the codes of practice will not in themselves give rise to any kind of court or tribunal-based liability.[218]

If that structure of co-regulation sounds like an appropriately balanced and principled relationship between platforms and the state, then we should note that government has not been able to resist the temptation to reserve the right to intervene, albeit indirectly, on a political basis. In a development worthy of any self-respecting authoritarian regime, the Secretary of State is empowered—Singapore style[219]—to direct the regulator to modify a Code of Conduct if they believe a modification is required, 'to ensure that the code of practice reflects government policy', as well as in cases where they believe a modification is required 'for reasons of national security or public safety'.[220] It is, to say the least, disappointing that government has seen fit to place so little trust in the regulator itself to take the measure of government policy at any given point, and make its own independent judgement of what action (if any) is required and when. I now turn to the nature of the user-to-user service provider's duties.

(ii) The illegal content duties

As far as 'illegal content' is concerned, there is an overarching duty on providers, under clause 9(2), 'to take proportionate steps to mitigate and effectively manage

212 Victoria Nash (2019), 23.

213 See e.g. OECD, 'Soft Law', https://www.oecd.org/gov/regulatory-policy/irc10.htm (last accessed 19/04/2021).

214 Jean-Baptiste Jeangène Vilmer (2018), 170. This approach can be described as one of 'co-regulation', as opposed to self-regulation: see Michèle Finck (2017).

215 Online Safety Bill, clause 36.

216 Online Safety Bill, clause 36.

217 Online Safety Bill, clause 85(1).

218 Online Safety Bill, clause 36(7).

219 See section 2.5 above.

220 Online Safety Bill, clause 33. It should be noted, though, that the Secretary of State cannot recommend that any 'particular step' is adopted in a code of practice for providers: clause 33(2).

the risks of harm to individuals', in so far as such risks have been identified in a (recent) 'illegal content risk assessment' of the service. In discharging their illegal content risk assessment duties, under clause 7(8), all platforms must have specific regard to the following kinds of content:

(i) terrorism content,
(ii) CSEA content,[221]
(iii) 'priority' illegal content,
(iv) other illegal content.[222]

In relation to (iii), under clause 9(3) providers must use 'proportionate systems and processes' designed to:

(a) minimise the presence of priority illegal content;
(b) minimise the length of time for which priority illegal content is present;
(c) minimise the dissemination of priority illegal content;
(d) where the provider is alerted by a person to the presence of any illegal content, or becomes aware of it in any other way, swiftly take down such content.[223]

In that regard, 'priority' illegal content is content specified as such in regulations to be created by the Secretary of State (under clause 44(1)), taking into account (a) the prevalence on the internet service of the content amounting to an offence, (b) the degree of risk of harm being caused to individuals by the presence of that content on the service, and (c) the severity of the harm in question.

It seems obvious that platform policy on harm ought to be guided by a graduated approach. In other words, effort and resources should be directed according to the seriousness of harm, and the degree of risk that it may occur, if particular content is posted, remains visible, and is spread. Does the UK government's approach achieve this? Arguably, only to a limited extent. Let it be granted that all terrorist and CSEA content warrants the highest degree of priority, when it comes to measures aimed at preventing the dissemination of such material. What about the thousands of other offences in English law? We should start by noting the politicization of the process by which illegal content is to be prioritized. The decision is

[221] Content involving child sexual exploitation or abuse.

[222] Although not all illegal content falls within this residuary heading. A criminal offence must be an offence against one or more individuals: clause 41(4).

[223] As far as duties (a) to (d) are concerned, Graham Smith notes that, 'duties (a) to (c) would have fallen foul of the ECommerce Directive's Article 15 ban on imposing general monitoring obligations on hosting providers. Section 9(3) thus departs from 20 years of EU and UK policy aimed at protecting the freedom of expression and privacy of online users': 'Harm Version 3.0: the draft Online Safety Bill' (2021), https://www.cyberleagle.com/2021/05/harm-version-30-draft-online-safety-bill.html (last accessed 21/06/2021).

for the Secretary of State, who (as indicated above) is already permitted to require that codes of conduct reflect 'government policy'. Whilst, in making the decision, the Secretary of State is obliged to take into account factors such as the seriousness of the harm, the prevalence of the offence, and the degree of risk, the Secretary of State is not confined to consideration of these factors: political policy may be factored in here too. It would be better for such decisions to be a matter for the regulator, in consultation with relevant bodies, with the Secretary of State empowered to request a review by the regulator. Even if one puts the potential for politicization on one side, a significant difficulty about assessing whether there will be a principled, graduated approach to illegal content is posed by the lop-sided nature of the requirements binding on platforms.

On the one hand, the approach to priority illegal content is dominated by value judgements the significance of which is unlikely to become apparent for some time: platforms must have 'proportionate' systems and processes, designed to 'minimize' the extent to which priority illegal content is posted, viewed, and spread. That approach might be considered over-generous towards platforms, even though it seeks to avoid the widespread adoption of a 'block first and ask questions later' platform policy. In relation, for example, to the more serious kinds of illegal content, why is there not a duty to go beyond mere 'minimization' of the posting and spread of such content and, in so far as is reasonably possible, employ proportionate measures to *eliminate* such content?[224] The duty to 'minimize' the most serious kinds content is really a kind of 'fall-back' duty, a secondary duty that comes into play only if what ought to be the primary duty—the duty to prevent such content being posted, and to remove it if it is—cannot reasonably be discharged. As John Gardner has aptly explained (albeit in a different context): 'the secondary obligation is a rational echo of the primary obligation, for it exists to serve, so far as may still be done, the reasons for the primary obligation that was not performed when its performance was due.'[225]

Under a properly graduated or tiered approach to online harms, the secondary duty of 'minimization' would apply only in special cases. It might be applied only to harmful content which is not only so widespread but also so difficult (in many cases) to identify and categorize correctly, that to impose an unqualified obligation to prevent it being posted at all, or to remove it all, would be hopelessly unrealistic as well as disproportionate. Hate or abusive content—in so far as it crosses the boundary into offences against individuals—might fall into this category. To illustrate why, we should note that from January to June 2020, of the 1,927,063 items of content removed by Twitter, some 1,564,465 items were categorized by Twitter

[224] In the way that, for example, clause 10(3) places platforms under a duty to employ proportionate measures to prevent children coming into contact with priority illegal content that is harmful to them.

[225] John Gardner (2011).

as 'abuse/harassment' or as 'hate'.[226] That is not to say, of course, that a platform which breaches its primary duty—to remove or prevent the posting of content of the worst kinds—should thereby automatically find itself exposed to penalties. In point of liability, it is perfectly justified to focus, respecting the way in which a platform seeks to discharge the primary duty, on the nature and quality of the 'net' employed to restrain or catch such content, rather than on the fact that some prohibited content gets through the net.

In that regard, there will be a compelling case for including electoral participation offences within the scope of 'priority' illegal content, whether the primary duty is to stop it being posted and remove it if it is, or merely to minimize the posting and spread of such content. Electoral participation disinformation is already in effect treated as a 'priority harm' by some major platforms. During the 2018 US midterm elections, Twitter took enforcement action under its civic integrity guidelines on nearly 6,000 tweets identified as voter-suppression attempts (many of which originated in the US itself).[227] Facebook's policy on the removal of content includes the view that 'there are some extreme forms of disinformation that we remove from our platform, including disinformation that leads to offline violence and disinformation that leads to voter suppression'.[228] It is absolutely correct to make this equation between hate speech and electoral participation disinformation, and it is proportionate to regard take-down (or at the very least, severe restriction) as the appropriate remedy.[229]

Returning to the general policy towards illegal content, under clause 9(3), when any kind of illegal content—whether prioritized or not—comes to the attention of a platform, it must 'swiftly' take it down: no element of value judgement is involved. This nod towards the EU 'notice-and-take-down' model, discussed earlier, sits uneasily alongside the 'value-judgment' approach to be employed for dealing with priority illegal content. For example, suppose two rival election candidates independently notify a platform that, during a campaign, their rival has made a false statement (posted through the platform) about their personal conduct or character, falling within the offence under section 106 of the 1983 Act.[230] Then, subject to the platform's free-speech obligations (discussed below), it would seem any content including one or both of these false statements must be taken down 'swiftly', because it is criminally illegal content notified to the platform. There is no

[226] https://transparency.twitter.com/en/reports/rules-enforcement.html#2020-jan-jun (last accessed 19/05/2021).

[227] https://blog.twitter.com/en_us/topics/company/2019/18_midterm_review.html (last accessed 09/06/2021).

[228] https://about.fb.com/news/2018/10/voter-suppression-policies/ (last accessed 19/04/2021); https://ec.europa.eu/digital-single-market/en/news/annual-self-assessment-reports-signatories-code-practice-disinformation-2019 (last accessed 19/04/2021).

[229] Indeed, as Facebook itself points out, some hate speech is directed at voter suppression, such as a claim that someone of a particular race or religion is unfit to vote or hold office: https://about.fb.com/news/2018/10/voter-suppression-policies/ (last accessed 19/04/2021).

[230] Discussed in Chapters 1 and 3.

scope for the platform to judge that, for example, the false statements cancel each other out, that one is far more serious than the other, or that they are too trivial to warrant censorship. Such an approach is too rigid, and unrealistic. Ordinary citizens have a 'discretion' whether or not to tolerate apparently illegal conduct that they have witnessed, without intervening, just as the police and prosecutors have a discretion, to be guided by public interest considerations, over whether or not to take action on evidence of illegal conduct. Platforms should be granted scope for exercising their own judgement, in cases when they have been alerted to the presence of illegal content.[231]

This final point demonstrates the inadequacy of a policy that fails to draw a distinction between political viewpoint and electoral participation information,[232] because the peremptory nature of 'notice and take-down' is, by way of contrast, eminently suited to forming part of a zero-tolerance approach to electoral participation disinformation. In a 2021 Private Member's Bill, the Online Harms Reduction Regulator Bill, Lord McNally sought to amend the Communications Act 2003 to impose a duty on Ofcom (the communications regulator) to report on platforms' obligations to prevent harm arising from, amongst other things, 'terrorism, racial hatred ... discrimination ... fraud or financial crime ... and threats which impede or prejudice the integrity and probity of the electoral process' (clause 2(A)(4)).[233] The Bill thus correctly and explicitly made electoral participation wrongdoing a harm equivalent to other serious harms or political silencing techniques, such as race hate or terrorism.[234]

(iii) Enhanced duties on major platforms: legal-but-harmful conduct

As indicated earlier, the Online Harms Bill places some important enhanced duties on larger platforms with greater diversity of content ('Category 1' service providers). One of these is the duty in clause 11 to formulate a policy towards legal-but-harmful content encountered by adults. As far as the meaning of 'harm' is concerned, for the purposes of clause 11, clause 46 defines it as follows:

[231] Of course, under the 'free-speech' approach defended in this book, platforms should not be taking down or restricting access to the kind of political viewpoint content just mentioned at all, in the absence of a need to respond to a court judgment—or a determination under their own complaint processes—that the content is defamatory. At most, they should be attaching unreliability warnings to it.

[232] See further section 2.7(v) below.

[233] https://publications.parliament.uk/pa/bills/lbill/58-01/022/5801022.pdf; https://bills.parliament.uk/bills/2546 (last accessed 12/05/2021).

[234] Although the extension of clause 2(A)(4) to 'any other harms that Ofcom deem appropriate' raises the risk of political viewpoint disinformation wrongly being included in the list.

> Content is within this subsection if the provider of the service has reasonable grounds to believe that the nature of the content is such that there is a material risk of the content having, or indirectly having, a significant adverse physical or psychological impact on an adult of ordinary sensibilities.[235]

As in the case of priority illegal content, harm is subject under clause 46(2) to potentially politicized intervention by the Secretary of State, who may designate illegal-but-harmful content as 'priority' content. Can political viewpoint speech fall within the scope of 'harm', thus understood? The relatively restrictive definition of 'harm' in clause 46 may allay the fears of some commentators on earlier government consultations that the proposals involved the risk of 'a significant chilling of freedom of expression'.[236] Further, in its response to consultation the government said:

> the duty of care will apply to content or activity which could cause significant physical or psychological harm to an individual, including disinformation and misinformation. Where disinformation is unlikely to cause this type of harm it will not fall in scope of regulation. Ofcom should not be involved in decisions relating to political opinions or campaigning, shared by domestic actors within the law.[237]

This appears to indicate that political viewpoint disinformation is not within scope other than (controversially, of course) when it already amounts to an offence: as under section 106 of the 1983 Act.[238] In any event, the duties on platforms in respect of legal-but-harmful content are less onerous than in the case of (priority) illegal content. The principal duty, in clause 11(2), is a duty merely 'to specify in the terms of service— (a) how priority content that is harmful to adults is to be dealt with by the service (with each such kind of priority content separately covered)'. Bearing in mind the broadly 'First Amendment' approach adopted by platforms to political viewpoint speech, it would be open to platforms to say that the way in which such speech will be 'dealt with' is to allow its posting and spread, other than when there is (say) a clear and obvious risk of harm occurring.

[235] The 'adult of ordinary sensibilities' standard is then modified to address cases in which someone has particular characteristics affected by content, but that issue will not be addressed here.
[236] Damian Tambini (2019), 30.
[237] HM Government (2019), para 2.81.
[238] See text at n. 232.

(iv) Speech policy online: qualified freedoms and politicization

That brings me directly to the Bill's policy on free (political) speech. In one important respect, the Bill treats speech less favourably than other kinds of conduct. In devising policies to discharge their duties in relation to illegal content, platforms will ordinary be concerned simply with regulated conduct that in law meets the definition of the relevant offence (clause 41(2)). However, when the issue is whether 'words, sounds, images or speech' (on their own or in combination with other conduct) amount to a relevant offence, a platform's duties will extend to content that 'the provider of the service *has reasonable grounds to believe*' (emphasis added) amounts to a relevant offence (clause 41(3)). That extension of what is to count as content amounting to a 'relevant offence' will inevitably encourage an over-extensive 'safety-first' blocking policy, in relation to words, sounds, images, and speech. Can such a singling out of speech content for less favourable treatment than non-speech content, in relation to its status as 'illegal content', really be regarded as consistent with obligations under Article 10?

Under clause 12, all platforms will be under a duty 'to have regard to the importance of ... protecting users' rights to freedom of expression within the law'. This relatively weak expression of an Article 10 obligation is, though, supplemented by a number of further obligations applicable only to the larger platforms with greater diversity of content (the Category 1 service providers). The latter will be under a duty, *inter alia*, to carry out impact assessments concerning the effects of their safety policies on freedom of speech (clause 12(3)), a duty to make public the steps they have taken in response to their impact assessments (clause 12(5)), and a further duty 'to protect content of democratic importance': the 'CDI' duty (clause 13).[239] The CDI duty is a duty to ensure that a major platform's systems and processes take account of 'the importance of the free expression of content of democratic importance', in so far as the systems and processes bear on take-down policies and action against particular users. The CDI duty is hence a duty, within the general duty to take account of the importance of free-speech rights, to take particular care with how 'political' speech is treated, as compared with (say) the freedom to post frivolous content. Category 1 service providers will be under two further duties. First, there will be a duty to make their systems and processes sensitive to the importance of a 'diversity of political opinion' (clause 12(3)). Second, by virtue of clause 14, there will be a duty on such providers to operate a service using systems and processes designed to ensure that 'the importance of the free

[239] Such content is defined in clause 13(6) as either 'news publisher content', or 'content [that] is or appears to be specifically intended to contribute to democratic political debate in the United Kingdom or a part or area of the United Kingdom'.

expression of journalistic content is taken into account', when making decisions about take-down or about action against particular users.[240]

The first point that ought to be emphasized about all these duties is that they are duties merely to take free expression, political diversity, and journalistic content 'into account', rather than duties to uphold these values as such. So, the duties are effectively side-constraints on the pursuit of the principal safety duties imposed on platforms. That tells us that the pursuit of safety is generally to be prioritized over the protection of free speech.[241] Such a 'safety-first' policy, in respect of the most dangerous kinds of content, may not seem wrong, and I will not comment further on it here. More pertinent, in the present context, are the duties to make systems and processes sensitive (i) to content of democratic importance, (ii) to the importance of a diversity of political content, and (iii) to the importance of the free expression of journalistic content. Can political viewpoint disinformation be counted as 'CDI' (content of democratic importance)? On a rationalistic or militant democratic account of defensible political speech, of the kind that has been defended in the House of Lords,[242] the answer to might appear to be 'no'. However, it must be kept in mind that CDI under the Bill is extended in blanket fashion to 'news publisher content'. Accordingly, news publisher content involving disinformation,[243] even though in all probability likely to be more widely shared than disinformation posted by other users, is protected by the CDI duty. By contrast, users seeking to spread political disinformation who are not 'news publishers' must rely principally for their freedom to do so on a platform's clause 12 general duty to take into account free speech, and (perhaps) to make its systems and processes sensitive to the importance of a diversity of political opinion.

As far as the latter is concerned, clause 13 imposes a duty to ensure that a provider's systems and processes take account of the importance of a 'diversity of political opinion' when making take-down or restriction decisions. This is a particularly surprising addition to the requirements placed on platforms, because it requires them to abandon content-neutrality. In theory, online platforms are not themselves broadcasters and so, in relation to political content, they cannot reasonably be expected to take steps to ensure that such content and coverage is varied or balanced overall, even if one could come up with an uncontentious understanding of what counts as 'a diversity of political opinion' (unlikely).[244] For some, perhaps, such a step might nonetheless seem justified by the risk that politics will

[240] There are stringent provisions in clause 14 giving rights to a 'dedicated and expedited' complaints procedure in relation to take-down decisions, in the case of journalistic content. Journalistic content is regulated UK media content. So, neither 'citizen journalism' nor foreign journalism is covered: see the discussion in Chapter 1.

[241] Other than in the case of legal-but-potentially-harmful content for adults, when platforms are under duty simply to explain how they propose to deal with it.

[242] See the discussion in Chapter 1, section 1.4(ii).

[243] See, for example, https://mediabiasfactcheck.com/daily-mail/ (last accessed 18/05/2021).

[244] See, by contrast, the obligations enforced on broadcasters by the UK regulator, Ofcom (2009).

otherwise become more polarized and difficult to 'manage' if, when forming political viewpoints, people rely only on so news 'echo chambers', where their views are affirmed rather than challenged.[245] The centrist bias in such thinking was criticized in Chapter 1, but the thinking is also empirically flawed. There is clear evidence that encountering *opposing* political opinions does as much, or more, than listening to politically like-minded thinkers, to drive people into the comfort zone of their political echo chamber.[246]

Having said that, there is a covert justification for the inclusion of this provision that is more likely to have been more influential than any worry about echo chambers. This is the (partisan) concern that, in taking down or restricting extreme content, platforms will find themselves concerned mainly with politically right-wing posts.[247] Would it be right, then, for a platform to leave publicly available a tranche of extreme (dis)information, in the interests of respect for a 'diversity of political opinion'? If that is, in effect, what clause 13 requires, then it risks a betrayal of the free-speech ideals highlighted at the outset of this chapter. Evidence indicates that the more extreme or detached from reality disinformation is, the more it is likely to involve intimidation or hate speech.[248] Jurisdictions committed to a flourishing free-speech culture, rather than to an undifferentiated notion of 'free speech', do not tolerate speech that itself involves the (effective) silencing of others, like the intimidatory or hate speech characteristic of extreme disinformation.

(v) Elections and the freedom to disinform

Clause 98 of the Bill provides that the regulator must set up an Advisory Committee on disinformation and misinformation. The function of the Advisory Committee will be to provide advice to the regulator about:

(a) how providers of regulated services should deal with—
  (i) in the case of regulated user-to-user services, disinformation and misinformation present on such services; and
  (ii) in the case of regulated search services, disinformation and misinformation that may be encountered in or via search results.

More particularly, the Advisory Committee will, first, advise the regulator on the kinds of information the regulator should seek from providers (under clause

245 https://www.theguardian.com/science/blog/2017/dec/04/echo-chambers-are-dangerous-we-must-try-to-break-free-of-our-online-bubbles (last accessed 19/04/2021).
246 Jay D. Hmielowski et al. (2020).
247 Deen Freelon, Alice Marwick, and Daniel Kreiss (2020).
248 Michael Hameleers et al. (2021).

49), when the regulator is determining what is to be included in a provider's annual 'transparency reports' on user activity (required as part of the reporting and record-keeping duties referred to earlier). Second, the Advisory Committee will advise the regulator, in relation to disinformation and misinformation, on the development of the regulator's 'media literacy' strategy, a strategy the development of which is also something that must feature in a provider's transparency report. As mentioned in Chapter 1, the duty on the regulator to promote media literacy under the Communications Act 2003 is now to be extended to cover 'the reliability and accuracy' of material online. The pursuit of a media literacy strategy is thus a 'more-speech' counterweight to disinformation that, in line with the argument of this chapter, is to be welcomed in so far as it enhances critical engagement by users online.

What kind of approach to disinformation is likely to be—or should be—adopted by the Advisory Committee? Clearly, there ought to be a clear distinction between the approach to political viewpoint information and the approach to electoral participation disinformation. As a more-speech solution, a media literacy strategy can be concerned with all kinds of disinformation; but the distinction between the types of disinformation becomes much more significant, if the work of the Advisory Committee and the regulator on disinformation leads to strategies (effectively) compelling platforms to take down or to restrict access to political disinformation. In the White Paper that preceded the Bill, the Government showed enthusiasm for what it called a 'news quality obligation', to be imposed on companies, to ensure that they 'improve how their users understand the origin of a news article and the trustworthiness of its source'.[249] The contentious point here is not so much the desirability of ensuring that users understand the source of news, but what the role of platforms should be in 'grading' news for trustworthiness. In the case of political viewpoint disinformation, that should be a matter for fact-checking organizations which use platforms, and not for platforms themselves.

The government went on in the White Paper to suggest that platforms must address the issue of 'making content which has been disputed by reputable fact-checking services less visible to users';[250] but the mere fact that there has been such a challenge from a fact-checker cannot by itself justify a restriction on access to political viewpoint content. To take such an approach in restricting access to such content, a platform would be abandoning moral toleration of political viewpoint disinformation. That is something which platforms have hitherto been reluctant to do, and rightly so, if the argument of this chapter is accepted. If and when the Advisory Committee turns its attention to election disinformation, as well as affirming the importance of tolerating political viewpoint disinformation, there needs to be a specific focus on how to address electoral participation

[249] HM Government (2019), para 7.29, citing Cairncross Review (2019).
[250] Department for Digital, Culture, Media and Sport, and Home Office (2020), para 7.28.

disinformation. For example, the Advisory Committee ought to commend Twitter's elections-specific support portal, which is designed to provide faster responses to alleged election abuses.[251]

2.8 The EU Code of Practice on Disinformation

In contrast to approach of the jurisdictions considered above, there has been at least one official attempt to mark some kind of distinction, for soft regulatory purposes, between political viewpoint and electoral participation disinformation. This is the EU Code of Practice, agreed with social media platforms in 2018.[252] The Code of Practice expresses its concern as being with disinformation in the sense of 'verifiably false or misleading information' which, cumulatively, '(a) is created, presented and disseminated . . . to intentionally deceive the public', and (b) 'may cause public harm'. The notion of harm includes (amongst other things such as threats to health or security) 'threats to democratic political and policymaking processes'.[253] The Code of Practice goes on to say that, by way of contrast, it is not concerned with, 'misleading advertising, reporting errors, satire and parody, or *clearly identified partisan news and commentary*'.[254] Through the contrasts that it draws, this policy statement at least gestures towards the distinction that I have argued to be fundamental in this area of law, between political viewpoint information ('partisan news and commentary') and electoral participation information ('threats to democratic political . . . processes').[255] However, it is badly flawed in the way that its terms are defined, even though the definitions given are not legal ones.

To begin with, what is to count as verifiably false, and in particular, verifiably *misleading* information? To leave this point hanging is to invite the criticism that verification is, by default if not by design, the domain of rationalistic centrists, and is hence the means through which they may seek to shape the character of political discourse to suit their own ends.[256] Facebook seeks to cut through this problem algorithmically, to some extent, by 'using various signals, including feedback from our community, to inform a machine learning model that predicts which stories

[251] https://blog.twitter.com/en_us/topics/company/2018/an-update-on-our-elections-integrity-work.html (Last accessed 19/04/2021).
[252] https://ec.europa.eu/digital-single-market/en/code-practice-disinformation (last accessed 19/04/2021).
[253] European Commission (2018a), Preamble.
[254] Ibid. (my emphasis).
[255] To some extent, it mirrors the distinctions drawn in Twitter's community guidelines, considered in Chapter 1.
[256] See e.g. Martin Montgomery (2017). Facebook has the following understanding of this notion: 'Facebook prohibits ads that include claims debunked by third-party fact checkers or, in certain circumstances, claims debunked by organizations with particular expertise'. https://www.facebook.com/policies/ads/prohibited_content/misinformation (last accessed 16/11/2021).

may be false.'[257] However, this is unlikely to help in identifying what is verifiably misleading, as opposed to false, and in any event the policy lacks credibility without clarity about how the 'signals' and the 'feedback from our community' are analysed and used as a basis for decision-making. Second, there is the extensive definition of 'harm'. Under the code, it is enough to trigger the justification for taking restrictive or censoring action that speech 'may' cause harm, a test that is excessively broad in scope when applied to all types of harm, great and small. There is a need to distinguish between harms on the basis of severity or gravity, when considering what degree of likelihood is sufficient to justify intervention to restrict speech. Whilst it might be acceptable to restrict access to or ban false information that 'may' cause serious harm, there ought to be a requirement of imminence or high risk in the case of more minor harms. It is obvious, but should have been spelled out that, for example, spreading false information which, if acted on, might conceivably in some cases lead someone's hair to thin slightly ought not to be treated in the same way as false information which, if acted on, greatly increases the chance of a serious cancer becoming aggressive.

Less obviously controversial, but controversial nonetheless, is the inclusion within the scope of the relevant harms of 'policymaking' processes, alongside 'democratic' processes. The idea of 'democratic processes' brings to mind the electoral process, threats to which (from false information) online are rightly targeted for take-down and restriction. Google's policy on misrepresentation could not, in this respect, be much clearer. It forbids paid-for content that 'makes claims that are demonstrably false and could significantly undermine participation or trust in an electoral or democratic process. Examples: information about public voting procedures, political candidate eligibility based on age or birthplace, election results, or census participation that contradicts official government records.'[258] No doubt influenced by First Amendment thinking,[259] this analysis seems fairly unequivocally to rule out political viewpoint disinformation from the scope of its take-down policy. The focus is the narrow one that I have described as electoral participation disinformation. By contrast, what is it that the Code of Practice has in mind by 'policymaking processes' that, it seems, are equally justifiably targeted for take-down or restriction (even though excluded from the scope of Google's policy)?

There must be a strong suspicion that this is a nod towards the controversial and much-criticized existence of criminal defamation or insult laws designed to protect officials that exist in a number of (otherwise democratic) EU jurisdictions. For example, in German law, Article 188 of the Criminal Code creates an offence of (publicly or through the media) defaming 'a person involved in popular political

[257] https://www.facebook.com/communitystandards/false_news (last accessed 19/04/2021). Facebook also commits itself to working with academics to address the issues, but the commitment is vague.

[258] https://blog.google/technology/ads/update-our-political-ads-policy/ (last accessed 19/04/2021).

[259] See the discussion in Thomas Wischmeyer (2018).

life [in a way that] may make [the person's] public activities substantially more difficult'.[260] The penalty is imprisonment for three months to five years. As far as criminal insult is concerned, an example can be found in the Criminal Code of Denmark, Article 121:

> Any person who attacks any of the persons referred to in Section 119 of this Act [public officials] with insults, abusive language or other offensive words or gestures, while they are executing their office or function or on occasion of such office or function, shall be liable to a fine or to imprisonment for any term not exceeding six months.

These provisions would be largely indefensible, even if they were confined to defamatory content: they are simply unnecessary in a democratic society.[261] Whilst there are a significant number of US states that retain criminal defamation laws that can protect officials while in office, they are narrowly construed through confinement to knowing or reckless defamation (and there is no Federal offence of defamation).[262] It is noticeable that Google's publisher policies contain no explicit reference to restrictions on defamatory content.

However, the publisher policies do forbid, in a generic way, the posting of 'illegal' content,[263] which makes them compliant with the EU's mantra that 'what is illegal offline is also illegal online'.[264] However, this mantra ought to be read not simply against the background of the wording of statutes criminalizing speech (such as those just mentioned). It must be considered against the human rights jurisprudence developed by the courts that construes such wording in a narrow way, especially when the speech in question is political. In *Otegi Mondragon v Spain*,[265] the court was concerned with a false allegation by an elected representative and spokesperson for a parliamentary group, who said at a press conference that the Spanish King 'protects torture and imposes his monarchical regime on our people through torture and violence'. The elected representative was convicted of insulting the Spanish King, but the conviction was held to be inconsistent with Article 10. The court held that:

[260] Article 32 of the Press Law 1881 (France) defines criminal defamation as 'any allegation or accusation of a fact that causes an attack on the honour or consideration of a person', and permits a maximum fine of 45,000 euros when the victim is a public official, as compared with 12,000 euros when the victim is a private individual.

[261] Tarlach McGonagle (2016), s. 3.3.

[262] https://cpj.org/reports/2016/03/north-america/ (last accessed 19/04/2021).

[263] https://support.google.com/adsense/answer/9335564?hl=en&visit_id=637491849670431104-1481837764&rd=1 (last accessed 19/04/2021).

[264] https://www.facebook.com/EuropeanCommission/posts/what-is-illegal-offline-is-also-illegal-online-we-made-security-a-top-priority-f/1695022480545225/ (last accessed 19.04/2021).

[265] *Otegi Mondragon v Spain* (Application no. 2034/07) 15 March 2011, para 50.

> There is little scope under Article 10 for restrictions on freedom of expression in the area of political speech or debate—where freedom of expression is of the utmost importance—or in matters of public interest. While freedom of expression is important for everybody, it is especially so for an elected representative of the people.[266]

These are not easy waters for an internet platform to negotiate, caught between the ever-growing threat of state regulation, the (conflicting) demands of users, and changing understandings of how best to commercialize content in order to maintain economic viability, invest in innovation, and sustain growth. Nonetheless, for a platform to adopt a purely 'legislative intent' approach to the meaning of illegal content is for the platform to become a mere gateway to authoritarian or militant democratic suppression of political speech. We should note, in that regard, that out of more than 9 million videos removed from YouTube between April and June 2019 across all of Google's community guidelines, more than 7.8 million were flagged by automated systems, and that more than 80 per cent of those were then removed before receiving any views.[267] Whilst automated systems constantly improve and become more sophisticated, we are a long way from the point where they can give interpretive priority to a strong presumption that political speech should not be censored, and to the view that a narrow construction should be given to offences criminalizing—or capable of being used to suppress—political speech.

2.9 The Need for Principles Governing Online Election Disinformation

No one doubts the significance of the role of internet platforms, in shaping the way that citizens, organizations (public and private), candidates, and officials understand, participate in, consume, and seek to influence politics. To give just one illuminating snapshot, from late March 2019 (when Facebook launched the ads transparency tools for the EU) to 9 September 2019, there were around 444,000 political ads on Facebook in the EU totalling around 31.5 million euros of political ads spend.[268] In this chapter, the themes pursued give rise to the suggestion that state regulation poses unacceptable risks to free speech in a number of ways. First, some jurisdictions—both liberal and illiberal—have adopted regulatory or criminal strategies in relation to the posting of political disinformation online that are designed either to chill some kinds of political viewpoint expression more or

266 Ibid. See further *Castells v Spain* (Application no. 11798/85) 23 April 1992, para 50.
267 https://transparencyreport.google.com/youtube-policy/removals (last accessed 19/04/2021).
268 Facebook annual report (2019), https://digital-strategy.ec.europa.eu/en/news/annual-self-assessment-reports-signatories-code-practice-disinformation-2019 (last accessed 19/04/2021).

less directly, or to do so indirectly through the encouraging of over-blocking of political content. Second, there has been a consistent failure on the part of states to distinguish between electoral participation disinformation and political viewpoint disinformation, and thus a lack of developed principle insisting that only 'more-speech' solutions are an appropriate remedy for the latter. Third, states have failed to look beyond the mantra that 'what is illegal offline is illegal online'. This means that individuals whose hard-hitting political speech is alleged to be criminally defamatory will find that their human rights arguments, in favour of permission to speak, are left in the (virtual) hands of automated blocking systems and—if they are lucky—unknown platform moderators.

Finally, there is still—albeit, understandably—a lack of clarity about the role of platforms as potential moral, and not just legal, tolerators of political disinformation. We saw in Chapter 1 that platforms, coming from a First Amendment perspective, are in general morally tolerant of hyper-partisan content and political viewpoint disinformation, but both morally and legally intolerant of electoral participation disinformation. This commendable approach is threatened not just by Germany's Network Enforcement Act 2017 but also by the UK proposal to place platforms under 'news quality obligations' that range indifferently across both categories of disinformation. In any event, requiring platforms to observe broadcaster-style obligations to ensure users come into contact with 'varied' and 'trustworthy' news content is not only politically contentious, but takes platforms too far away from just being 'platforms'. They are user-hosts, who can be asked to commercialize content responsibly, but should not also be asked to politicize it in order to serve liberal-centrist rationalist preferences concerning that way political conversations are conducted. The UK risks overlooking the fact that, in relation to news content obligations, 'any purely governmental response ... is bound to be regarded as biased and propagandist'.[269]

Andrej Lang has divided approaches to platform regulation into the following categories: (1) the non-legal approach, which instead encourages education and 'counter-speech'; (2) the liberal approach, which immunizes intermediaries and only holds the speakers responsible by means of civil and criminal law; (3) the bureaucratic model, in which an administrative agency takes responsibility for supervising the content on social networks; and (4) the 'intermediary approach' followed in Germany, which introduces new responsibilities for intermediaries and for the state.[270] Seen in terms of the argument offered here, the approach to be taken depends on the nature of the speech.

Category (1) is the right approach for political viewpoint speech. Category 2 is unacceptable, because the state is under a duty to control and regulate vehicles for crime, hate, harassment, and the like, just as much as it is under a duty to prevent

[269] Jean-Baptiste Jeangène Vilmer (2018), 170.
[270] Andrej Lang (2018), 222–4, cited by Thomas Wischmeyer (2018), 5 n. 27.

or minimize these kinds of conduct in themselves. Category 3, a version of which we saw enacted in Singapore, involves an approach most likely to lead to inappropriate censorship and state repression of political counter-narratives. Category 4, the 'guided regulation' approach in Germany and in England and Wales, is the most promising approach, in general terms, placing duties on platforms to commercialize content responsibly. However, only in England and Wales has a serious effort been made to ensure that the issue of how wide-ranging and stringent the duties need to be depends on the character of the content in question. Even then, not enough has yet been done to indicate when 'more-speech' solutions ought to be preferred to take-down and restriction, and to give serious attention to the policies that platforms should adopt towards political speech during elections.

3
Personal Attacks and Political Disinformation in UK Law

Imposing a [criminal] penalty where care is not taken in making a statement . . . in relation to the personal character of a candidate, can only enhance the standard of political debate and thus strengthen the way in which a democratic legislature is elected.

R (on the application of Woolas) v The Parliamentary Election Court [2010] EWHC 3169 (Admin), para 124.

3.1 Introduction

As we saw in Chapter 1, free-speech issues are always liable to render controversial the use of criminal laws to deter individuals from making false political viewpoint claims. As the passage cited above from the judgment in the *Woolas* case indicates, there is a strong judicial (as well as political) attachment to the idea that rationalism in political debate is legitimately supported through state coercion.[1] Yet, as indicated in Chapter 1, the spectre of criminal liability may chill provocative speech, draw officials tasked with adjudication on such matters into political controversy, and inappropriately serve to protect members of the government or of officialdom more broadly from hard-hitting criticism. As Lord Thomas remarked, in support of the abolition of the crimes of seditious and criminal libel:

> The ability of individuals to criticise the state is crucial to maintaining freedom. In this day and age, when we have so many journalists, bloggers and so forth who give us their views all the time, we should get rid of anything that may in any way curb their criticisms of the state. We need a vigorous culture of free speech in order to keep government up to the mark.[2]

[1] See the discussion of rationalism in Chapter 1.

[2] https://publications.parliament.uk/pa/ld200809/ldhansrd/text/90709-0013.htm (last accessed 20/04/2021), col. 849.

Criminal Fraud and Election Disinformation. Jeremy Horder, Oxford University Press. © Jeremy Horder 2022.
DOI: 10.1093/oso/9780192844545.003.0004

Seditious and general criminal libel offences were abolished in England and Wales after 2009.[3] The analogous offence of *scandalum magnatum* under the 1275 Statute of Westminster was abolished as long ago as 1887.[4] However, in common with many other jurisdictions, it continues to be an offence in the UK (i.e. not only in England and Wales) to make some kinds of false political viewpoint claims. In some instances, what matters about such claims, from a criminal law point of view, is that, even if they do not involve actual hate speech, they have caused or are liable to cause more or less serious mental distress. I give some consideration to such cases in section 3.2. More central to my concerns in this chapter is what remains of criminal defamation, in spite of the abolition of the general offence. This is what can be called the 'election defamation offence', set out in Chapter 1, section 1(ii), in section 106 of the Representation of the People Act 1983. This offence is committed when someone makes a false statement of fact about the personal conduct or character of an election candidate, with intent to affect the voting return of that candidate. I shall be concerned here neither with the question whether a finding that such a statement has been made should have public law consequences[5] nor with the question whether the private law remedies available to a victim of election defamation are adequate.[6] My question is, is the criminalization of electoral defamation consistent with spirit of Lord Thomas's critique of the abolition of the general criminal libel offence, and with the case made for legal and moral tolerance of false political viewpoint information made in Chapters 1 and 2? I suggest that it is not. Before turning to that issue, though, I will briefly consider some of the broader picture, where the continuing criminalization of false statements is concerned.

3.2 Communicating Political Threats and Lies in UK Criminal Law

There is no doubt that the protection of election candidates from serious mistreatment is a legitimate aim of the criminal law. Indeed, offering such protection is necessary in any democratic state.[7] However, a current weakness of English law (and it is not alone in this) is that, in seeking to tackle abusive behaviour, a distinction is not always drawn between on one hand harmful hate speech, threats,

[3] Coroners and Justice Act 2009, s. 73.

[4] The 34th chapter of the Statute of Westminster formed part of the statutory basis for the crime of *scandalum magnatum*: 'that from henceforth none be so hardy to tell or publish any false news or tales, whereby discord, or occasion of discord or slander may grow between the King and his people, or the great men of the realm'. A version of the offence was incorporated into modern Canadian law in 1892: see *R v Zundel* [1992] 2 SCR 731.

[5] Such as the mandatory removal from office (if successful in the election) of a candidate who has made the relevant kind of false statement. For further discussion, see Jeremy Horder (2021a).

[6] See the brief discussion in Jacob Rowbottom (2012).

[7] See Committee on Standards in Public Life (2017).

and harassment, and on the other hand false (political) information.[8] First, for example, section 127(2) of the Communications Act 2003 says, in relation to improper use of a public electronic communications network:

> A person is guilty of an offence if he—
> (1) sends by means of a public electronic communications network a message or other matter that is grossly offensive or of an indecent, obscene or menacing character;
> (2) for the purpose of causing annoyance, inconvenience or needless anxiety to another
> (a) sends by means of a public electronic communications network, a message that he knows to be false, [or]
> (b) causes such a message to be sent . . . .[9]

There were 254 charges under section 127 in 2017.[10] Second, alongside this offence, is a more serious one created by section 1(1)(a) of the Malicious Communications Act 1988.[11] This makes it an offence to a send a letter, electronic communication, or article of any description which conveys an indecent or grossly offensive message, which involves a threat, or which—under section 1(1)(a)(iii)—conveys, 'information which is false and known or believed to be false by the sender', in circumstances where one of D's purposes in communicating in the proscribed way was 'that it should . . . cause distress or anxiety to the recipient or to any other person to whom he intends that its contents or nature should be communicated'.[12] There were 2,626 charges under section 1(1)(a) in 2017,[13] most of these being likely to have concerned 'grossly offensive' or 'threatening' communications.

How legitimate is the application of these offences to false statements made in political contexts? It is important to start by noting that the false statements prohibited by the 1988 and 2003 Acts are not statements aimed at doing damage that is essentially reputational in nature (by way of contrast with the now abolished offence of criminal libel). The 1988 and 2003 Acts apply, amongst other things, only to false statements aimed at having a negative impact on a specific victim's mind, by causing (say) distress or needless anxiety. That being so, at least in serious cases,

[8] The following analysis draws on Jeremy Horder (2021a).

[9] The penalty upon summary conviction is a sentence of imprisonment for a term not exceeding six months or a fine not exceeding level 5 on the standard scale, or both. See, further, Law Commission for England and Wales (2018).

[10] Law Commission (2018), para 4.55.

[11] See also the Public Order Act 1986, ss 4a and 5, as qualified by section 29J (of part IIIA).

[12] See the discussion in Law Commission (2018), Chapter 4. An offence may be met with a fine and or a sentence of imprisonment for up to two years.

[13] Law Commission (2018), para 4.7.

these offences can justifiably be used to protect the interests of election candidates or others involved in politics in not having false statements made about them. It is important not to underestimate the risk that some people or groups within society may be deterred from participating in politics because of the fear of exposure to vilification and threats when they do.[14] For example, evidence suggests that women more frequently make reference to the risk of being the target of public attack on their dignity as a deterrent to entering politics.[15] Such attacks may come through malicious falsehood, as well as by other means such as threats or grossly offensive messages.

However, even in a case where someone intends by making a false statement to cause one of the states of mind set out in the 1988 and 2003 Acts, is it not necessarily justified to make such conduct a criminal offence. Almost any kind of false statement made publicly about someone is liable to cause annoyance and inconvenience (one may have to take steps to deny it publicly), and perhaps some degree of distress. So, to use the criminal law to prioritize people's insulation from being caused to endure these mental states is, perforce, to chill speech, even when the speaker has set out to cause such a state of mind. To be sure, no one should be expected to react with President Biden's insouciance to a false allegation of being a paedophile and rapist;[16] but to criminalize the making of such statements simply because they were intended to cause, say, 'annoyance or inconvenience' is in effect to countenance the continuation of a kind of defamation offence. If X, who is by nature sensitive and somewhat thin-skinned, stands for office on a platform of extreme right- or left-wings views, X may expect to become personally the target of hostile political commentary, be it well- or ill-informed. Should a jurisdiction committed to free political speech be countenancing the use of the criminal law to protect X from false or misleading comments intended to cause X *merely* some distress, annoyance, or inconvenience?

A thorough critique of the breadth of the 1988 and 2003 Acts is beyond the scope of this work, but it is important to consider recent proposals for change. In a 2018 Scoping Report, considering the direction of reform of the scope of liability for online communication of false statements, the Law Commission emphasized the need for reforms in which 'legitimate speech that should not be criminalized would be more clearly excluded'.[17] Do its 2020 provisional proposals live up to this ambition?[18] The Commission begins by pointing out that the kind of 'harm' required to be caused under the 1988 and 2003 is insufficient (and, one might add, an unwarranted threat to what is merely provocative or acerbic speech). The

[14] See e.g. the valuable discussion in Law Commission (2020), paras 4.38–4.66.
[15] Law Commission (2020), paras 4.42–4.45; Committee on Standards in Public Life (2017), para 4.1.6.
[16] See Chapter 2, section 2.2.
[17] Law Commission (2018), para 13.21.
[18] Law Commission (2020).

Commission says, 'annoyance' and 'inconvenience', in particular, 'seem to be insufficiently harmful to meet the threshold of criminality'.[19] Consequently, the Commission proposes to replace section 127(2)(a) and (b) of the 2003 Act—the false statement provisions—with the following offence, triable only summarily:

> [T]he defendant sent a communication that he or she knew to be false;
> (2) in sending the communication, the defendant intended to cause non-trivial emotional, psychological, or physical harm to a likely audience; and
> (3) the defendant sent the communication without reasonable excuse.
> (4) For the purposes of this offence, definitions are as follows:
> (a) a communication is an electronic communication, letter, or article; and
> (b) a likely audience is someone who, at the point at which the communication was sent by the defendant, was likely to see, hear, or otherwise encounter it.[20]

The offence is designed to rein in the scope of the false statement offence in the 2003 Act by (i) continuing the concentration only on statements known to be false, and (ii) introducing a requirement that there be an intention, in sending the communication, to cause non-trivial harm to a likely audience. In the Law Commission's view, these restrictions make it possible to have a relatively broad understanding of harm. What is required is not necessarily that D intend to cause 'serious' emotional distress, but that D intend to cause 'non-trivial' emotional, psychological, or physical harm.[21] The Commission goes on to say: 'We mean for 'non-trivial emotional, psychological, or physical harm' to include, for example, distress and anxiety, but not annoyance or inconvenience which in our provisional view do not justify the imposition of a criminal sanction.'[22] So, for example, suppose that D, intending to cause inconvenience and annoyance, makes a call to a take-away ordering a delivery to a non-existent address. Such conduct is covered in principle by the existing law. However, in all probability, it would not be covered by the proposed offence, because there is no intention to cause non-trivial harm. By contrast, if D calls V posing as a police officer, and falsely tells V that his or her daughter has been killed in a car accident, leading V to suffer great distress, such conduct would be covered by the proposed offence if D intended to bring about that result. In so far, though, as the proposed restrictions on the scope of the existing offence may

[19] Law Commission (2020), para 6.24.
[20] Law Commission (2020), para 6.32.
[21] The Law Commission acknowledges that there is a distinction between, on one hand, 'serious' emotional harm, and on the other, emotional, psychological, or physical harm that is merely 'non-trivial': Law Commission (2020), para 6.29.
[22] Law Commission (2020), para 6.46.

nonetheless still be insufficient to protect free speech, the inclusion of a defence of 'reasonable excuse' is designed as a safety-net provision, 'to protect freedom of expression and to ensure compatibility with Article 10 of the European Convention on Human Rights'.[23]

How would these changes impact on the freedom to spread political viewpoint information, especially in the run-up to elections? The Law Commission's proposals do not draw distinctions between political viewpoint speech and other kinds of speech. It would be for an accused person, in an individual case, to claim that his or her known-to-be-false political viewpoint statement was made with a reasonable excuse in the circumstances, even though it was intended to cause non-trivial harm. However, there must a concern about the way in which the provisions may impact on, say, a bitter election campaign in which each of two thin-skinned candidates deliberately maligns and traduces the other, in a tit-for-tat mud-slinging exercise. Unedifying though the prospect of such campaigns undoubtedly is, in the absence of hate speech, harassment, or intimidation, is it right to provide recourse to the criminal law as a remedy when candidates simply set out to cause distress to one another in the course of campaigning? As indicated in Chapter 1,[24] it must be kept in mind that use of the law can itself become weaponized for political purposes in this kind of case. An allegation that the making of a known-to-be-false claim was intended to cause non-trivial emotional harm (an allegation easy to make) can straightforwardly become simply another piece of mud to throw, putting the police and prosecution services into a difficult and potentially politicized position.[25]

For example, consider the commonplace allegation that someone's policy proposals mean that they have (say) 'signed up to a Nazi agenda'.[26] Such a claim might be regarded as nothing more than the expression of an opinion or the making of a value judgement directly protected by Article 10, and hence outside the scope of the current law, and of the Law Commission's proposed offence. However, the European Court of Human Rights has taken the view that where an opinion or value judgement is based on some underlying (false) factual claim, then the expression of the opinion or judgement also involves a false statement.[27] Consequently, it may legitimately be the subject of (a proportionate) criminal prohibition. Even so, the European Court has also acknowledged that in relation to, for example, a claim that someone is a 'closet Nazi', 'the assessment of whether a certain statement

[23] Law Commission (2020), para 6.66. For criticism, see Article 19 (2020).

[24] See also the discussion in Chapter 4.

[25] One way to restrict the scope of any new law restricting freedom of speech, in this regard, would be to require proof not only of an intention to cause non-trivial harm, but of actual non-trivial harm caused: see Article 19 (2020).

[26] David Molloy, 'Why Does Everyone Keep Making Nazi Comparisons?' (24 November, 2017), https://www.bbc.co.uk/news/world-39266863 (last accessed 20/04/2021).

[27] *Lingens v Austria* (1986) 8 EHRR 407; *Oberschlick v Austria No. 1* (Application no. 11662/85), of 23 May 1991.

constitutes a value judgement or a statement of fact might in many cases be difficult'.[28] That reinforces the worry that when such allegations are made, in some cases they will be—ironically—a political gift to person against whom they are made, something they can use to bring media and public attention to an issue in their campaign, or simply to suggest that their opponent has resorted to criminal means to win the election.[29] In that regard, it is important to recall the views, cited in Chapter 1, of the French Institute for Strategic Research (Ministry for the Armed Forces) and Policy Planning Staff (Ministry for Europe and Foreign Affairs): 'Overregulation is a real danger, and even a trap set by our adversaries: far from being bothered with overzealous regulations, they will actually benefit from the controversy and divisions that it will create.'[30]

There is a way to create space specifically for protected campaign speech under the 1988 and 2003 Acts, or under replacement legislation. An amendment could indicate, first, that a known-to-be-false statement intended to cause annoyance or inconvenience (2003 Act), distress or needless anxiety (1988 Act), or non-trivial harm (Law Commission proposals) will fall in principle *outside* the scope of the relevant offence, if it involved the expression of a false political viewpoint directed by one election candidate (or their agents) at another during the course of a campaign.[31] This in-principle exclusion would do something to meet the Law Commission's aim of giving a high priority to the protection of free political speech from the application of the criminal law in political campaign cases; but it would also confine the exemption to those directly involved in an election —candidates or agents—thus keeping the scope of the exclusion narrow. Such a change would bring to criminal law something of the policy of section 29J of the Public Order Act 1986, which is designed to protect those who are intemperate in their language, or simply outspoken, from victimization by a criminal law in thrall to oversensitive people:

> Nothing in this Part [hate offences] shall be read or given effect in a way which prohibits or restricts discussion, criticism or expressions of antipathy, dislike, ridicule, insult or abuse of particular religions or the beliefs or practices of their adherents, or of any other belief system or the beliefs or practices of its adherents, or proselytising or urging adherents of a different religion or belief system to cease practising their religion or belief system.

[28] *Scharsach and News Verlagsgesellschaft mbH v Austria* (Application no. 39394/98), 13 November 2003. In this case, which involved journalistic content, the assertion that someone was a 'closet Nazi' was held to be a value judgement, in the particular context, rather than a claim of fact.

[29] An example that comes to mind is that of *Susan B Anthony List v Dreihaus* 45 F Supp 3d 765, 769 (2014), in which the allegedly false claim—'Candidate X's voting record shows she is anti-abortion'—did as much simply to raise the issue as it did to blacken the complainant's name.

[30] Jean-Baptiste Jeangène Vilmer et al. (2018), 176.

[31] Subject to a key exception, set out below.

However, second, there ought to be an exception, where the offences in the 1988 and 2003 Acts (or the Law Commission proposals) should still apply, if a relevant statement was directed at an election candidate and:

(i) the statement was intended to, and did, have a seriously adverse effect on the victim's state of mind, and
(ii) there was no opportunity adequately to counter the effect of the statement.

In this exception, the point of (i) is to go beyond the Law Commission's restriction of the communication offences to cases in which the relevant harm—a seriously adverse effect on the victim's mind—was intended, by further restricting political speech-crime to cases in which the relevant harm was in fact caused.[32] The point of (ii) is to accommodate the 'Brandeis gap' in the efficacy of more-speech solutions, discussed in Chapter 1,[33] where there is no adequate opportunity to counter a false allegation through more speech.[34] The inclusion of (ii) acknowledges that there is an important political context to acts intended to set back the interests of electoral campaign opponents. This is a context in which someone who is victimized by false claims can nonetheless reasonably be expected—if possible—to fight back against such allegations, not just for their own sake but (crucially) for the sake of would-be voters and those who support their campaign.[35] The point of (i) is, as with the Law Commission proposals, to link the criminality of making a false statement with an intended impact on 'negative' political freedom. This is freedom from obstacles to doing as one wishes: including certain internal obstacles, such as fear.[36] Even in election contexts, criminalization can be justified when, through the serious effect it is meant to have—and does have—on V's mind, a false statement does not simply cause significant distress but—in virtue of causing such distress—undermines V's effective participation in the campaign.

Some defamatory statements—including some false political viewpoint statements—might fall within the scope of such a prohibition. Even so, they would only stand to be criminalized because they were intended to have—and did have—a seriously harmful effect of the kind just mentioned (and not because they were defamatory). However, a case could fall within the proposed amendment without

[32] See further, Article 19 (2020).

[33] See Chapter 1, section 1.6(ii) for discussion of the Brandeis gap. It would probably be right to provide that the defendant should bear the evidential burden, in relation to (ii). Prosecution guidance should indicate that a prosecution should not be undertaken when the absence of an adequate opportunity to counter the effect of the statement came from a spreading of the statement through the public domain that D could not reasonably have foreseen as the effect of his or her conduct.

[34] Under the Law Commission's proposals, the absence of a 'Brandeis gap'—in other words, when there is a 'more-speech' opportunity for an opponent to counter an attack by a rival—might go towards establishing a reasonable excuse for making the statement.

[35] So, this is not a point involving 'victim blaming'. It is about the public responsibilities of those standing for public office.

[36] See the discussion in George Crowder (1988).

the false statement being defamatory. An example might be a false but credible statement, sent at a crucial point in the campaign, suggesting that a candidate or campaigner's only child has been killed in an accident in circumstances, perhaps, where the truth was difficult to ascertain. The proposal from the Committee on Standards in Public Life for an offence of intimidating parliamentary candidates or campaigners follows this general line of argument.[37] Intimidation is defined by the Committee as words or behaviour intended or likely to block or deter participation, which could reasonably lead to an individual wanting to withdraw from public life.[38] The point is that criminalization is not justified simply because, for example, a false statement is intended to make V needlessly anxious about whether or not the merits of his or her candidacy or arguments will be accurately understood by voters. To target such cases would involve the criminal law in, in effect, protecting someone from false political viewpoint statements—an inappropriate task (I argued in Chapter 1) for which it is ill-suited.

3.3 The UK's 'Electoral Defamation' Offence in Outline

The provisions of the Coroners and Justice Act 2009 dealing with homicide, and with the reform of coroners' inquests, understandably attracted the lion's share of scholars' critical attention when the Act came into force; but a reform of constitutional significance was also brought about by section 73 of the 2009 Act. This was the abolition of the offences of obscene, seditious, and defamatory libel, a reform which followed on from the abolition of blasphemy and blasphemous libel by section 79 of the Criminal Justice and Immigration Act 2008. The Law Commission[39] had supported the retention of defamation's criminalization in some form, in spite of the fact that there had been no successful prosecutions since the 1970s.[40] The offence was nonetheless abolished by the Labour government in the 2009 Act, on the grounds that such offences 'stem from a bygone age when freedom of expression was not seen as the right that it is today'.[41]

In constitutional terms, the abolition of those offences (together with the abolition of the public order offence of 'insulting' behaviour[42]) made English criminal

[37] Committee on Standards in Public Life (2017).

[38] Ibid., at 26. In cases of *intimidation* (as opposed to false viewpoint information), understood as involving an express or implied threat of physical or psychiatric harm, there is a justification for focusing purely on D's intent, rather than requiring that the intimidation have led to harm done.

[39] Law Commission for England and Wales (1985).

[40] See also John Spencer (1983).

[41] Lord Bach, HL debate on the Coroners and Justice Bill, https://hansard.parliament.uk/Lords/2009-10-28/debates/09102836000557/CoronersAndJusticeBill?highlight=coroners%20justice%20bill#contribution-09102836000245, column 1173 (last accessed 20/04/2021).

[42] Public Order Act 1986, s. 5, as amended by the Crime and the Courts Act 2013, s. 57.

law in an important respect more overtly republican in its attitude to speech.[43] These steps did something to curb overweening or arbitrary official power over speech, by restricting the circumstances in which the commission of a wrong involving an affront to the reputation or dignity of a public official was, in itself, sufficient to justify the intervention of the criminal law. As the Law Commission rightly remarked in its critique, '[t]he history of criminal libel shows that one of its principal uses was once to protect the government from criticism'.[44] So, the abolition of the offence is a republican step, in that, in the words of leading republican theorist Philip Pettit, 'traditionally, republicans have concerned themselves mainly with how to stop the protective state becoming itself a threat to freedom'.[45]

It is important to bear in mind that protection from insult or 'unfair' criticism is still widely afforded to government officials in other democratic countries bound by Article 10 of the ECHR, such as Germany. As we saw in Chapter 2, section 2.6, in spite of the fact that Article 5(1) of Germany's basic law stipulates that 'everyone shall have the right freely to express and disseminate his opinion by speech, writing, and pictures', it is nonetheless an offence under the German Criminal Code to engage criminal insult (Article 185), malicious gossip (Article 186), defamation (Article 187), defamation of the President of the Federation (Section 90), and defamation of the state and its symbols (Section 90a). Whilst the European Court of Human Rights construes such provisions narrowly, especially when they are alleged to have been committed in the course of political debate, offences of this kind are not, as such, contrary to Article 10.[46] Even in the USA, the First Amendment does not prevent states prosecuting cases of criminal defamation, when officials have taken umbrage at attacks on their reputation that they regard as involving untrue statements.[47] In *Garrison v Lousiana*,[48] Garrison was prosecuted for libel when he suggested that delays in the court system could be explained by the fact that the judges were lazy and inefficient. His conviction was overturned by the Supreme Court, in part because the libel offence in question did not require proof of 'malice' (intention or wilful disregard), but Justice Brennan said:

> The use of calculated falsehood, however, would put a different cast on the constitutional question. Although honest utterance, even if inaccurate, may further the fruitful exercise of the right of free speech, it does not follow that the lie,

[43] https://plato.stanford.edu/entries/republicanism/ (last accessed 20/04/2021).There are, of course, other respects in which English criminal law falls well short of the republican ideal as far as free speech is concerned, as in its prohibition on the glorification of terrorism: Terrorism Act 2006, s. 1.

[44] Law Commission (1985), para 5.2.

[45] Philip Pettit (1996), 321.

[46] *Otegi Mondragon v Spain* (Application no. 2034/07) 15 March 2011, para 54; *Lindon, Otchakovsky-Laurens and July v France* (Application nos 21279/02 and 36448/02) 22 October 2007.

[47] Eugene Volokh (2019).

[48] (1964) 379 US 64.

knowingly and deliberately published about a public official, should enjoy a like immunity.[49]

Against this background, we can turn to what appears to be an important exception to this republican turn in English criminal law jurisprudence governing state–citizen relations. This is the continued applicability of what it is convenient—if somewhat misleading—to call the 'electoral defamation' offence in section 106 of the Representation of the People Act 1983.[50] Section 106 (set out in a shorter form in Chapter 1, section 1.1(ii)) reads as follows.

A person who, or any director of any body or association corporate which—

(a) before or during an election,
(b) for the purpose of affecting the return of any candidate at the election, makes or publishes any false statement of fact in relation to the candidate's personal character or conduct shall be guilty of an illegal practice, unless he can show that he had reasonable grounds for believing, and did believe, that statement to be true.[51]

The section 106 offence model—focused on false statements of a personal nature about candidates, and aimed at affecting the candidate' vote return—is mirrored in a number of jurisdictions around the world, including the USA.[52] However, it is important to note that—Brennan J's statement in *Garrison v Louisiana* notwithstanding[53]—the US Supreme Court has cast doubt on the compatibility of such provisions with the First Amendment (unless, perhaps, they are very narrowly drawn), because they impinge on the scope to engage in political speech.[54] Some jurisdictions have broader and some narrower provisions outlawing false statements meant to affect voting at elections,[55] but I will concern myself initially with the section 106 type of offence, focused on false personal claims about candidates.

[49] *Garrison v Louisiana* (1964) 379 US 64, 75. For a contrary view about the constitutionality of prohibiting false statements, in a different context, see *R v Zundel* [1992] 2 SCR 731.

[50] For comprehensive analysis of this provision, see Jacob Rowbottom (2012); Jeremy Horder (2021a).

[51] The conduct described in section 106 is made a criminal offence under s. 169 of the 1983 Act. The offence is punishable upon summary conviction by a fine up to level 5 on the standard scale.

[52] See, for example, Elections Act 1991 (St John's Newfoundland and Labrador), s. 197; Alberta Election Act 2000, s. 160; Prevention of Electoral Abuses Act (Ireland) 1923, s. 11; Mississippi Code: Title 23-Elections, 23-15-875.

[53] Text at n. 49 above.

[54] See the discussion in Stuart P. Green (2018), 491–2.

[55] For broader provisions, see e.g. Colorado Revised Code: Title 1-Elections, 1-13-109(1)-(3); Florida Statutes: Title IX-Electors and Elections, 104.271(2); Minnesota Statutes 2020, 211B.06. For narrower provisions, see e.g. Canada Elections Act 2003, s. 91, as amended by the Elections Modernisation Act 2018, s. 61.

Clearly, the section 106 offence is not a straightforward offence of defamation. To begin with, it is not confined to attacks on or defamation of a candidate, but extends to falsely positive statements about candidates intended to affect their vote return.[56] This is an issue that affects the overall justification for the offence, but I will not be further concerned here with the significance of false positive statements.[57] Second, when a negative false statement about a candidate is involved, section 106 substitutes for the terminology commonly used to describe such a wrong in the civil law of defamation[58] the notion of 'a false statement of fact in relation to the candidate's personal character or conduct'. I examine this notion in detail in section 3.6 below, but one point about its narrowness can be highlighted now. Notably, this notion does not extend to 'misleading' statements about personal character or conduct, even though such statements may be just as damaging to an election candidate as false statements. As indicated in Chapter 1, section 1.3(ii), someone might disseminate a perfectly correct claim that a candidate has been convicted of murder, whilst failing to mention that the conviction was later overturned and the candidate completely exonerated when someone else was proved to have committed the crime. It might be argued that the greater apparent element of value judgement involved in deciding whether a politically motivated statement is 'misleading', as opposed to whether it is simply 'false', makes it less appropriate for judicial determination, but courts are routinely asked to adjudicate on whether statements are 'misleading', for the purposes of criminal liability.[59] Further, as we saw in Chapter 1, difficult questions of value judgement may also arise in cases where the prosecution alleges that D 'knew proposition X was false', in circumstances where D knew others regarded it as false, but did not him or herself accept the standards of truth and falsity applied by the prosecution.

Third, the making or publication of such a false statement about personal conduct or character is not an offence contrary to section 106 unless it is made or published 'for the purpose of affecting the return of any candidate at the election'. The offence is thus one of ulterior intent, something that gives it both greater certainty, in terms of its compliance with the guidance demands of the rule of law, whilst tying it to an important public law purpose: protection of the political and moral integrity of the election contest. Even so, on the face of it, section 106 would not pass muster under the First Amendment to the US Constitution, because there is no requirement for the prosecution to prove 'actual malice' (intention or recklessness).

[56] *Petition of Timothy Denis Morrison and Others against Alistair Carmichael MP and another* [2015] ECIH 71.

[57] See, for further discussion, Jacob Rowbottom (2012); Jeremy Horder (2021a).

[58] Broadly, an untrue imputation against the reputation of individuals, companies, or firms which serves to undermine such reputation in the eyes of right-thinking members of society generally, by exposing the victim to hatred, contempt, or ridicule.

[59] See e.g. Fraud Act 2006, s. 2, and the discussion in Chapter 1, section 1.3. For a defence of the view that misleading statements should not come within the scope of section 106-style offences, see Richard L. Hasen (2013), 71–2.

The offence is satisfied when D publishes a false statement of the relevant kind, believing it to be true but having no reasonable grounds for that belief (section 106(b)).[60] The problem with that, as Lord Diplock memorably put it, is that:

> In ordinary life it is rare indeed for people to form their beliefs by a process of logical deduction from facts ascertained by a rigorous search for all available evidence and a judicious assessment of its probative value. In greater or in less degree according to their temperaments, their training, their intelligence, they are swayed by prejudice, rely on intuition instead of reasoning, leap to conclusions on inadequate evidence and fail to recognize the cogency of material which might cast doubt on the validity of the conclusions they reach.[61]

Any democratic state has what is referred to in US case law as a 'compelling interest' in ensuring that elections are not compromised by illegality in the form of fraud.[62] However, it is not necessary to criminalize false political viewpoint statements in order to serve that interest adequately. The conduct described in section 106 is not only a criminal offence but also amounts to an 'illegal practice' under electoral law. Proof in an electoral court (a hearing before two High Court judges[63]) that someone has engaged in this illegal practice will lead to the banning of the offender from holding elected office for three years.[64] Moreover, section 164 of the 1983 Act empowers an election court to declare an election void when, amongst other things, illegal (or corrupt) practices—such as fraud—have so extensively prevailed that they may reasonably be supposed to have affected the result. My suggestion will be that the existence of electoral sanctions should—other than in exceptional cases—be regarded as sufficient to address what we will see is in fact a broad-ranging wrong created by section 106, covering defamatory remarks unlikely to have much electoral impact.[65]

[60] See *R (on the application of Woolas) v The Parliamentary Election Court* [2010] EWHC 3169 (Admin), para 124; Jacob Rowbottom (2012), 529–30.

[61] *Horrocks v Lowe* [1975] 1 AC 135, 150.

[62] *Crawford v Marion County Election Board* (2008) 553 US 181; *Brown v Hartlage* (1982) 456 US 45; https://www.mtsu.edu/first-amendment/article/31/compelling-state-interest (last accessed 20/04/2021).

[63] Representation of the People Act 1983, s. 123(1).

[64] Representation of the People Act 1983, s. 160(5)(b). Further, if it was the winning candidate who engaged in the illegal practice, the election will be declared void, and re-run: see s. 159 of the 1983 Act. For criticism of the inflexible terms in which s. 159 is expressed, see Jeremy Horder (2021a).

[65] Of course, the electoral sanctions would be no deterrent to someone not entitled to stand for election in the UK, but it ought to be sufficient to deal with the unlikely circumstances in which such a case arose to provide that any UK-based individual who assisted or encouraged such a person would themselves be guilty of an illegal practice.

3.4 Propagating Disinformation: The Origins of Section 106

An election campaign is obviously the key opportunity for parties and candidates not merely to present themselves as fit for government, but also – perfectly legitimately - to explain why other parties and candidates are unfit for government.[66] Whilst that is uncontroversial in itself, as we saw in Chapter 1, research shows that individual voters commonly give more weight to negative than to positive political information, and negative political information is treated as more newsworthy by the media.[67] Of course, complaints about the use of fraud (and other wrongdoing) in the course of elections are nothing new;[68] but from where has come the concern of English criminal law with attacks, through the use of false information, on the conduct and character of election candidates?

In 1895, in debating what was to become the ancestor of section 106,[69] Mr T. H. Bolton (Solicitor, and MP for St Pancras North) complained of 'an illegal practice ... which, he was sorry to say, was too common in elections—the making of false and libellous statements with regard to the personal character and conduct of candidates'.[70] What explained the (perceived) rise in the making of such false statements—'a flagrant offence which stood prominently before the public'[71]—and the increasingly combative nature of elections more generally? The UK franchise was expanded from 720,000 people after 1832 to over 5.7 million people in 1885.[72] At an earlier time, with a much smaller captive electorate to woo in constituencies, and no secret ballot until 1872, it was chiefly bribery, corruption, and intimidation on the part of candidates that preoccupied legislators and reformers who turned their minds to abuses of the system.[73] In 1865, the results in no less than 61 separate constituencies were challenged, on the basis of bribery or other corrupt practices having been employed.[74] Such challenges continued to show up the system in a poor light for years to come: there were 39 challenges following the 1880 election, of which 15 were successful.[75] However, from 1883, there were new restrictions in place on overall expenditure on electioneering,[76] too many potential voters for most candidates to bribe in a cost-effective manner,[77] and no way

66 William G. Mayer (1996).

67 See e.g. Martin Haselmayer (2019), 361 and 364.

68 In 64 BC, Cicero said of election times, 'Deception, intrigue, and treachery are everywhere': Q. T. Cicero, 'On Running for the Consulship', in E. S. Shuckburgh (2015), section 11.

69 The Corrupt and Illegal Practices Prevention Act 1895, s. 1.

70 HC Deb 1 May 1895 vol 33, 219.

71 Ibid.

72 Karen Rix (2017).

73 Ibid. 76. For comparable analysis considering the United States, see Peter H. Argersinger (1985).

74 Caroline Morris and Stuart Wilks-Heeg (2019), 33.

75 Kathryn Rix (2008), 82. In 1860, Sir Frederick Slade QC remarked, 'I do not think that you will ever prevent bribery. You might as well try to prevent the sexes coming together as try to prevent bribery': *Proceedings of Parliament* (1860), vol x, 1–7, 191.

76 Instituted by the Corrupt and Illegal Practices Prevention Act 1883.

77 The 1865 election had revealed the extent of the problem: candidates spent £705,429 on their campaigns, compared with £403,852 in 1859: https://thehistoryofparliament.wordpress.com/2018/07/31/

of checking which way people voted once the ballot had become secret. So, trying to undermine the credentials of rival candidates, by fair means or foul, must have become a tempting alternative short-cut to an election advantage.[78] The strength of the temptation would have come, in part, from the fact that the very idea that a candidate's credentials, or their fitness of office, could and should make a difference in electoral terms—making the telling of lies about such matters politically significant—is itself a product of a changing political environment. The political environment in which the 1895 debate took place was one in which the 'right to rule' of a narrow political class was being replaced by the perceived need for candidates to win over public opinion.[79] What was now needed, said Conservative election agent John Gorst, was argument over 'the character, qualifications, and political views of the candidates'.[80] So, there was now fertile ground for the generation and spread of false claims about election hopefuls.

In that regard, there was no shortage of indignation at what was perceived as a 'gloves-off' approach being taken by some people to campaigning. Sir Frederick Milner, Conservative MP for Bassetlaw, fulminated:

> What right had a candidate, or his agent, to go fishing about and try to take up some rumour about the gentleman who was opposing him? They ought to fight their battles like men, on purely political issues, and if they did try to fish up scandals, whether they believed them or not, they ought to receive just retribution.[81]

Drawing a veil over what might be involved in fighting political battles 'like men', I will come back in due course to Milner's important point about the meaning and desirability of fighting election battles on 'purely political issues'. My focus for now will be the way in which it was feared that the making of false claims about the personal character and conduct of election candidates was becoming such a significant menace that it required the intervention of the criminal law.

By the 1880s, it was common for candidates to employ agents, clerks, investigators, canvassers, and messengers during campaigns, sometimes in their hundreds. The Corrupt and Illegal Practices Prevention Act 1883 (to which the Corrupt and

tackling-electoral-corruption-how-victorian-britain-reformed-the-trial-of-election-petitions-in-1868/ (last accessed 20/04/2021). By 1880, expenditure had reached an astronomic £1,737,300.

[78] Of course, whilst reducing the attractiveness of bribing voters, secret ballots may create incentives to bribe election officials to skew results instead, and may lead to new kinds of fraud, such as the manipulation of voter registration lists and interference with ballot boxes. For discussion, see Susan Rose-Ackerman and Bonnie J. Palifka (2016), 364–7.

[79] See James Thompson (2013), 5–6. I am not claiming, by implication, that electoral corruption was eliminated after 1883.

[80] Hansard, cclxviii (24 April 1882), 1346, cited by Kathryn Rix (2017), 73. See further, E. J. Feuchtwanger (1959).

[81] HC Deb 1 May 1895 vol 33, 227. He went on to complain of 'unmanly and un-English tactics' (such as revealing a candidate's wealth) now being deployed to discredit rivals.

Illegal Practices Prevention Act 1895[82] was an amendment) had sought to impose strict limits on this practice, as it was considered to be simply a cover for vote-buying, but these employees were also put to use in the perpetration of corrupt and illegal practices. It was, said Sydney Buxton (Liberal MP for Peterborough) in 1881, all too easy for a candidate to be 'lured from his lofty eminence of purity down the easy incline of illegalities and colourable employment which lead to the dangerous precipice of corruption'.[83] A way around the financial restrictions of the 1883 Act was to use volunteers as canvassers or in other roles, something beginning to be organized by Party Associations: some 3,000 volunteers were allegedly fielded by the Birmingham Liberal Association in 1880.[84] The importance of this is that, whether they were volunteers or being paid, politically engaged voters were being used to spread disinformation about candidates: '[an] evil ... greatly increased by the growing practice at by-elections of flooding the constituencies with irresponsible outsiders'.[85]

An election agent—some of whom were solicitors—was commonly the culprit, in cases where there was an organized attempt to spread disinformation. The Law Society's President had at one point felt compelled to issue a warning to solicitors not to engage in 'dirty work' when acting as election agents.[86] One instance mentioned in the debates leading to the passing of the 1895 Act was a 'deliberately planned' distribution of placards by the Liberal Agent throughout Evesham, falsely claiming that a candidate, Colonel Charles Long, 'had passed a most cruel and unjust sentence upon a labouring man, because he had taken a handful of corn to give to his little children's rabbits'.[87] On other occasions, as indicated above, men were hired—commonly from outside the constituency—to spread false rumours. An example was the false claim spread at the 1892 general election about the Liberal MP for Gateshead, William Allen, by 'a great number of hireling scoundrels [who] went about the constituency—they came from Sheffield, Birmingham, and other places'.[88] The colourful claim was that Allen was a pirate who had sunk English ships and marooned their crews.[89] There were other instances, as when a false claim was spread when:

> an election agent on the other side engaged a number of men to parade the town on the morning of the poll with large placards stating [the false claims].... It was

[82] See n. 69 above.

[83] S. C. Buxton (1881).

[84] Francis Schnadhorst (1882), cited by Kathryn Rix (2008), 79.

[85] Sir Henry Hobhouse, HC Deb 1 May 1895 vol 33, 238. The Attorney General, Sir Robert Reid, agreed: 'It was a matter of comparatively recent growth, but wherever an election took place, a swarm of people, mostly paid, descended upon the constituency': HC Deb 1 May 1895 vol 33, 246.

[86] Harry Kirk (1976), 193, cited by Kathryn Rix (2008), 81.

[87] HC Deb 1 May 1895 vol 33, 227 (Sir Frederick Milner).

[88] Mr W. Allen, MP for Gateshead, HC Deb 1 May 1895 vol 33, 240.

[89] HC Deb 1 May 1895 vol 33, 241. Allen was elected, in spite of—or perhaps because of—such lurid claims being made.

> stated that the device won many votes for the opposition candidate.... But the truth could not be brought out in time; the injury was done, and was without remedy.[90]

Political 'placarding' was, of course, the Victorian equivalent of using electronic media to spread claims amongst voters as widely as possible. In that regard, it is important to note that some contributors to the debate leading up to the 1895 Act drew a distinction between such coordinated election-spoiling tactics, and the mere voicing of (false) claims:

> No law could be devised which would have the effect of curbing the excited imagination of many political pamphleteers; it would be impossible to check the glib tongue of the frothy stump orator; but it ought to be easy to prohibit the use of placards such as he had exhibited, and the resorts to practices such as had been mentioned.[91]

Yet, neither the 1895 Act, nor its successor, section 106 of the 1983 Act, drew a distinction between these two kinds of situations. It is as much an offence contrary to section 106 for someone spontaneously—say, in angry response to some personal barb during a public debate—to make a false statement about an opposing candidate's personal conduct or character (with intent to affect the voting return) as it for someone premeditatedly to flood the constituency with such statements through the use mailshots, bot-generated online communications, and other like devices. Of course, in human rights terms, there may be as much (or more) that is worthy of protection in the activities of organized political groups as there is in the speech of the solo orator. However, the Victorian politicians' concerns discussed in this section raise the issue of whether the law's approach is proportionate, in terms of the conduct that is targeted. The question is whether the law should distinguish between attempts to influence the intentions of no more than a handful of voters through a false claim—something more likely to be the case with the 'frothy stump orator', or the pamphleteer with an 'excited imagination'—and attempts to ensure that a false claim is sufficiently widely spread and believed as to be liable to affect the election outcome itself.[92] I return to this issue below.

[90] Sir Henry Hobhouse, HC Deb 1 May 1895 vol 33, 239. The false claim in question concerned the (non-) ownership of co-operative stores.

[91] Sir Frederick Milner, HC Deb 1 May 1895 vol 33, 229.

[92] Of course, in a highly marginal constituency, the effective difference between these two situations narrows, but the difference in the nature of what is being attempted may not.

3.5 Free Speech and Viewpoint Disinformation under Section 106

Can the language of the section 106 offence wrongly permit the law to take what was argued in Chapter 1 to be the impermissible path of threatening coercion to deter the spread of political viewpoint disinformation, simply because—in a prosecutor or court's view—it is politically 'disinformative'? The courts have arguably been drawn down this path: for example, in seeking to negotiate the troublesome distinction (mentioned above) between statements of fact and statements of opinion, for the purposes of section 106.[93]

In 1995, Ismail Pirbhai was convicted of publishing a false statement of fact about the personal character of a candidate, contrary to section 106.[94] The statement concerned Jack Straw, who at the time the statement was made was a Parliamentary candidate in Blackburn at the 1992 general election. Pirbhai had published a single sheet that contained the following wording: 'Avoid Mr Straw who hates Muslim, because he is from a Jewish family and Jews are the enemy of Islam and he is a tyrant of Labour Party. No doubt he hates Muslim.' The Crown Court (hearing an appeal from the magistrates' court) found that this statement related to Straw's personal character (a matter to which I return below), and that it was made with the intention of affecting Straw's vote return. The Crown Court also ruled that it was untrue to say that Straw hated Muslims,[95] and that this was a purported statement of fact and not merely an expression of opinion.[96] On appeal to the Divisional Court, Pirbhai's conviction was upheld, on the basis that a statement concerning someone's state of mind (that, for example, they hated a particular group within society) could indeed be a statement of fact and was not necessarily merely the expression of an opinion.[97]

Further support for the conviction comes from the fact that the serious allegations involved in the remarks in *Pirbhai* formed no part of any ongoing political debate: the remark constituted a gratuitous attack on Mr Straw.[98] However, against the court's view, it seems clear that an allegation—however odious and incendiary it may be—that someone with Jewish heritage hates Muslims, involves a strong element of value judgement about that person. Courts should not be too ready to find that false statements involving value judgements made in political contexts

[93] For an election statement dispute involving the fact/opinion distinction, litigated in a civil law context, see *Waterson v Lloyd and Carr* [2013] EWCA (CIV) 136.
[94] *Pirbhai v DPP* [1995] C.O.D. 259 QBD.
[95] Jack Straw did have Jewish heritage, so that part of the statement was true.
[96] On the significance of a factual basis to value judgements under Article 10, see: *Otegi Mondragon v Spain* (Application no. 2034/07) 15 March 2011, para 54.
[97] See also *Angus v Clifford* (1891) 2 Ch 449, at 470.
[98] See by contrast, *Otegi Mondragon v Spain* (Application no. 2034/07) 15 March 2011; *Oberschlick v Austria (no. 2)* (47/1996/666/852) 1 July 1997, where the speech in question was part of an ongoing political debate.

can be subject to criminal sanctions, because political election contests invite the expression of strong opinion and (sometimes, ill-considered or biased) judgement.[99] For criminal law purposes, how clear can it ever be that speakers making claims such as that in *Pirbhai* have been put adequately on notice that their statements are not ones of opinion, but of fact, about the state of mind of the person targeted? There is a significant risk, in such cases, of judges who strongly object to what was said engaging in largely *ex post facto* rationalization of what is little more than emotionally charged politicking. Accordingly, decisions like *Pirbhai* might have a chilling effect on speakers wishing to make allegations in politically highly sensitive areas such as race, but not only in that area.

For example, in *Hoffer and Annen v Germany*,[100] the defendants distributed pamphlets outside a medical centre in Nuremburg which said, amongst other things, that 'Killing specialist for unborn children Dr F [is] on the premises of the Northern medical centre'. Is the allegation that a medical practitioner performing lawful abortions is a 'killing specialist' a misleading statement, a false statement of fact, an opinion, a true statement, or should it be characterized in some other way? When the making of such statements can be the object of criminal prosecution, there is a significant risk that people will be wrongly deterred from engaging in merely provocative and attention-grabbing speech. The courts should generally lean in favour of regarding such statements as statements of opinion that are to be tolerated, most especially when they occur in political contexts.[101] For, as the European Court of Human Rights put in it in *Lingens v Austria*:[102]

> The limits of acceptable criticism are ... wider as regards a politician as such than as regards a private individual. Unlike the latter, the former inevitably and knowingly lays himself open to close scrutiny of his every word and deed by both journalists and the public at large, and he must consequently display a greater degree of tolerance.[103]

3.6 Horns of a Dilemma: Distinguishing Personal from Political Attacks

That brings me to the distinction at the heart of section 106. This is the distinction between a false statement of fact about a candidate's 'personal' conduct or character

[99] See, in particular, *Oberschlick v Austria (no. 2)* (47/1996/666/852) 1 July 1997, and the discussion in Chapter 1.

[100] Application nos. 397/07 and 2322/07), 20 June 2011.

[101] This was the approach of the court in *Waterson v Lloyd & Carr* [2013] EWCA (CIV) 136.

[102] *Lingens v Austria* (Application no. 9815/82), 8 July 1986.

[103] Ibid., para 42. See also *Makraduli v The Former Yugoslav Republic of Macedonia* (Application no. 64659/11), 19 July 2018, paras 69–71.

(prohibited, when made with intent to affect a candidate's return), and a false statement about their political conduct or character (not prohibited).[104] The focus of section 106 on false statements about 'personal' character or conduct, as opposed to political character or conduct, is intended strike a balance between the protection of free political speech and the protection of candidates' reputations, a balancing act that is central to Article 10 of the ECHR. The distinction is also meant to avoid the need for the courts to become embroiled in passing judgment on political viewpoint disinformation. In *R (on the application of Woolas) v Parliamentary Election Court*,[105] the Administrative Court said this about the distinction:

> It was as self-evident in 1895 as it is today, given the practical experience of politics in a democracy, that unfounded allegations will be made about the political position of candidates in an election. The statutory language makes it clear that Parliament plainly did not intend the 1895 Act to apply to such statements.... In our judgment ... a court has to ... decide whether the statement is one as to the personal character or conduct or a statement as to the political position or character of the candidate. It cannot be both.[106]

Admirably clear though this analysis is, there is no avoiding the fact that, as Judge Andrew Saffman put it in *Banwait v Bettany*, 'the line on which a political attack becomes a personal one may not be well defined'.[107] The European Court of Human Rights has made a similar point, indicating that 'political invective often spills over into the personal sphere; such are the hazards of politics and the free debate of ideas, which are the guarantees of a democratic society'.[108] In *Woolas* itself, for example, the Election Court had found, amongst other things, that a false allegation that a candidate had reneged on a promise to live in the constituency was an allegation that related directly to the candidate's personal character: 'a person who breaks his promise is untrustworthy'.[109] However, the High Court overturned this part of the Election Court's decision, on the grounds that the false claim 'is in respect of his trustworthiness in relation to a *political* position. To hold that such a statement fell within the prohibition [section 106] would have a significant inhibiting effect on ordinary political debate'.[110]

[104] For detailed analysis see Jacob Rowbottom (2012); Jeremy Horder (2021a).

[105] [2010] EWHC 3169 (Admin). I will not review all the facts of that case, which has been extensively discussed elsewhere: see e.g. Jacob Rowbottom (2012).

[106] *R (on the application of Woolas) v Parliamentary Election Court* [2010] EWHC 3169 (Admin), paras 110 and 111.

[107] *Banwait v Bettany* [2018] EWHC 3263 QB, para 71.

[108] *Lopes Gomes da Silva v Portugal* (Application no. 37698/97) 28 September 2000, para 34.

[109] *Watkins v Woolas* [2010] EWHC 2702 (QB), at para 109.

[110] *R (on the application of Woolas) v The Parliamentary Election Court* [2010] EWHC 3169 (Admin), para 117 (my emphasis).

The difference of opinion between the judges on this point is understandable. Evidence that a candidate is untrustworthy is evidence that they may well not be fit to hold office—a political issue. As the Supreme Court put it, in *Garrison v Louisiana*: 'Few personal attributes are more germane to fitness for office than dishonesty, malfeasance, or improper motivation, even though these characteristics may also affect the official's private character.'[111] As this passage implies, though, some evidence of 'untrustworthiness'—and hence, of unfitness for office—may come from private conduct, such as evidence arising from a candidate's lifestyle preferences, including their preferences about where to live, that ought in principle not to be weaponized by political opponents. However, a claim (whether or not false) that a candidate has reneged on a promise to have a residential address in the constituency is not a claim relating to a wholly private matter. The claim involves the making of an inescapably political commitment (to the constituency). As the US Supreme Court said of this link between the personal and the political, in *Monitor Patriot Co v Roy*:[112] 'A candidate who, for example, seeks to further his cause through the prominent display of his wife and children can hardly argue that his qualities as a husband or father remain of "purely private" concern.'[113]

In *Woolas*, the High Court said, 'Statements about a candidate which relate, for example, to his family, religion, sexual conduct, business or finances are generally likely to relate to the personal character of a candidate'.[114] By using the qualifier 'generally', the High Court understandably hedges its bets on this issue; but this does suggest that the High Court would have approved of the decision in *Pirbhai*, considered above.[115] The problem, though, is that when an allegation is made—however damaging or outrageous—that an election candidate with Jewish heritage hates Muslims, that is, in context, likely to be an allegation with a strongly *political* character to it, especially in a constituency like Jack Straw's that has a significant minority ethnic population.[116] It does not appear to be an allegation that is purely personal in character. It would, perhaps, have been a different matter if the defendant in *Pirbhai* had falsely claimed that, in virtue of his Jewish heritage, Jack Straw had indicated that he would never employ someone who was a Muslim in his household. That is more unequivocally a false statement relating purely to the candidate's personal character. As the High Court itself in *Woolas* made clear, it is not open to a court to find against a defendant under section 106 on the basis that the false statement in question is a mixture of the personal and the political: it must rule that the statement is one, or the other, and act accordingly. When it is criminal

[111] (1964) 379 US 64, 76–77.
[112] (1971) 401 US 265.
[113] *Monitor Patriot Co v Roy* 401 US 265 (1971), 275 (per Stuart J).
[114] *R (on the application of Woolas) v The Parliamentary Election Court* [2010] EWHC 3169 (Admin), para 112.
[115] See text at n. 94 above.
[116] https://www.lancashire.gov.uk/lancashire-insight/population-and-households/population-and-households-2011-census/population-by-ethnicity/ (last accessed 20/04/2021).

conviction for disseminating false information that is in issue, as in *Pirbhai*, a court ought surely to lean in favour of finding that a statement was political in character, in cases where there is any doubt.[117]

In *Rahman v Earlham*,[118] during a mayoral election campaign, Rahman falsely claimed of his Labour Party opponent, John Biggs:

(a) that Biggs opposed renaming the ward of Spitalfields as Banglatown;
(b) that Biggs's Labour group had wrongly suggested that housing allocations had been biased in favour of Rahman's supporters; and
(c) that Biggs had claimed Rahman only intended to serve the Bangladeshi community in Tower Hamlets, thus inflaming racial tensions by encouraging protests by white racists in the borough.

The trial judge, Richard Mawrey QC, found that these false allegations went beyond claims that Biggs was guilty of making merely 'racially insensitive remarks' (as Rahman's Counsel was prepared to concede[119]), and instead amounted to an allegation of out-and-out racism against Biggs.[120] The judge concluded:

> There can be no doubt that to call a man a racist is to make 'a statement of fact in relation to [his] personal character or conduct' [s. 106] In the multi-racial, multicultural society that is twenty-first-century Britain there can be few more damaging statements to make about anyone.[121]

What should one make of this conclusion, in relation specifically to the false allegations about Biggs? The judge treats the claims as involving an express or implied assertion that Biggs was a racist, and then treats this assertion as a false claim being made about Biggs's personal character. However, first, whilst people might well *infer* that Biggs held racist views from one or more of Rahman's (false) claims, the known likelihood that a particular inference will be drawn from a statement is not the same as an implied assertion to that effect in the statement.[122] So, it is not clear that Rahman made, as section 106 requires, false statements 'in relation to the candidate's personal character or conduct'. Further, the trial judge did not consider whether the false claims related exclusively to Biggs's personal character or conduct (as *Woolas* requires), or were intended to reflect also—or instead—on his political character or conduct. Disgraceful though Rahman's conduct may have been, it is submitted that his false claims should have been regarded as at least partly

117 See e.g. *Oberschlick v. Austria (no. 2)* (47/1996/666/852) 1 July 1997.
118 *R (on the application of Rahman) v Erlam & Ors* [2015] EWHC 4186 (Admin).
119 Ibid., at para 382.
120 Ibid., at para 435.
121 Ibid., at para 38.
122 For discussion, in an evidentiary context, see Paul Kirgis (2001), 283–4.

political in nature, and thus outside the scope of section 106: there is no doubt, for example, that the renaming of the Spitalfields ward was an issue that had been under political discussion.[123] The European Court has clearly indicated that where claims relate to extant political controversy (and are not purely gratuitous attacks), they are deserving of special protection.[124] The court in *Rahman v Erlam* failed to construe section 106 in a narrow and restrictive way, to avoid being called on to pass a judgment—on which the justifiability of a criminal conviction may otherwise hang—on a political viewpoint controversy.

3.7 Reform of the Section 106 Offence?

There is probably no way to provide complete clarity, whilst avoiding arbitrariness, with regard to the limits of false statement offences in this context. However, an alternative approach to the section 106 offence, one more consistent with the approach to free speech developed in Chapter 1, is to start by abandoning the reliance on inclusionary definitions of what the false statement must concern, such as 'personal conduct or character'.[125] Broadly following the approach of section 3 of the Corporate Manslaughter and Corporate Homicide Act 2007 to the limits of the duty of care owed by public authorities,[126] it would be possible instead to adopt an exclusionary approach. For example, section 106 could be reformed to focus on false statements about candidates that are *not* statements about (the candidate's approach to) political, economic, or social policy. This would mean, for example, that a false claim that a candidate was guilty of an offence[127] or of some other non-criminal wrongdoing,[128] or was not eligible to stand for election,[129] could—if made with the relevant intent (considered below)—be subject to criminal prosecution. By way of contrast, false allegations that candidates had supported or implemented racially biased policies,[130] or were disposed to do so,[131] would be protected statements (vile though the allegations might be). It must be kept in mind, so far as protected statements are concerned, that it will still be open to the candidate-victim to

[123] *Erlam v Rahman* [2015] EWHC 1215, para 410; https://www.change.org/p/local-government-boundary-commission-for-england-save-the-spitalfields-and-banglatown-ward-name (last accessed 20/04/2021).

[124] *Otegi Mondragon v Spain* (Application no. 2034/07) 15 March 2011.

[125] For the argument that follows, see Jeremy Horder (2021a).

[126] See e.g. s.3(1): 'Any duty of care owed by a public authority in respect of a decision as to matters of public policy (including in particular the allocation of public resources or the weighing of competing public interests) is not a "relevant duty of care"'.

[127] *The North Division of the County of Louth* (1911) 6 O'M and H 103. See also *Ocala Star-Banner Co v Damron* 401 US 295 (1971), and the unreported case of Miranda Grell (discussed below).

[128] *Waterson v Lloyd and Carr* [2013] EWCA (CIV) 136.

[129] https://www.nytimes.com/topic/subject/birther-movement-obama-birth-certificate (last accessed 20/04/2021).

[130] *R (on the application of Rahman) v Erlam & Ors* [2015] EWHC 4186 (Admin).

[131] *Pirbhai v DPP* [1995] C.O.D. 259 QBD: text at n. 94 above.

sue in private law for defamation, where different canons of construction govern the courts' interpretation of what has been said.

If, though, section 106 is to remain, alongside the introduction of an 'exclusionary' approach to the kind of statements covered, the specific intention with which D must have acted in making a false statement—'the purpose of affecting the return of any candidate at the election'—should also be given a different focus. This element is controversial, in part because it does not involve wrongdoing in itself. Whilst personal intimidation and abuse may involve a wider range of motives, almost all election-related statements about candidates made by their supporters or rivals—whether involving true, misleading, or false statements—are likely to be intended to affect the candidates' vote return: the existence of the intent simply reveals the political explanation for the making of the statements. Further, the specific intent covers too many trivial cases, and involves the law in the criminalization of false statements that would not even be prohibited by the civil law of defamation. As far as this second issue is concerned, the problem is that an intention to affect a candidate's return may be evinced by an intention to influence the way in which a single person votes—for example, someone's spouse. Can it really be right that section 106 applies, for example, to a remark made privately to a spouse or friend?

As far as the first issue is concerned (trivial cases), the problem is that the law looks no further than the fate of the individual candidate affected by the false statement, and is not concerned with the electoral impact of the false statement overall. So, in an election in which 80,000 votes are cast, to use a false statement in order to take one vote from an outsider candidate, whose modest aim was to garner a few hundred votes, is as much an offence as using a false statement intended to deprive an otherwise likely winner of tens of thousands of votes.[132] A related problem, going back to the analysis of the history of section 106 in section 3.2 above, is that section 106 fails to draw any distinction between the spur-of-the-moment diatribes of the 'frothy stump orator'[133] and planned or systematic attempts (as, in the nineteenth century, through placarding) to affect the outcome of the election as a whole.[134] So, it can be argued that criminalization of the illegal practice in section 106 is disproportionately wide in scope, as a response to the problem of false statements about candidates at election times. In that regard, a useful case to discuss is the unreported case of Miranda Grell.[135]

Grell, a Labour Councillor, was fined £1,000, forced to vacate her Waltham Forest seat, and banned from holding public office for three years, following conviction for a breach of section 106. During the election campaign, she was found to have communicated to a number of local residents a false claim that her gay Liberal

[132] See the discussion in ch. 4 of *Sanders & Huggett v Chichester* [1994] EWHC 9 (QB).
[133] Text at n. 91 above. See also *Vitrenko v Ukraine* (Application no. 23510/02), 16 December 2008.
[134] See the helpful discussion in Staci Leiffring (2013), 1075.
[135] http://news.bbc.co.uk/1/hi/england/london/7006231.stm (last accessed 20/04/2021).

Democrat rival, Barry Smith, was dating a 19-year-old boy, and was a paedophile. Smith lost his seat to Grell, was abused and threatened in public, and moved to the North of England, fearing for his safety. Grell's conduct constituted, by any standard, a completely unacceptable personal attack on Smith that had nothing to do (going back to the distinctions made above) with his views on political, economic, or social policy. Nonetheless, as with *Pirbhai* considered earlier, how consistent is the possibility of criminal conviction in such a case with the rationale for the abolition of criminal defamation in England and Wales?[136] If D's intention is simply to defame V, and damage V politically in the eyes of one or more voters, then public law remedies—such as being forced to vacate one's seat, or endure a ban on holding public office[137]—ought to be regarded as easily sufficient.[138] It is perhaps arguable, by contrast, that the criminal law would be more justifiably invoked if D's intention went further, and was that the false statement should be widely and deeply influential, with the capacity to affect the outcome of the election as a whole; but there are difficulties about this residual role for the criminal law.

Section 164 of the 1983 Act empowers an election court to declare an election void when, amongst other things, illegal (or corrupt) practices have so extensively prevailed that they may reasonably be supposed to have affected the result. One way to make the criminalization of false statements about election candidates more proportionate, in line with the suggestion in the last paragraph, is to tie it to this set of circumstances. The aim of criminalization would be to deter and prevent the dissemination of false statements that are intended to be so extensively influential with voters as to be capable of affecting the result of the election itself. However, the difficulty with giving the criminal law a role on this kind of basis is that it would mean in practice offering protection only to candidates who stood a good chance of being elected. 'Fringe' candidates, with no realistic chance of winning the election, would not be protected, however widely disseminated the falsehoods about them. It would be best thus to abolish the criminal offence created by section 106, and rely on the public law remedy in section 164 to ensure that the use of fraud does not threaten to undermine compliance with Article 3 of Protocol 1 of the ECHR: 'The High Contracting Parties undertake to hold free elections at reasonable intervals by secret ballot, under conditions which will ensure the free expression of the opinion of the people in the choice of the legislature.'

[136] See section 1.1 above.

[137] Curiously, in virtue of section 160(5), these are only sanctions available when someone has committed an illegal practice contrary to section 106, even though the offence may be committed by someone who was not, and has no intention of, standing for office. It ought to be possible to impose a ban on voting in such cases, as a more potent electoral sanction.

[138] I say 'easily sufficient' because of course the victim of the false statement has remedies in private law. It should be kept in mind that it is possible to obtain an injunction to prevent the making or repetition of the false statement.

4

Election Fraud and Adjudication: UK Law and Beyond

The state does not possess an independent right to determine truth and falsity in public issues.

State of Washington v 119 Vote No! Committee 957 P 2nd 691 (1998), 698.

4.1 Introduction

When the UK Parliament passed the Election Petitions and Corrupt Practices at Elections Act 1868 ('the 1868 Act'), its provisions for dealing with electoral fraud and corruption were described to the Queen by Prime Minister Benjamin Disraeli as involving a constitutional principle of 'vast importance'.[1] Henceforth, electoral malpractice—a staple of Victorian elections[2]—would no longer be investigated by a committee of five MPs (prone to vote along partisan lines[3]), but would instead be resolved by a judge of the superior courts sitting in the relevant constituency.[4] Such a change was meant to stamp out abuses such as political 'log-rolling', in which parties would tacitly agree not to enquire closely into corruption in each other's constituencies, thus leaving tainted elections to stand.[5] And so, the long-standing practice of Members of Parliament having exclusive jurisdiction over the elected membership—'regarded by generations of statesmen as an indispensable privilege of an independent legislature'[6]—came, in this crucial area of contention, to an end.[7]

[1] Benjamin Disraeli to Queen Victoria, 31 January 1868, in M. W. Pharand et al., *Benjamin Disraeli Letters 1868: Volume X* (Ontario: University of Toronto Press, 2014), 40, cited by Kathryn Rix (2017), 65.

[2] See the discussion in Kathryn Rix (2008).

[3] See Andrew Eggers and Arthur Spirling (2014), 5.

[4] An 'election court' is now comprised of two High Court judges. The court established to try parliamentary election petitions was constituted by two judges from 1879 onwards, and was not referred to as an 'election court' until 1883: Law Commission for England and Wales (2012), para 1.10.

[5] Kathryn Rix (2017), 72. See also Cornelius O'Leary (1962), 20–1. In debating the Corrupt Practices Bill in 1854, Sir John Trollope remarked, 'It was quite clear that during the last Session a great number of petitions was presented with no other intention than that of pairing off': HC Deb 10 February 1854 vol 130 (10 February 1854), col 438. See also Law Commission for England and Wales (2012).

[6] *Annual Register*, 1868 (1869), 38, cited by Kathryn Rix (2017), 65.

[7] For broader discussion of how electoral disputes are and should be resolved, see L. Massicotte, A. Blais, and A. Yoshinaka (2004). See also the United States Constitution, Article 1, Section 5, Clause 1,

Criminal Fraud and Election Disinformation. Jeremy Horder, Oxford University Press. © Jeremy Horder 2022.
DOI: 10.1093/oso/9780192844545.003.0005

My main focus in this chapter, in terms of the powers of the courts to address electoral wrongdoing, is fraud in a broad sense, including the use not only of deception but of false pretences and trickery. I will begin with an examination of pioneering nineteenth-century legislation in England and Wales. I choose this starting point not only because the foundations of the approach I will defend can be found there, but also because that legislation has influenced, and continues to influence, jurisdictions outside England and Wales.[8] Electoral fraud was not, compared to the use of bribery and intimidation at elections, especially high on the list of concerns voiced by early Victorian franchise reformers.[9] Nonetheless, there were consistent complaints about personation—a classic election fraud—described as 'flagrant', and 'common in Parliamentary elections',[10] and about the associated abuse (in the form of sharp practice or trickery, rather than fraud) of 'faggot voting'.[11]

It had been common, at least since the 1830s, to refer to the practices in need of stamping out as 'bribery and undue influence',[12] where the latter was understood to include not only common-or-garden intimidatory threats from the laity[13] but also the (*ex hypothesi*) baneful influence of partisan priests suggesting that eternal damnation awaited anyone who voted the 'wrong' way.[14] By way of example, in relation to intimidation, in a debate in 1854 on the issuing of a new writ for the election of two Burgesses to serve for Cambridge, Mr H. Berkley MP remarked:

which states, 'Each House shall be the Judge of the elections, Returns, and Qualifications of its own Members . . .'.

[8] Canadian state and federal law being a prominent example. See e.g. Election Act 1996 (British Columbia) s. 256. See also Election Offences Act 1954 (Malaysia), s. 9; Massachusetts, General Laws, Part 1, Title VIII, ch 56, s. 42.

[9] In introducing the Corrupt Practices Bill in 1854, and the draft clause creating the relevant offences, Lord John Russell does not mention fraud at all as a basis for overturning an election result: HC Deb 10 February 1854 vol 130, col 412 ff.

[10] Select Committee on the Operation and Effect of Corrupt Practices Prevention Act 1854 (1860), paras 1960 and 2070. 'Personation agents' employed by each party at the polls in Ireland were meant to operate as a check against personation: ibid. 1679. See also Mr Liddell MP, who complained of 'an abuse which prevailed at election contests, more particularly in seaport towns—namely, the personation of voters': Hansard, 3rd Series, vol 135 (1854), 504.

[11] In which someone would claim to have met a property qualification to vote, in virtue of benefitting from the deliberate splitting of a beneficial interest in property solely in order to create more qualified voters: 'There were liverymen who had no connection with the City, beyond the fact that they were faggot voters . . . they were now living away from [the city] and their only qualification was that they had . . . bought their liveries at the cost of a small sum of money': HC Deb 12 July 1888, vol 328, col 1183. See also Hansard, 3rd Series, vol 184 (1866), col 439. Faggot voting was abolished by a combination of the effect of the Representation of the People Act 1867 and the Representation of the People Act 1884.

[12] See e.g. Mr George Faithful MP, HC Deb 6 May 1833, vol 17 col 964.

[13] A broad notion, including 'fear of incurring the displeasure of influential individuals', according to Lord Dudley Stuart, debating a motion to introduce a secret ballot to deter the use of undue influence: HC Deb 7 March 1850, vol 109 col 505.

[14] See, for example, *The Petition of Sir Francis Leopold M'Clintock* (1869) 1 O'M and H 252: Election voided when the person complained of (one Whitworth) was found to have organized a system of intimidation through the Roman Catholic clergy of the borough, Drogheda. It is worth noting that the Roman Catholic clergy was held to have the right to address their congregations more narrowly on the merits of the candidates: *The Petition of Thomas M'Govern* (1869) 1 O'M and H 303.

> In regard to the borough of Cambridge … wherever there was a university there was intimidation. The intimidation carried on by the University of Oxford was a palpable, notorious and crying evil. The same observation applied equally to Cambridge, which was as corrupt a place as any in the kingdom.[15]

The broadening of the franchise had given rise to such concerns, because—for example—once tenants and employees (servants) were permitted to vote, they could be threatened with eviction or dismissal if they failed to follow a landlord or employer's instructions on which way to vote.[16] John Stuart Mill further cautioned that if votes were to be given on paper rather than in person, 'every tenant may be taken to the drawing room of his landlord and there compelled to sign his voting paper'.[17] As this opinion reveals, there was a widespread assumption that that newly enfranchised voters were, unlike the traditional political classes, simply more susceptible to ill-motivated outside influences. As Robert Lowe MP famously put the point: 'If you want venality, if you want ignorance … and facility for being intimidated; or, if … you want impulsive, unreflecting and violent people, where do you look for them in the constituencies? Do you go to the top or to the bottom?'[18] No doubt, the assumption was that the new class of voter would be more susceptible to frauds, even of a comparatively venial kind.

Accordingly, the Corrupt Practices Prevention Act 1854 ('the 1854 Act'), substantially re-enacted in the 1868 Act and in all subsequent legislation,[19] wrapped fraud as a form of electoral malpractice into undue influence. The 1854 Act made the following conduct (along with bribery and intimidation) a criminal offence, as well as—if sufficiently widespread and potentially influential—a ground for declaring an election void:

> Undue Influence: Every person who shall … by … any fraudulent device or contrivance impede or prevent the exercise of the franchise of any elector, or shall thereby compel, induce, &c., any elector to give or refrain from giving his vote, shall be guilty of undue influence.[20]

[15] Hansard, 3rd Series, vol 135 (1854), 1543.

[16] See e.g. Richard Groom (1980), 19.

[17] John Stuart Mill, Hansard 3rd Series, vol 189 (1867), col 1192.

[18] Robert Lowe (1867), 74, cited by Robert Saunders (2007), 576 See also the remarks of solicitor William Gibson, giving evidence to the Select Committee on the Operation and Effect of Corrupt Practices Prevention Act (1854), 1675: 'I think very few of the lower class of voters would be free agents in the signature of … voting papers.'

[19] See now the Representation of the People Act 1983, s. 115.

[20] It is arguable that much earlier legislation may have covered the use of fraud in elections. For example, the Statute of Westminster 1275 declared 'Because elections ought to be free, the King commands, under pain of great forfeiture, that no great man or other, by force or arms, nor by *malice* or menacing, shall disturb any to make free election' (my emphasis).

The main object of the clause, said Spencer Walpole QC MP, 'was to guard the free exercise of the franchise'.[21] The wording has survived largely unchanged in the present law[22] (not only in England and Wales but in other jurisdictions too, as we will see), and may be found in section 115 of the 1983 Act (I shall refer to it as the 'section 115 offence'). In that regard, it is illuminating to consider some of the frauds that this provision was intended to address. One kind of election fraud had arisen in relation to the election of poor law overseers, where voting took place through the use of voting papers. These frauds were highlighted by a Parliamentary Committee, reviewing the 1854 Act in 1860, when the Committee came to consider the possible use of voting papers in parliamentary elections. The frauds in question were tampering with voting papers, along with the filling in of papers with fictitious details.[23] Another example of a 'fraudulent device'—one to which we will return—was the use of similar names for candidates or parties, to confuse voters (as in a Kidderminster Municipal election in 1877[24]). A final example comes from an objector in Parliament to the inclusion in the 1854 Act of the phrase, 'by ... *any* fraudulent device or contrivance' (my emphasis). Mr Vernon Smith MP, rightly observing that the law would thus operate with no *de minimis* principle, complained that:

> [T]he phrase might be applied to every minute interference, such as the harmless hoaxes sometimes resorted to of inducing voters to go into other counties by invitations to pretended entertainments or festivities, in order to prevent them from giving their votes .... [I]f people were foolish enough to be duped in this manner ... it was rather below the dignity of legislation to interfere for their protection.[25]

It is worth noting that, wide though the phrase 'any fraudulent device or contrivance' might thus appear in scope, it was found to be—and remains now—in one respect arguably too narrow. It does not cover trickery (as in the case of faggot voting[26]) involving no fraud. An example was a practice commented on by the famous colonist Edward Gibbon Wakefield (1796–1862). Wakefield remarked that some voters enfranchised in 1832 were then deprived of their vote when an unexpectedly early day was intentionally set for the payment of a tax, payment of the tax

21 Select Committee on the Operation and Effect of Corrupt Practices Prevention Act (1854), 1469.

22 The provision was expanded to include acting with 'intent' to impede or prevent etc, irrespective of whether the attempt was successful, in 2006. See Law Commission for England and Wales (2012), para 11.47.

23 Select Committee on the Operation and Effect of Corrupt Practices Prevention Act (1854), para 1089: 'In Ireland ... extensive frauds were committed in the filling up of papers, particularly in the cases of persons who could not write.' See also para 2070.

24 Richard Groom (1980), 297.

25 Hansard, 3rd Series, vol 134 (1854), 1469.

26 See text at n. 11 above.

being a condition of entitlement to vote. The result was that voters were taken by surprise and found themselves disqualified at the next election.[27] An act of 1843 sought to do something to counter this practice, by giving voters more time to pay their rates, but the scope of wrongdoing under the 1854 Act was not revisited.

Although commonly lumped together in offence definitions, electoral bribery and fraud are in important respects different. They are different morally, in that fraud—like intimidation—threatens to impinge on voter autonomy, whereas bribery does not.[28] Indeed, according to one school of thought (drawing on Edward Gibbon's famous remark that corruption is 'the most infallible symptom of constitutional liberty'[29]), the use of bribery-for-votes was an indication of rude constitutional health. It was taken to be a sign that voters could not be controlled or intimidated in voting, and so would have to be bought.[30] Bribery and fraud were also different politically in that electoral bribery, unlike fraud, was the palpable embodiment of the link between membership of Parliament and the privileges of wealth.[31] It has been said that the choice of a political candidate was at that time, 'almost entirely determined by his willingness and ability to spend money'.[32] However, legislation which outlaws bribery as an influence on voting ought, perforce, also to seek to prohibit at least some kinds of fraud, in order to avoid arbitrariness in the reach of offences. Consider an old case in which an allegation was raised that a deaf man had been promised a cure for his deafness in exchange for his vote.[33] The applicability of the relevant provision ought not to turn on whether the promise was sincere (in which case, it would involve bribery but not fraud), or insincere (in which case, it would involve fraud but not bribery).

Bearing in mind, though, that the wording of the provision set out above remains largely unchanged in the present law (the section 115 offence), an important question is: how widely was the prohibition on the use of a fraudulent 'device or contrivance' intended to go? Consistent with the theme developed throughout this book, my answer to that question will be that the prohibition was concerned with electoral participation fraud, and not with political viewpoint fraud. Having shown how the historical context demonstrates that this was so, I will then go on to examine the merits and demerits of expanding the scope of section 115-type

[27] Edward Gibbon Wakefield (1834), 115 See further, Law Commission for England and Wales; Scottish Law Commission; Law Commission for Northern Ireland (2014), para 11.50.

[28] Unless, of course, an offer of a bribe is perceived to carry with it an implied threat of unpleasant consequences if the bribe is not accepted.

[29] Edward Gibbon (1836 edition), ch. 21, pt V, 'We combat (says Hilary of Poitiers) against Constantius the Antichrist; who strokes the belly instead of scourging the back'.

[30] See e.g. Dr J. T. Ball MP, HC Deb 26 June 1871, vol 207 col 626. Whilst the use of bribery might not impinge on voters' autonomy, its use distorts the political process by making it possible heavily to influence or determine the outcome of elections through spending alone. In other words, it is forbidden for the same reason overall spending by parties on election campaigns is limited.

[31] See the passage cited from John Stuart Mill's contributions to the debate: text at n. 42 below.

[32] Charles Seymour (1915), 390.

[33] *Petition of Robert Richard Broad and Others* (1869) 1 O'M and H 127.

offences to cover political viewpoint fraud or disinformation. Following the suggestion made in Chapter 1, I will argue that such an expansion is wrong in principle. In that regard, I will focus not so much on the substantive political case for tolerating the dissemination of political viewpoint fraud (the main concern of Chapter 1), but on an argument that such an expansion wrongly places the judiciary in a position in which they have to take an overtly political approach to adjudication, in determining the applicability of criminal sanctions. To that end, I consider case law development in England, in Canada and in Australia, analysing the different approaches that have been taken.

What happens when courts extend section 115-type provisions to cover political viewpoint fraud, as we will see in due course that the Canadian Courts have done? Courts that proceed down that path purport to do so by applying supposedly neutral adjudicative principles, distinguishing 'factual' political claims (justiciable) from political value judgements (non-justiciable). However, courts making this distinction are in practice likely to be adopting a highly contentious political framework for adjudication, one that inappropriately furthers a rationalist, militant democratic political agenda.[34] The adoption of such a framework overexposes to the risk of criminalization certain kinds of political electioneering: for example, electioneering based on nationalistic myth-making[35] or on emotive distortions and misrepresentations of opponents' commitments.[36] Courts in liberal-democratic jurisdictions should eschew such an approach by confining their interventions in election fraud cases to instances of electoral participation fraud (as I have defined that notion).

4.2 Historical Foundations: Fraud as Electoral Malpractice

In order to answer the question of how wide a range of frauds what is now the section 115 offence was intended to cover, it is important to set Victorian law reforms in context. In the 1850s, when the Corrupt Practices Act 1854 (one of the 1983 Act's predecessors) was debated and enacted, a significant number of parliamentary seats were effectively controlled by wealthy and influential families who held sway over the small numbers of people eligible to vote.[37] Consequently, a remarkably small percentage of seats saw a contested election;[38] and even in

[34] Se Chapter 1 for an explanation of these terms.
[35] Arash Abizadeh (2004).
[36] See, for example, *The State of Washington on the relation of Public Disclosure Commission v 119 Vote No! Committee* 135 Wn 2d 618 (1998), in which the Washington Supreme Court refused to uphold the constitutionality of a statute that forbade falsehoods of this type.
[37] E. Miall (1848), 34, speaks of 'the extraordinary and paramount influence of the hereditary nobility'. See also Norman Gash (1977), Appendix D.
[38] In his survey of small-town voting practices, Edwin Jaggard notes that between 1832 and 1865, only 57 per cent of the elections were contested, although that was a great increase on the period

constituencies where a vote took place, there were 115 small boroughs in 1852 (boroughs with 1,000 voters or fewer), which sent some 176 MPs to Westminster.[39] The small-scale nature of such electorates made bribery in exchange for electorally significant numbers of votes a very realistic possibility, and hence one that was frequently exploited.[40] In 1859, the enormous sum of £403,852 was expended on bribes in the general election.[41] It was one of John Stuart Mill's hopes, as Liberal MP for Westminster, that the 1868 Act would, by deterring bribery, lead to a different breed of MP in the House of Commons: MPs more concerned with politics than with—as he snidely remarked—gaining a position in the social hierarchy that might otherwise not be open to them:

> They [the reformers] desired to diminish the number of men in this House, who came in, not for the purpose of maintaining any political opinions whatever, but solely for the purpose, by a lavish expenditure, of acquiring the social position which attended a seat in this House, and which, perhaps, was not otherwise to be attained by them.[42]

What does this tell us? To be sure, debates about electoral reform were heavily influenced by partisanship on all sides: how would a particular party's electoral prospects fare if the franchise was extended, or a secret ballot introduced, and so on?[43] However, whilst debates on matters of political principle were far from irrelevant to mid-nineteenth-century voters in many constituencies,[44] reliance on popularizing substantive political viewpoints (and the political credentials of the candidates) did not play anything like the crucial role in electioneering that it does today. It follows that, in seeking to reform the process in the mid-nineteenth century by deterring and punishing electoral dirty tricks, Parliament was emphatically not seeking primarily to ensure that voters were not misled or deceived as to the political positions being adopted by candidates or as to the candidates' conduct and character. In the UK, a high-level concern with political disinformation about

1800–31 when the figure was 11 per cent. By contrast, between 1868 and 1880, 84 per cent were contested: Edwin Jaggard (2004), 14.

[39] Edwin Jaggard (2004), 15.

[40] A secret ballot was not compulsory in the UK until 1872. Bribery was also perceived to be a 'big city' problem. In the debates leading up to the passing of the 1854 Act, Sir Fitzroy Kelly, Tory MP for East Suffolk, complained that 'In Liverpool, Hull, Norwich, among the largest, wealthiest, and most populous towns of the British Empire, corruption had been found most extensively to prevail': HC Deb 16 February 1854, vol 130 col 737.

[41] That is approximately £32 million, in modern terms. Gladstone complained that, whilst it had not necessarily become more intense, bribery had 'grown far more patent, and therefore more scandalous, of late years': *Hansard*, HC Deb, 3rd ser., 5 February 1867, clxxxv, cols 71–2, cited by Kathryn Rix (2017), 66.

[42] HC Deb, 21 May 1868, col 686, cited by Andrew Eggers and Arthur Stirling (2014), 8.

[43] See e.g. Laura Bronner (2014).

[44] See Edwin Jaggard (2004); Frank O'Gorman (1989).

candidates and their values only came later, when the franchise had been greatly expanded, and winning over public opinion counted for much more.[45] An example of that latter concern, considered in Chapter 3, was the enactment for the first time, in 1895, of a prohibition on the making of false claims about a candidate's personal conduct or character.[46]

If not to deter and punish political viewpoint fraud, what, then, was the concern of Parliament in 1854 in enacting what is now section 115 of the 1983 Act? In the 1875 case of *Re East Northumberland Election* (Ontario),[47] a circular was published wrongfully alleging that one of the candidates had despaired of winning and, therefore, wanted his friends to vote for one of the other candidates. In applying the relevant provision (in much the same terms as its English equivalent), Mr Justice Gwynne drew an important distinction. First, he identified cases—and he thought the current case was one—in which candidates 'were by a falsehood appealing to the electors to exercise their judgment in voting for the friend of the parties issuing the circular'.[48] Such cases, cases of 'political viewpoint' fraud (in my terms), would not be justiciable. Second, there were cases in which

> the act complained of ... would have been calculated to have the effect of misleading persons, *without any exercise of judgment*, to place their mark on the ballot paper opposite the respondent's name only, and so have been calculated to make persons, by a trick and deception, vote for a candidate for whom at the time of voting they did not intend to vote.[49]

By contrast, the latter kinds of cases were to be regarded as justiciable. The most important class of justiciable frauds in election cases—those which mislead 'without any exercise of (political) judgment'—are what I have been calling electoral participation frauds.[50]

Political viewpoint frauds and electoral participation frauds are not the only species of fraud addressed by electoral law (as we will see), but my argument has been that the contrast between them is of great importance. The wording of the version of the 1854 Act now embodied in section 282.8 of Canada's Elections Act 2000 supports the distinction between them, and the understanding of the limits to justiciability to which that distinction gives rise. Section 282.8 forbids the use of 'pretence or contrivance' to influence someone (not) to vote, or (not) to vote for a particular candidate, 'including by representing that the ballot or special ballot

45 James Thompson (2013), 5–6. The numbers entitled to vote were 1.43 million in the early 1860s, 2.5 million after the Parliamentary Reform Act 1867, and 8 million after the Reform Act 1884.

46 Corrupt and Illegal Practices Prevention Act 1895, s. 1, discussed in Chapter 3.

47 (1875) 1 HEC 387 (Ontario).

48 Ibid. 391.

49 Ibid. (my emphasis).

50 See Chapter 1 and Staci Leiffring (2013), 1078.

or the manner of voting at an election is not secret'.[51] The specific inclusion of this indicative example is telling, because fraud concerning the secrecy of the ballot is fraud concerned with an issue bearing on voter participation, and not a political viewpoint fraud.[52] Section 282.8 of Canada's Election Act 2000 makes a contribution to that end, because the secrecy of the ballot is of the essence in any systematic attempt to prevent intimidation as a threat to autonomy in voting.

4.3 Electoral Participation Frauds and Political Viewpoint Frauds

I indicated above that the wording of the 1854 Act (or something close to it), with regard to the use of fraud to interfere in the electoral process, is now to be found in section 115 of the 1983 Act, as well in the electoral codes of other jurisdictions. We now know that the clear intention of the legislature, with regards to the wording of the section 115 offence, was to target the use of fraud (or intimidation) to interfere with the participation element of the electoral process. The participation element has two dimensions to it, a liberty and an equality dimension.[53]

The liberty dimension involves a kind of negative liberty,[54] freedom 'from' certain kinds of threat to one's autonomy in political decision-making (fraud; intimidation). The threat, where intimidation is concerned, may seem obvious. Even so, it is worth noting that—as we have seen—the law has always imposed only loose conditions on what amounted to the kind of intimidation regarded as sufficient to impede or prevent the free exercise of the franchise in any individual case.[55] As Sir Fitzroy Kelly put it, in suggesting that voters should be required to pronounce their independence of mind in voting: '[T]he voter, besides abjuring bribery and any species of corruption, should declare, in direct and solemn terms, that he gave his vote freely and willingly, and according to the best of his judgment and conscience, and not under any intimidation or coercion or undue influence whatsoever.'[56]

The same point can be made about fraud. For example, in their late-nineteenth-century commentary on 1854 Act provisions, Mattinson and Macaskie suggest that it would be sufficient to bring someone—A—within the scope of the 1854 Act

[51] It broadly reflects the concerns of the nineteenth-century case of *Down* 3 O'M and H 122, in which the court divided on the question of whether the offence was committed, when an election agent distributed 10,000 copies of a newspaper falsely claiming that the agent would be able to discover how electors had cast their votes. See the discussion in M. W. Mattinson and S. C. Macaskie (1883), 55.

[52] Historically, after voter registration was first introduced in England and Wales in 1832, voter registration was frequently subject to politically motivated, partisan meddling and fraud: Cornelius O'Leary (1962), 16; J. A. Thomas (1950).

[53] See Jeremy Horder (2021a).

[54] George Crowder (1988).

[55] As Mr Milner Gibson MP put it, 'why, they all knew that sometimes a look or a frown was sufficient to influence a voter': HC Deb 10 February 1854, vol 130 col 419.

[56] HC Deb 16 February 1854, vol 130, cols 750–751.

that they formed an agreement with B that neither would vote, when A secretly intended all along to go ahead and vote.[57] What this suggests is that, in relation to the liberty dimension to electoral participation, the law was not especially concerned with whether or not the will of an individual voter was wholly subverted by fraud, or overborne by a threat to the person—a traditional test for the legal effect of duress or fraud in private law.[58] As long as a causal link with the voter's behaviour was established, the law was more concerned with the culpability of the intimidating or defrauding offender, operating in that respect as a traditional *malum in se* offence.

By way of contrast, as we saw in Chapter 1, securing the equality dimension to electoral participation more closely resembles a regulatory enterprise, albeit that proof of fault in relation to fraud or intimidation may be required. The equality dimension to participation involves securing every voter's 'positive liberty' in the electoral sphere: freedoms to engage in valued political activities connected to the franchise.[59] The enjoyment of positive liberties commonly requires organized—often, state sponsored—support.[60] As we saw in Chapter 1, these liberties are secured when, for example, adequate facilities are provided for voting, when there is adequate time provided to reach the polls, when voters are not deterred by complex schemes for proof of identity or registration, and also when voters can be confident that their votes will be securely and impartially counted. Further, albeit more controversially, certain essential kinds of reliable information must also be provided about political parties and their candidates, if positive electoral liberty is adequately to be protected. A right to vote is deprived of its value when the voter has no basis on which to distinguish between the identities of parties and candidates. However, crucially, this argument does not extend to the elaboration of political viewpoints. To begin with, no candidate is obliged to disclose their political standpoint. A candidate is perfectly entitled to say merely 'Vote for me, the mystery candidate'. So, there is no right to know what policies a candidate, or a party, will pursue, even if few votes will in practice be secured by candidates or parties that keep their political cards close to their chests. Let us consider how this distinction stands up, in the light of an examination of the case law.

In *Sanders & Huggett v Chichester*,[61] a European Parliament election was held in the Devon and East Plymouth constituency on 9 June 1994. The election was won by Bryan Chichester, the Conservative Party candidate, with 74,953 votes. His nearest rival, the Liberal Democrat Party candidate, Adrian Sanders, received 74,253 votes. Also listed on the ballot paper was Richard Huggett, who

[57] M. W. Mattinson and S. C. Macaskie (1883) 63.

[58] See, for example, the plea of duress to goods rejected in the much-criticized contract case of *Skeate v Beale* (1840) 11 Ad & El 983.

[59] See Jeremy Horder (2021a)

[60] See the discussion in Chapter 1.

[61] [1994] EWHC 9 (QB).

garnered 10,203 votes on behalf of what was described on the ballot paper as the '*Literal* Democrat Party' (my emphasis). Bearing in mind the narrow margin of Chichester's victory, Sanders launched an election petition with a view to having the election overturned, on the grounds that a large number of voters must—in Sanders's view—have been misled into voting for the 'Literal Democrat Party' rather than his own Liberal Democrat Party. Sanders' claim was not that an offence contrary to section 115 of the 1983 Act had been committed by Huggett, although he certainly could have made such an allegation, given the court itself observed that: 'It might be thought obvious that the description "Literal Democrat" was calculated to confuse the voters and mislead supporters of Mr Sanders into thinking that Mr Huggett was Mr Sanders.'[62] I will come back to this point below. Sanders's claim was, instead, that the election result should be overturned because the returning officer ought to have insisted that Huggett change the name of his party to something less easily confused with the Liberal Democrat Party. The legal basis for this claim was that Huggett's description of himself as a 'Literal Democrat' was not a description 'as required by law', within the meaning of Rule 12(2)(a) of the Parliamentary Election Rules ('the Rules') in Schedule 1 of the 1983 Act (as applied by the European Parliamentary Regulations 1986, Regulation 5(1) and Schedule 1). Sanders claimed that the description was not 'as required by law', because it did not satisfy the requirements of Rule 6(3), namely that this description, together with his other particulars on the nomination paper, should be sufficient to identify the candidate.

The court rejected Sanders's petition. The basis on which it did so was a simple one, namely that the relevant rules required only that a candidate be identified by full name and address, and Huggett had complied with that requirement. Further, it was clear from the debates leading up to the 1983 Act that Parliament had quite intentionally passed up the opportunity to insist that any further description given by a candidate of him or herself (which, if given, by law must be no more than six words), beyond name and address, must avoid being misleading or inaccurate.[63] Even so, the court went on to consider the applicability of an important *obiter dictum* of Wright J in *Harford v Linskey*.[64] In relation to a municipal election under the Municipal Corporations Act 1882, Wright J said:

> If the nomination paper is, on the face of it, a mere abuse of the right of nomination or an obvious unreality, as, for instance, if it purported to nominate a

[62] *Sanders & Huggett v Chichester* [1994] EWHC 9 (QB). The Law Commission has noted a case in which, when a would-be candidate tried to stand for what he described as 'New Labour', an injunction was obtained to prevent this, as involving an offence contrary to section 115: Law Commission for England Wales; Scottish Law Commission; Northern Ireland Law Commission (2016), para 11.33. See also the discussion of *Bank v Lewis* (unreported), text at n. 73 below.

[63] *Sanders & Huggett v Chichester* [1994] EWHC 9 (QB), para 20.

[64] [1899] 1 QB 852.

woman or a deceased sovereign, there can be no doubt that it ought to be rejected, and no petition could be maintained in respect of its rejection.[65]

The Court in *Sanders* doubted the applicability of this dictum to cases in which, as under the 1983 Act, the grounds on which a nomination can be rejected by the returning officer are specified by law. Nonetheless, the court went on to find that Huggett's nomination was neither an abuse of the right of nomination nor an obvious unreality.

In that regard, the court contrasted the facts with those of an earlier unreported case in which a Mr Hanoman, of 83 Northfield House, London SE15, changed his name by deed poll to, 'Margaret Thatcher', and changed his address to 'Downing Street Mansions, 83 Northfield House'.[66] The returning officer rejected his nomination on the grounds given in *Harford v Linskey*, namely that it was an abuse of the right of nomination and an obvious unreality. The Court of Appeal, in upholding the returning officer's decision in the exercise of its discretion to refuse relief, gave as its grounds for doing so that Hanoman's application constituted an abuse of process since he was seeking to confuse the electorate: 'It was a case where the candidate obviously intended to confuse the electorate. Eveleigh LJ (transcript at page 12E) referred to his "unlawful object of confusing the people and making the electoral process a farce"'.[67] By contrast, the court in *Sanders* took the view that the description 'Literal Democrat' was no more, but probably rather less, likely to mislead than the description, 'Liberal Democrat', and that 'there was no exclusive right in Mr Sanders to the description "Liberal Democrat"'.[68] Whether or not that claim is right (considered below), the court latches on to an important point. The mere fact, for example, that one group is standing for election representing (say) the 'People's Front of Judea' should not be permitted to prevent another group standing for the 'Judean People's Front', or the 'Judean Popular People's Front'.[69]

Leading election fraud expert Richard Mawrey QC has described to the Law Commission the decision in *Sanders v Chichester* as 'scandalous'.[70] However, whilst the decision is certainly controversial, it is perfectly defensible, in terms of the analysis being provided here. Put aside the precise question with which the court was concerned—the scope of the returning officer's powers. Was there, contrary to section 115 of the 1983 Act, a criminal use of a fraudulent 'device or artifice' that induced 'any elector to give or refrain from giving his vote'? The answer ought to be made to depend on whether Huggett engaged in, on one hand, a kind of electoral

65 [1899] 1 QB 852, 862.
66 *R v Bennet ex parte Margaret Thatcher*, 3 June 1983 (CA, unreported).
67 *Sanders & Huggett v Chichester* [1994] EWHC 9 (QB).
68 Ibid.
69 https://en.wikipedia.org/wiki/Monty_Python%27s_Life_of_Brian#Political_satire.
70 Law Commission for England and Wales; Scottish Law Commission; Northern Ireland Law Commission (2016), para 11.33.

participation fraud, or on the other hand, a political viewpoint fraud. On my account, only the former kind of fraud ought to be regarded as falling within the purview of section 115. Huggett was guilty of an electoral participation fraud falling under section 115, if his intention, in registering as a 'Literal Democrat' candidate, was to confuse voters intending to vote for the Liberal Democrats. This is an intention to deny voters what I described as an important aspect of the positive freedom dimension to the right to vote: knowing enough about candidates and parties to be able to distinguish between them.[71] By contrast, if Huggett's intention in calling himself a 'Literal Democrat' was to give a short descriptive summary of his political thinking (analogous to 'Labour', 'Conservative', or 'Liberal Democrat'), then he was justified in using the description, even if he knew perfectly well that it was likely it was to cause confusion.

In essence, the court in *Sanders* appears to have adopted the latter analysis. The court took the view that Huggett's and Sanders's descriptions of themselves respectively as 'Literal' and 'Liberal' democrats were evaluative political claims. Contrary to the court's blithe treatment of the issue, it was surely true that the 'Literal Democrat' label was more likely to mislead than the 'Liberal Democrat' label. Voters could be assumed to be much more familiar with the name and broad policy outlook of the Liberal Democrats, and would expect to see that name on the ballot paper, whereas, the presence of a lesser-known 'Literal Democrat' on the ballot paper would have taken many voters by surprise. However, the court's error here is beside the point. What matters is that, in both cases, the court in effect found that the name on the ballot paper amounted to the expression of a political viewpoint. By contrast, in the *Bennett* case,[72] the candidate Hanoman's attempt to register himself in his own (changed) name as 'Margaret Thatcher' could have had no purpose, when entered onto the list of candidates, other than to mislead, and thus perpetrate a participation fraud. Hanoman's action, unlike that of Huggett, could not plausibly be regarded as expressing a political viewpoint at all. It could thus legitimately be regarded as falling within the purview of section 115 as a participation fraud.

In that regard, it is worth considering a further UK case. In the unreported case of *Bank v Lewis*,[73] the defendant had been a long-standing Labour MP who was deselected at the 1983 General Election. In consequence, he stood against his replacement as an independent, describing himself as the 'Official Labour Party Candidate'. An injunction to prevent him using this description was refused by the Court of Appeal. Curiously, the application for an injunction was made on the grounds that the defendant's description of himself amounted to a breach of section 106 of the 1983 Act (considered in Chapter 3), rather than a breach of section 115.

71 See text following n 60 above.

72 *R v Bennet ex parte Margaret Thatcher*, 3 June 1983 (CA, unreported).

73 (unreported). The decision is described in H. F. Rawlings (1988), 185–6.

The application for an injunction was refused because the court decided that the defendant did not make—expressly or impliedly—a false claim about his personal conduct or character, as required by section 106. What if the application for an injunction had been made to prevent the commission of an offence contrary to section 115? Then, in terms of the analysis defended here, it seems right to say that it falls on the 'electoral participation fraud' side of the line, and the issuing of an injunction would have been appropriate. Had the defendant described himself as the 'True' Labour candidate, the 'Proper' Labour candidate, the 'Traditional' labour candidate, or something along these lines, then, as in *Sanders*, such labelling would have been appropriately regarded as permissible (albeit misleading), because it would be political viewpoint information. However, for the defendant to describe himself as the 'Official' Labour Party candidate is to give little or no political viewpoint information. Instead, the predominant aim appears to be (impermissibly) confusing voters as to which candidate and party they are voting for.

Hard case though it may have been, the *Sanders* decision can accordingly be defended, in so far as the decision was intended to disallow a use of the returning officer's discretion to prevent the dissemination of information that amounted to political viewpoint information, misleading though the information certainly was.[74] Without more,[75] such (mis)information should no more be subject to suppression by administrative fiat than it should be subject to criminal prohibition. This distinction can help us to understand other cases. For example, consider the facts of *Re East Northumberland Election*,[76] the nineteenth-century Ontario case, discussed earlier. In that case, according to the judge's ruling, a false claim that a candidate 'despaired of winning and, therefore, wanted his friends to vote for one of the other candidates' was not a justiciable fraud. That seems right. A false claim that a candidate has simply given up hope, and voters would do better to vote for other candidates, is a political viewpoint fraud.

However, we must also consider a common provision in electoral law, dealing with a closely analogous case, making it a criminal offence falsely to claim that a candidate has withdrawn.[77] Such a false claim is not a political *viewpoint* fraud, but neither is it a fraud 'calculated to make persons, by a trick and deception, vote for a candidate for whom at the time of voting they did not intend to vote', to recall the

[74] Although the matter is not entirely clear, it seems likely that a section 115 offence can be committed when D is reckless as to the possible effect a fraudulent device or contrivance may have on one or more voters. In accordance with ordinary fault principles, when the prosecution seeks to rely on an allegation of recklessness, D may deny the charge on the grounds that s/he was justified in acting in such a way as to impede or prevent etc the exercise of the franchise.

[75] Such as proof of hate content, or of an intimidatory purpose.

[76] (1875) 1 HEC 387 (Ont).

[77] See, for example, Representation of the People Act 1983, s. 106(5), 'Any person who, before or during an election, knowingly publishes a false statement of a candidate's withdrawal at the election for the purpose of promoting or procuring the election of another candidate shall be guilty of an illegal practice.'

works of Mr Justice Gwynne in *Re East Northumberland Election* (Ontario).[78] In a democracy, a voter who is falsely led to believe that a candidate has withdrawn is still free to choose between other candidates or to decide that none of the others merits his or her vote. The fact that such a fraud is *not* a political viewpoint fraud makes it justiciable in principle, as if it were a participation fraud, although the fact that is not a participation fraud makes justiciability—and criminalization, in particular—more controversial. However, an important reason for making such false claims justiciable and prohibiting them[79] is not just that they pose an improper threat to the chances of the candidate in question, and mislead voters: that is also true of political viewpoint frauds. It is that the fraudulent claim involves a relatively uncontentious claim of fact, appropriate for an independent body (a court; an election commission) to adjudicate on.

A limited number of political viewpoint frauds—concerned with the suitability of someone to hold office—also have this character, such as a candidate's false claim to have served in the military. An example is the following provision from the election laws of Massachusetts:

> No person, except a veteran, as defined by section one of chapter thirty-one, who is a candidate for nomination or election to any public office shall use the word 'veteran' as applied to himself, in any circular, poster, card, handbill, placard, picture or other printed matter unless the word 'veteran' is accompanied by other words indicating the country for which he served.[80]

However, well-intentioned though such provisions may be, as far as protecting rival candidates and voters is concerned they should be regarded with suspicion. Not only are they likely to contravene the First Amendment,[81] but they intervene in an inevitably arbitrary way in the area of political viewpoint articulation. For example, why should a false claim to have been a 'veteran' be justiciable and prohibited, but a false claim *not* to have been a veteran (of, say, a particular conflict) be tolerated?

An English test case is *Ex Parte Mainwaring*.[82] Just before polling day in a local election in 1990, the Liberal Democrat group circulated in key wards a leaflet entitled 'Labour News', designed to look as if it came from their Labour Party opponents. The leaflet contained a carefully chosen selection of statements genuinely made previously by Labour politicians in the past, but put together in what the court described as a 'politically tendentious' way, to make the statements appear

[78] (1875) 1 HEC 387 (Ont).

[79] Other, similar examples would be ones in which it was falsely claimed that a candidate was dead, or was legally disqualified.

[80] Massachusetts, General Laws: Title VIII—Elections, ch. 56, s. 43A.

[81] See *US v Alvarez* 132 S. Ct. 2537 (2012), discussed in Staci Leiffring (2013).

[82] *R v Rowe Ex parte Mainwaring* [1992] 1 WLR 1059.

unappealing to voters in the wards in question.[83] An election petition was launched to overturn the election of successful Liberal Democrat candidates, on the grounds that they were guilty of undue influence—through fraud—contrary to section 115. At first instance, the Election Commissioner dismissed the petition on the grounds that nothing false was contained in the leaflets, even if they were—deliberately—misleading.[84] On this point, the Court of Appeal disagreed. The element of false pretence, for the purposes of section 115, lay in the pretence that the leaflets were official Labour Party documents, and not in the precise content of the documents.[85]

If the leaflets had merely contained false viewpoint information about Labour Party policy, a section 115 charge would have been improper, on my account. As Robert Reid MP remarked over 100 years ago:

> [A]nything that savoured of a political character should not be made a ground for interference with an election. As long as human nature remained what it was, [I believe] that in elections there would be exaggerations and unfounded statements as to the opinions of people with whom other people did not agree which it would be impossible to avoid, and all they could do was to hope that the electors would have the good sense to take the necessary discount off such statements.[86]

However, a fraud as to the political *source* of a document is not a fraud concerning substantive political viewpoints, even if also not a participation fraud. So, the grounds on which the Court of Appeal intervened—looking to the form, and not the substance—are defensible. Putting the point another way, the petition in *Ex parte Mainwaring* could have been defended as a proper use of section 115, given the source-based nature of the fraud, even if the Liberal Democrats had mistakenly placed in the leaflet full and entirely accurate summaries of Labour Party policy.

4.4 Electoral Fraud: The Legislature and the Courts

Harold Laski records that, between 1832 and 1906, out of 139 judges appointed, 80 were MPs at the time of nomination, with a further 11 having been candidates for Parliament.[87] Out of the 80, 63 were appointed by their own party while in office, and 33 had been either Attorney-General or Solicitor-General.[88] Far from being an

[83] Ibid. 1061f.

[84] The Commissioner also found no evidence that any voter had in fact been impeded or prevented in exercising the franchise by the leaflets.

[85] Nonetheless, the Court of Appeal did not remit the case for re-hearing, because it accepted the validity of the Commissioner's finding that no voter had in fact been impeded or prevented from exercising the franchise by the fraud.

[86] House of Commons Debate, 01 May 1895 vol 33 col 244, cited by Alex Parsons (2016), 5.

[87] H. J. Laski (1932), 170

[88] H. J. Laski (1932), 180, cited by J. A. G. Griffith (1977), 20.

embarrassment, this close connection between a political background and judicial appointment was considered at a high level to amount to something like a constitutional convention. Lord Salisbury, when Prime Minister, said in writing to the Lord Chancellor in August 1895: '[T]here is no clearer statute in [the unwritten law of our party system] than the rule that party claims should always weigh very heavily in the disposal of the highest legal appointments.'[89] How, if at all, did this background affect the way in which judges were considered likely to approach the interpretation of the 1895 Act, and subsequent amending and incorporating legislation? It seems that, when they moved from the political to the judicial realm, judges saw themselves as, if not beyond politically motivated decision-making,[90] then at least beyond the kind of partisan, disrespectful, belittling treatment that commonly accompanies criticism of such decision-making; and that development shaped their understanding of the kind of decisions that ought to fall for judicial determination.

When it was first proposed that judges should take over jurisdiction in election petition cases from Parliament (as explained at the outset of this chapter), the Lord Chief Justice was vehemently opposed, on the grounds that this would unacceptably politicize the role of the judge. Cockburn LCJ, himself a former Liberal MP and both Solicitor-General and Attorney-General, complained to the Lord Chancellor that:

> The decision of the Judge given under such circumstances will too often fail to secure the respect which judicial decisions command on other occasions. Angry and excited partisans will not be unlikely to question the motives which have led to the judgment. Their sentiments may be echoed by the press. Such is the influence of party conflict, that it is apt to inspire distrust and dislike of whatever interferes with party objects and party triumphs.[91]

Cockburn LCJ's objections did not affect the outcome, of course, in that jurisdiction was passed to the courts; but the issue of politicization did not go away. In a debate on the Parliamentary Elections (Corrupt and Illegal Practices) Bill 1883, Patrick Martin, County Kilkenny MP for the Home Rule League, objected to the breadth of the wording of the 1854 Act (particularly 'intimidation'), because of the degree of discretion it would give to judges to make controversial decisions in sensitive election cases:

[89] Cited by J. A. G. Griffith (1977), 23.
[90] Ibid.
[91] Cited by Thomas LCJ, in *R (on the application of Woolas) v The Parliamentary Election Court* [2010] EWHC 3169 (Admin), para 23. For further discussion of this point, see e.g. Alan Renwick and Michela Palese (2019), ch. 2.

> Judges, though he did not question their desire to do justice, had widely divergent views as to the right claimed by public men to denounce what they considered abuses in strong and emphatic language. What one considered permissible and fair, another held as an abuse and violation of the right of free speech .... The vagueness in the words would lead to unpleasant and injurious comments as to the motives which influenced those election tribunals in their decisions.[92]

These considerations are important, because the way in which the election offences are interpreted—the fraud offence in particular—has implications for whether or not judges will indeed leave themselves open to questioning of their motives and the (justified) criticism of 'partisans'.

For the most part, the relevant election fraud offences across the common law world are sufficiently open-textured to make it possible for courts to interpret them so that the offences cover political viewpoint frauds. In that regard, as we will see in the next section, courts in different jurisdictions have varied in their approach, with courts in some jurisdictions taking an expansive interpretive view, impervious to the kinds of considerations in favour of judicial restraint articulated (above) in the nineteenth century. In Chapters 1 and 2, I made the case for restraint and tolerance on the part of legislatures and platform regulators in relation to political viewpoint falsehoods, in the face of populist and identity politicians' rejection of traditionally shared understandings about the limits of acceptable political viewpoint speech. In this section, I will make a brief case for judicial restraint and tolerance, probing the insights underpinning Cockburn LCJ's remarks about the threat, posed by their role in election disputes, to the understanding of judges as impartial and 'above' politically motivated criticism.

An evaluation of Cockburn LCJ's fear, that respect for the judiciary might be undermined by their involvement in election disputes, turns on the degree of fit between the nature of those disputes and the skills particularly (even if not uniquely) associated with judicial decision-making. For example, this is what H. L. A. Hart had to say about what he called the 'judicial virtues' on display in constitutional cases, where a choice between conflicting values had to be made.

> These virtues are: impartiality and neutrality in surveying the alternatives; consideration for the interests of all who will be affected and a concern to deploy some acceptable general principle as a reasoned basis for decision .... In all this we have the 'weighing' and 'balancing' characteristic of the effort to do justice to competing interests.[93]

92 HC Deb 15 June 1883, vol 280 cols 702–3.
93 H. L. A. Hart (2012), 204–5.

Jeremy Waldron paints a similar picture of the virtues of judicial decision-making, although—like Hart—he does not entertain the expansive role for such decision-making developed by, for example, Ronald Dworkin. Waldron suggests that when judges are called on to take decisions with moral import, the institutional constraints they are under mean that they can at least be relied upon to approach the issues in (what appears to be) an apolitical manner:

> They [judges] define their terms, they separate different lines of reasoning, they pay attention to the logical force of the arguments they consider, they distinguish issues and discuss them in a certain order, they entertain objections to their own lines of reasoning and try to respond to them, and so on.[94]

In particular, says Waldron, judges do not decide cases by reliance on 'tendentious popular slogans or ... the bargaining and horse-trading that characterize electoral politics'.[95]

Nonetheless, a question arises about the aptness of this decision-making method for different kinds of election dispute. For example, suppose that the only two parties standing in an election, Party X and Party Y, garner exactly the same number of votes. The question of which party should be elected is referred to a court, which is empowered to resolve the case 'as it sees fit'. The court proceeds by applying the reasoning techniques described by Hart and Waldron to the parties' election manifestos, to try to decide which manifesto best makes the case for the party in question being given the chance to govern. This way of proceeding would be fundamentally unsound, and not solely because elections ought ideally to be decided by voters rather than courts (sometimes, courts—or other unelected bodies—must decide the outcome of disputed elections). It would be unsound because judicial reasoning techniques do not give houseroom to every warp and weft of electoral politics: appeals to emotion, prejudice, petty hatreds, point-scoring, local rivalries, much-vaunted goals their proponents know it will be impossible to attain, what Waldron calls 'tendentious popular slogans', and so on. Tossing a coin to decide the matter would make more sense,[96] because that at least leaves intact and unadulterated the role of the electorate's political viewpoint preferences, whatever the outcome.

Now consider the Election Court's important role under section 164 of the Representation of the People Act 1983. Section 164 empowers the court to declare

[94] Jeremy Waldron (2009), 4.

[95] Ibid. I should note that Waldron's broader argument is a highly sophisticated one to which I cannot (and do not need to) do justice to here.

[96] https://www.bbc.co.uk/news/av/uk-england-39818052 (last accessed 24/04/2021); https://www.independent.co.uk/news/uk/politics/local-election-results-northumberland-council-majority-drawing-straws-a7719241.html (last accessed 24/04/2021); https://www.theatlantic.com/politics/archive/2012/11/when-a-state-election-can-be-literally-determined-by-a-coin-toss/265413/ (last accessed 24/04/2021).

an election void when, amongst other things, illegal or corrupt practices (including fraud) have so extensively prevailed that they may reasonably be supposed to have affected the result. As I explained earlier, this important constitutional power was given to the courts, because members of Parliament could not be trusted to conduct investigations into corruption and fraud in elections on a non-partisan basis. A section 164 enquiry clearly involves a mixture of largely factual enquiry—how prevalent was corruption or other illegality?—and value judgement—can the corruption or illegality reasonably be supposed to have affected the result? Can a section 164 enquiry involve a court in the invalidation of political viewpoint judgements? If electoral 'fraud' is deemed to include political viewpoint fraud, then this is indeed a possibility. In the next section I will consider court rulings that have taken some jurisdictions down this interpretive road. As we will see, courts sometimes explain their adoption of this broad view of electoral fraud—encompassing viewpoint as well as participation fraud—on the grounds that a knowing misrepresentation of the 'facts' is just as much a fraud when it concerns, say, a claim about resources available for public sector investment, as when it concerns people's entitlement to vote. It is important not to be gulled by such appeals to (a fictitious) neutrality in the legal approach to electoral fraud. As argued in Chapter 1, the attempt to confine 'legitimate' viewpoint politics to political programmes based on the 'facts' is itself a form of (rationalist, liberal-minded) politics, that is hence open to the inevitable consequences for judges of politicization of their role feared by Cockburn LCJ.

In defending a (as I would have it, politicized) role for the courts in liberal societies more broadly, Joseph Raz has suggested that:

> The courts are, or at least they should be, above the rough and tumble of everyday political pressures. They should be relatively immune to passing fashions. In constitutional matters they may succeed in representing a lasting consensus, even at times when prevailing trends disguise its existence from the majority of the public, and even in the face of a government whose reforming zeal blinds it to the need to preserve the fabric of the political culture.[97]

We see here a clear echo of the issues raised in Chapter 1 about the politicized nature of claims to neutrality. Raz does not allow for the possibility that (to use his words) the 'fabric of [a nation's] political culture', its 'lasting consensus' (that prevailing trends are wrongly disguising from the majority), is in fact itself an idealized political vision shared only by some, and contested by others. For example, to what extent can it said that, if the UK has a rights-based culture, that culture has evolved to become global in character, now drawing on and being shaped

[97] Joseph Raz (1986), 260.

predominantly by international norms and aspirations;[98] or, contrariwise, that this culture is best understood as linked to a latent but distinctively British (or English) national identity, with its own distinctive hierarchy and understanding of rights and responsibilities that are actually threatened by internationalization?[99] Whilst the latter view may seem implausible, to choose between these rival visions of the 'fabric of [our] political culture' is to *enter* the political domain. It is not to stand back from that domain, on some Archimedean point representing neutrality and impartiality between political visions.

As I indicated above, the same is true of attempts to hold political viewpoint controversies accountable to a (supposedly) shared understanding of what are to count as the political, social, and economic 'facts'. We can trace the roots of such an approach—a 'rationalized' politics—to the unconscious adoption by the judiciary of a Weberian commitment to 'distinguish between empirical knowledge [factual truth] and value-judgments [our own ideals]',[100] a drive towards a legal world in which one can 'master all things by calculation'.[101] We can now see how some courts have appointed themselves guardians of rationalized Weberian politics, the politics of 'calculation', in the resolution of disputes about election fraud.

4.5 Politicizing the Judiciary in Canada: *Friesen v Hammell*

While the issue remains unclear in the UK, some courts overseas have rejected the drawing of any distinction between political viewpoint and electoral participation fraud in election cases, for the purposes of restricting the judicial role and avoiding politicization. In that regard, a key focus is the decision of the Court of Appeal for British Columbia in *Friesen v Hammell & Clark*.[102]

Friesen (and other petitioners) launched a petition seeking to overturn the election of no less than 39 New Democratic Party ('NDP') Members of the Legislative Assembly ('MLAs'). The basis of their petition was an alleged breach of the British Columbian descendent of the 1854 Act: section 256 of the Election Act (British Columbia) 1996,[103] which provides that:

> An individual or organization must not, by abduction, duress or fraudulent means, do any of the following:

[98] See, for example, the House of Lords European Union Committee (2015–16).

[99] Conservative Party, *Strong Leadership, a Clear Economic Plan, a Brighter, More Secure Future: The Conservative Party Manifesto 2015*: https://www.theresavilliers.co.uk/sites/www.theresavilliers.co.uk/files/conservativemanifesto2015.pdf, 73 (last accessed 18/11/2021).

[100] Max Weber (1904), 58.

[101] Max Weber (1919), 8.

[102] (1999) BCCA 23.

[103] The British Columbian ancestor of this provision can be found in the Corrupt Practices Act (British Columbia) 1871.

(a) impede, prevent or otherwise interfere with an individual's right to vote;
(b) compel, persuade or otherwise cause an individual to vote or refrain from voting;
(c) compel, persuade or otherwise cause an individual to vote or refrain from voting for a particular candidate or for a candidate of a particular political party.

As under the equivalent UK provisions, breach of section 256 is not only a basis for challenging an election but also a criminal offence, with a maximum penalty—in British Columbia—of two years' imprisonment. So, the court's interpretation of its breadth is of direct relevance to the argument here.

The petitioners' section 256 claim was that they had been led to vote for NDP candidates in the wake of false NDP claims that the 1995–6 and 1996–7 provincial budgets would have a surplus, a surplus sufficient to ensure that the government would have a $250 million capital development programme to back a number of construction projects. The petition also alleged that the MLAs and the NDP (at least, the Premier and some of his colleagues) intentionally concealed the information necessary to ascertain the truth of these representations. For its part, the government said that its projected surplus was based on private industry economic forecasting. Whilst the government had admittedly chosen one of the most optimistic of the budget forecasts available, it was nonetheless a projection based on independent economic analysis. The petitioners countered—successfully, at first instance—that, even if this was true, the extent to which the financial situation had deteriorated by the time of the election meant that the NDP must have been aware that its financial projections were likely to be false.[104] Clearly, the petitions concerned political viewpoint matters. The question of whether there is, or will be, a (sufficient) budget surplus that can be used to support a development programme is a central example of such a matter.

Even so, the BC Court of Appeal rejected the MLAs' invitation to confine section 256 to what I have been calling election participation frauds—frauds concerned with (in the court's words) 'the act of voting [rather than] … the formation of the political judgment for whom to vote'.[105] Instead, in relation to section 256, the BC Court of Appeal found that

> the Legislature intended to safeguard the public from fraudulent conduct on the part of, or on behalf of, a candidate or a political party, which was of sufficient import that it influenced the judgment of potential voters by causing them to vote other than they would have but for the fraudulent conduct.[106]

[104] See, further, Andrew Heard (1997).
[105] (1999) BCCA 23, para 72.
[106] Ibid., para 74.

In this kind of case, said the court, the value of free speech is not diminished by construing section 256 broadly, to include false political viewpoint claims.[107]

The court briefly reviewed the development of the provisions of English law, set out in detail above, that influenced similar Canadian legislation.[108] However, the court did not seek to set that development in the context of political history, and in particular, against a background in which procedural unfairness took precedence over the misrepresentation of political viewpoints, in shaping the legislation. A major plank of the court's justification for its expansive view of the scope for judicial intervention in election fraud cases came from its reading of previous authorities, such as *Re East Northumberland*[109] and *Ex parte Mainwaring*.[110] As we saw in *Re East Northumberland*, a clear distinction was drawn by Mr Justice Gwynne between political participation and political viewpoint fraud; but other than noting that the decision favoured the arguments of counsel for the MLAs, the court simply failed to engage with the arguments put forward by Mr Justice Gwynne. As far as *Ex parte Mainwaring* is concerned, the court found support for its expansive reading of section 256 in that decision: 'The *Mainwaring* decision lends support to the interpretation of the legislation preceding s. 256 urged on us by the petitioners. Although not binding on us, as a decision of the English Court of Appeal, it is of persuasive precedential value.'[111] The analysis of *Ex parte Mainwaring* given above simply does not support this interpretation. The case concerns a fraud concerning the *source* of political documents, and is not a case about political viewpoint fraud.

The court in *Friesen v Hammell* also had to confront the important decision of the Australian High Court in *Evans v Crichton-Browne*.[112] In this case, the validity of the election of Crichton-Browne (and others) to the Western Australian Senate was challenged on the grounds that Crichton-Browne had published advertisements in breach of section 161 of the Commonwealth Electoral Act 1918, which prohibited as an illegal practice: 'Printing, publishing, or distributing any electoral advertisement, notice, handbill, pamphlet, or card containing any untrue or incorrect statement intended or likely to mislead or improperly interfere with any elector in or *in relation to* the casting of his vote' (my emphasis). Evans, an unsuccessful candidate representing the Australian Democrats, complained that Crichton-Browne breached this provision by falsely suggesting that Australian Democrat senators had in the last parliament voted with the Labor Party eight times out of ten, that a vote for the Australian Democrats could be a vote for the Labor Party and could give the Labor Party control of the Senate, and that the Australian Democrat senators in the last parliament had been absent for 52 votes

[107] Ibid., para 77.
[108] Ibid., paras 35–38.
[109] (1875) 1 HEC 387 (Ont), discussed at n 47 above.
[110] *R v Rowe Ex parte Mainwaring* [1992] 1 WLR 1059, discussed in the text at n. 86 above.
[111] (1999) BCCA 23, para 59.
[112] [1981] 147 CLR 169.

out of 192 occasions. Other allegedly false or misleading statements made by their opponents included claims that the Labor Party was committed to the introduction of a wealth tax or capital gains tax which would affect not only the wealthy, but a much wider range of people who made savings intended to provide for their old age or for their children, along with hundreds of thousands of Australians who owned modest homes which had risen in value. It was also stated, or implied, that the policies of the Labor Party would lead to a rate of inflation of 20 per cent.

Making knowingly false, misleading, or exaggerated claims of these kinds is the bread and butter of politics conducted in a full-throated and unashamedly partisan manner, commonly fuelled by anger and rage as much as it is driven by reason,[113] with the overriding aim of defeating an opponent at the polls.[114] As argued in the previous section, judicial methods of dispute resolution are ill-suited to manufacturing the exclusion or deterrence of this kind of politics, because they are founded on a kind of public sector decision-making that it is part of the very point of emotive, identity politics to oppose. Accordingly, the court in *Evans* observed, in relation to section 161 of the 1918 Act, that

> even if the paragraph were thought to apply only to those statements affecting a voter's choice of candidate which appear to be statements of fact, that construction would require an election campaign to be conducted in anticipation of proceedings brought to test the truth or correctness of any statement made in the campaign. Indeed any person who published an electoral advertisement containing an incorrect statement of fact might be exposed to criminal proceedings. In a campaign ranging over a wide variety of matters, many of the issues canvassed are likely to be unsuited to resolution in legal proceedings; and a court should not attribute to the Parliament an intention to expose election issues to the potential requirement of legal proof in the absence of clear words.[115]

The court, following the line of argument being developed here, thus construed the words of section 161 ('in relation to the casting of [a] vote') narrowly to refer to 'the act of recording or expressing the political judgment which the elector has made rather than to the formation of that judgment'.[116] This is a distinction, in essence, between political participation fraud and political viewpoint fraud.

However, in *Friesen v Hammel*, this approach was rejected.[117] Finding that the MLAs' allegedly fraudulent statements about budgetary resources fell within the scope of the prohibition in section 256 of the Election Act 1996, the court said: 'Freedom of speech is a cherished value in our society, but we are unable to

[113] Debra Thompson (2017); Chapter 1, section 1.3(iii) above.
[114] Chantal Mouffe (2005), 20–3.
[115] [1981] 147 CLR 169, para 12.
[116] Ibid.
[117] For a similar approach, see *Cameron v Becker* (1995) 64 SASR 238 (South Australia SC).

conclude that this value is diminished by an interpretation of s. 256 which penalizes fraudulent misrepresentations concerning material facts which go to the heart of the voter's decision for whom to vote.'[118] The decision thus plunges courts directly into controversies over the representation of figures and statistics underpinning political viewpoints.[119] Moreover, the decision fails to recognize that, to use the time-honoured language of the court, adequately to 'cherish' the value of free speech is to recognize that a different approach must be taken to judicial—and indeed legislative—(non-)intervention, depending on the context in which the speech takes place. *Political* speech, in particular, requires an exceptionally high level of tolerance and restraint, in terms of legal intervention, something the Court in *Friesen v Hammel* fails to acknowledge.

4.6 Politicizing the Judiciary in Canada: *Todd v Coleridge*

The Canadian courts have continued to follow the path established in *Friesen v Hammell*. In *Todd v Coleridge*,[120] the BC Supreme Court considered a local government petition, arising in relation to section 152(3)(b) of the BC Local Government Act, which reads as follows:

> 152 …
>
> (3) A person must not, by abduction, duress or fraudulent means, do any of the following…
> (b) compel, persuade or otherwise cause a person to vote or refrain from voting.

The defendant, Coleridge, had defeated Todd in an election to the council in the city of White Rock. According to the court, as part of his election campaign, Coleridge agreed that he had 'described himself to the electorate in his campaign materials as a person someone could come to for straight answers. During the election, he was endorsed by the White Rock Citizens for Positive Renewal, which has one of its goals to "Restore Public Trust".[121] One could scarcely imagine a more routine or predictable political claim to be worthy of an elector's vote. The idea that such a claim might give rise to legal consequences seems quite extraordinary; but that is not how it appeared to the BC Supreme Court. The court contrasted Coleridge's claim, in this respect, with an incident in the course of the campaign, which arose

[118] *Friesen v Hammel* (1999) BCCA 23, para 77.
[119] See, by way of comparison, the fraught debate (discussed in Chapter 1, section 1.2(ii) above) over the savings that might be made by the UK if it were to leave the EU, and whether particular representations of these figures amounted to fraud or falsehood.
[120] (2009) BCSC 688.
[121] *Todd v Coleridge* (2009) BCSC 688, 690.

when—using an assumed name—Coleridge's wife sent an email linking Todd with a pro-development list of candidates for the council. Coleridge responded to the email as if it came from one of his supporters, and Todd was criticized in the course of the email chain. When asked by reporters if he knew the source of the email, Coleridge lied, saying he had no idea and then, when the source of the email was discovered, he falsely claimed to have been the victim of identity theft.

The attempt by Coleridge and his wife to establish a false or misleading connection between his rival and the pro-development list of candidates is a political viewpoint fraud. That Coleridge lied about his wife's role in setting up this fraud certainly reflects badly on Coleridge's political credibility, but this too is a matter of political viewpoint: can a proven liar be trusted with public office? Nonetheless, the BC Supreme Court declared Coleridge's election to be invalid and ordered him to pay $20,000 to the City of White Rock to contribute towards the expenses of running another by-election. The court justified this by saying:

> The question ... is whether Mr Coleridge persuaded or caused anyone to vote for him by stating that in his campaign material that he was someone the electorate could come to for a straight answer, i.e. that he was someone you could trust. Mr Coleridge displayed a willingness to continue to lie and deceive the public .... [I]f a candidate puts his character in issue and runs on his integrity and honesty, then his character, including his integrity and honesty, is a material fact.[122]

Here we see the court turning an issue of what ought to be seen as a broad matter of political judgement—can politician X be trusted?—into a narrow issue of fact (did politician X make a false claim about himself?), thus facilitating what I have been describing as the rationalistic approach to the regulation of political disputation. The court, thus, frustrated the voting intentions of those—perhaps the majority—who voted for Coleridge on the basis that they identified with the political narrative he was developing (he provided them with a sense of 'belonging' in politics[123]), irrespective of the truth or falsity of any particular claim he made about himself or his opponents. In no position to distinguish this group of voters from those motivated by more rationalistic considerations, the court should have refused to intervene.

We have seen that the Australian High Court rightly observed in *Evans v Crichton-Browne* that, even if a court confined its powers of review to cases in which there was an alleged false statement of political fact that influenced voters, '[such a] construction would require an election campaign to be conducted in anticipation of proceedings brought to test the truth or correctness of any statement made in the campaign'.[124] Even so, the *Evans* court does not quite get to the heart of the political

[122] Ibid.
[123] Chantal Mouffe (2005), 25.
[124] [1980] 147 CLR 169, 207.

issues at stake. To be sure, a proper regard for tolerance and free political speech requires, on rule-of-law grounds, that would-be speakers should not be deterred from speaking by the unpredictable threat of legal sanctions following an *ex post facto* court judgment that they were guilty of political viewpoint falsehoods. The judgment in *Evans* nonetheless presupposes that political speakers are motivated by rule-of-law concerns of this kind. The judgment takes it for granted that speakers are imbued with a commitment to a broad concept of truth-telling in politics that is shared and (*ex hypothesi* legitimately) applied by the judiciary as much as by politicians and activists. Even the *Evans* court thus fails properly to appreciate the importance of toleration of political viewpoint falsehoods, in a world in which confrontational, identity politics seeks to bypass or challenge the very idea that the conduct of politics should be bounded by (supposedly) shared understandings of truth and falsity.

Bibliography

Abizadeh, Arash, 'Historical Truth, National Myths and Liberal Democracy: On the Coherence of Liberal Nationalism' (2004) 12 Journal of Political Philosophy 291.

Advertising Standards Authority, Annual Report (1999), https://www.asa.org.uk/asset/40D37406-BDD0-48A4-BF46C68DE81C1E39/.

Alexander, Larry, and Sherwin, Emily, 'Deception in Morality and Law' (2003) 22 Law and Philosophy 393.

Allcot, Hunt, and Gentzkow, Matthew, 'Social Media and Fake News in the 2016 Election' (2017) 31 Journal of Economic Perspectives 211.

Alterman, Eric, *Lying in State: Why Presidents Lie, and Why Trump is Worse* (New York: Basic Books, 2020).

Ardèvol-Abreu, Alberto, and De Zúñiga, Homero Gil, '"Obstinate Partisanship": Political Discussion Attributes Effects' (2020) 14 International Journal of Communication 324.

Arendt, Hannah, *Crises of the Republic* (San Diego: Harvest, 1972).

Argersinger, Peter H., 'New Perspectives on Election Fraud in the Gilded Age' (1985) 100 Political Science Quarterly 669.

Article 19, *Defining Defamation: Principles on Freedom of Expression and Protection of Reputation* (2000), https://www.article19.org/wp-content/uploads/2018/02/defining-defamation.pdf.

Article 19, *Right to Online Anonymity* (2015), https://www.article19.org/data/files/medialibrary/38006/Anonymity_and_encryption_report_A5_final-web.pdf.

Article 19, *Germany: The Act to Improve Enforcement of the Law in Social Networks* (2017), https://www.article19.org/wp-content/uploads/2017/09/170901-Legal-Analysis-German-NetzDG-Act.pdf.

Article 19, *Social Media Councils: Consultation* (2019a), https://www.article19.org/resources/social-media-councils-consultation/.

Article 19, *Media Regulation in the United Kingdom* (2019b), https://www.article19.org/data/files/pdfs/publications/uk-media-regulation.pdf.

Article 19, *Law Commission Consultation on Reform of the Communications Offences* (2020), https://www.article19.org/wp-content/uploads/2020/12/UK-Law-Commission-response-Communications-Offences-December-22-Dec-2020.pdf.

Asean Law Association, *The Singapore Legal System* (2018), https://www.aseanlawassociation.org/wp-content/uploads/2019/11/ALA-SG-legal-system-Part-2.pdf.

Badouard, Romain, *Le Désenchantement de l'Internet. Désinformation, Rumeur et Propagande* (Paris: FYP Editions, 2017).

Barendt, Eric, *Freedom of Speech*, (2nd edition, Oxford: Oxford University Press, 2007).

Barendt, Eric, 'Bad News for Bloggers' (2009) 1 Journal of Media Law 14.

Barr, Robert R., 'Populists, Outsiders, and Anti-Establishment Politics' (2009) 15 Party Politics 29.

Birch, Sarah, 'Electoral Systems and Electoral Misconduct' (2007) 40(12) Comparative Political Studies 1533.

Bradshaw, Samantha, and Howard, Phillip, 'The Global Organisation of Social Media Disinformation Campaigns' (2018) 71 Journal of International Affairs 23.

Bronner, Laura, 'Property and Power: MPs' Assets and Support for Democratisation in the 1867 Reform Act' (2014) 39 Legislative Studies Quarterly 439.

Brownlee, Kimberley, 'What's the Value of Teamwork?' (2019) 19(1) Jerusalem Review of Legal Studies 173.

Bullock, J., 'The Enduring Power of False Information' (unpublished manuscript), cited in Sniderman, Paul M., and Levendusky, Matthew S., 'An Institutional Theory of Political Choice', in Dalton, Russell J., and Klingemann, Hans-Dieter (eds), *Oxford Handbook of Political Behaviour* (Oxford: Oxford University Press, 2007).

Buxton, S. C., 'The Attorney General's Corrupt Practices Bill' (1881) xxxix Contemporary Review 758.

Bychawska-Siniarska, Dominika, *Protecting the Right to Freedom of Expression under the European Convention on Human Rights* (Council of Europe, 2017).

Cabinet Office, *Protecting the Debate: Intimidation, Influence and Information, Government Response* (London: Cabinet Office, 2019).

Cairncross Review: A Sustainable Future for Journalism (2019), https://assets.publishing.service.gov.uk/government/uploads/system/uploads/attachment_data/file/779882/021919_DCMS_Cairncross_Review_.pdf.

Carswell, Douglas, and Hannan, Daniel, *The Plan: Twelve Months to Renew Britain* (London: Douglas Carswell and Daniel Hannan, 2008).

Cassam, Quassim, *Vices of the Mind* (Oxford: Oxford University Press, 2019).

Chandler, Jennifer A., 'A Right to Reach an Audience: An Approach to Intermediary Bias on the Internet' (2007) 35 Hofstra Law Review 1095.

Committee on Standards in Public Life, *Intimidation in Public Life*, 17th Report, CM 9543 (London, 2017).

Council of Europe, *Defamation and Freedom of Expression* (Strasbourg: Council of Europe, 2003).

Cram, Ian, 'Keeping the Demos out of Liberal Democracy? Participatory Politics, "Fake News", and the Online Speaker' (2019) 11 Journal of Media Law 113.

Craufurd-Smith, Rachel, 'Fake news, French Law and Democratic Legitimacy: Lessons for the United Kingdom?' (2019) 11 Journal of Media Law 52.

Crowder, George, 'Negative and Positive Liberty' (1988) 40 Political Science 57.

Crowley, John, 'Paradoxes in the Politicisation of Race: A Comparison of the UK and France' (1993) 19 New Community 627.

Davis, Aeron, 'Journalist–Source Relations, Mediated Reflexivity and the Politics of Politics' (2009) 10 Journalism Studies 204.

De la Torre, Carlos, *Populist Seduction in Latin America* (Athens, OH: Ohio University Press, 2010).

Department for Digital, Culture, Media and Sport, and Home Office, *Online Harms White Paper: Full government Response to the White Paper* (2020), https://www.gov.uk/government/consultations/online-harms-white-paper/outcome/online-harms-white-paper-full-government-response#fnref:21.

Duff, Antony, *Answering for Crime* (Oxford: Hart Publishing, 2007).

Dworkin, Ronald, *Taking Rights Seriously* (Cambridge: Harvard University Press, 1977).

Eddington, Arthur, *The Nature of the Physical World: The Gifford Lectures* (New York: Macmillan, 1928).

Edgar, Robin, 'Are Hate Speech Provisions Antidemocratic? An International Perspective' (2010) 26(1) Am U Int LR 119.

Eggers, Andrew, and Spirling, Arthur (2014), 'Guarding the Guardians: Legislative Self-Policing and Electoral Corruption in Victorian Britain', https://www.nyu.edu/projects/spirling/documents/pets.pdf.

Electoral Commission, *Digital Campaigning: Increasing Transparency for Voters* (Electoral Commission, London, 2018).

Electoral Commission, *Candidate Imprints: England and Wales, May 2021* (2021), https://www.electoralcommission.org.uk/sites/default/files/2021-08/Candidates%20imprints%20factsheet%20EWNI.pdf.

Ellehuus, Rachel, and Ruy, Donatienne (2020), 'Did Russian Influence Brexit?', https://www.csis.org/blogs/brexit-bits-bobs-and-blogs/did-russia-influence-brexit.

Engesser, Sven, Fawsi, Nayla, and Larsson, Anders Olof, 'Populist Online Communication' (2017) 20 Information, Communication and Society 1279.

Erbschloe, Michael, *Extremist Propaganda in Social Media: A Threat to Homeland Security* (Boca Raton, FL: BRC Press, 2019).

European Audiovisual Observatory, *Disinformation in the Media under Russian Law* (2019), https://rm.coe.int/disinformation-in-the-media-under-russian-law/1680967369.

European Commission Staff Working Document (2012), 'Online services including e-commerce in the Single Market', https://op.europa.eu/en/publication-detail/-/publication/2d17d3dd-4f00-4e3c-b75c-98c03b135047/language-en.

European Commission (2018a), 'Tackling Illegal Content Online: Meeting with Online Platforms', https://digital-strategy.ec.europa.eu/en/policies/illegal-content-online-platforms#:~:text=The%20Commission%20issued%20a%20Recommendation,more%20responsible%20in%20content%20governance.

European Commission, Code of Practice on Disinformation (2018b), https://ec.europa.eu/digital-single-market/en/code-practice-disinformation.

European Data Protection Supervisor, *EDPS Opinion on Online Manipulation and Personal Data* (2018), https://edps.europa.eu/sites/edp/files/publication/18-03-19_online_manipulation_en.pdf.

European Union High Representative of the Union for Foreign Affairs and Security Policy, *Action Plan Against Disinformation* (JOIN 2018, 36 Final).

Fabre, Cécile, 'The Case for Foreign Electoral Subversion' (2018) 32(3) Ethics and International Affairs 283.

Facebook, *Facebook's Policies on Elections and Voting: What You Need to Know* (2020), https://about.fb.com/wp-content/uploads/2020/10/Facebooks-Policies-for-Elections-and-Voting.pdf.

Faris, Robert, et al. (2017), 'Partisanship, Propaganda, and Disinformation: Online Media and the 2016 US Presidential Election,' https://dash.harvard.edu/handle/1/33759251.

Feuchtwanger, E. J., 'J. E. Gorst and the Central Organisation of the Conservative Party 1870–82' (1959) 32 Historical Research 192.

Finck, Michèle, 'Digital Regulation: Designing a Supranational Legal Framework for the Platform Economy' (2017), http://eprints.lse.ac.uk/87568/1/Finck_Digital%20Co-Regulation_Author.pdf.

Fraser, Nancy, 'Rethinking the Public Sphere: A Contribution to the Critique of Actually Existing Democracy' (1990) 25/26 Social Text 56.

Freelon, Dean, Marwick, Alice, and Kreiss, Daniel, 'False Equivalences: Online Activism from Left to Right' (2020) 369 Science (6508) 1197.

Full Fact, *Research into Public Views on Truth and Untruth in the 2019 General Election* (December 2019), https://fullfact.org/media/uploads/ff_election_research_report_final_version_16.12.19.pdf.

Funke, Daniel, and Flamini, Daniela, *A Guide to Anti-Disinformation Actions Around the World* (2018), https://www.poynter.org/ifcn/anti-misinformation-actions/.

Gardner, John, 'Wrongs and Faults' in A. P. Simester (ed.), *Appraising Strict Liability* (Oxford: Oxford University Press, 2005) 51.

Gardner, John, 'What is Tort Law for? Part 1. The Place of Corrective Justice' (2011) 30 Law and Philosophy 1.

Gash, Norman, *Politics in the Age of Peel* (Brighton: Harvester Press, 1977).

Gibbon, Edward, *The History of the Decline and fall of the Roman Empire* (revised edition, New York: Harper, 1836).

Glasgow Media Group, *Bad News* (London: Routledge and Kegan Paul, 1976).

Google, *EC EU Code of Practice on Disinformation Annual Report* (2019), https://ec.europa.eu/digital-single-market/en/news/annual-self-assessment-reports-signatories-code-practice-disinformation-2019.

Gorell, Genevieve, et al. (2019), *Online Abuse toward Candidates during the UK General Election 2019: Working Paper*, https://arxiv.org/pdf/2001.08686.pdf.

Gorton, William, 'Manipulating Citizens: How Political Campaigns Use of Behavioural Social Science Harms Democracy' (2016) 38(1) New Political Science 61.

Green, Stuart P., *Lying, Cheating and Stealing: A Moral Theory of White-Collar Crime* (Oxford: Oxford University Press, 2007).

Green, Stuart P., 'Lying and the Law', in Jörg Meibauer (ed.), *The Oxford Handbook of Lying* (Oxford: Oxford University Press, 2018) 483–494.

Griffith, J. A. G., *The Politics of the Judiciary* (London: Fontana, 1977).

Grisez, Germain, Boyle, Joseph, and Finnis, John, 'Practical Principles, Moral Truth, and Ultimate Ends' (1987) 32 American Journal of Jurisprudence 99.

Groom, Richard, 'The Conduct of Parliamentary Elections in Kidderminster 1832–1880' (PhD, Coventry University, 1980).

Habermas, Jurgen, *Between Facts and Norms* (Cambridge, MA: MIT Press, 1996).

Habermas, Jurgen, 'Some Further Clarifications of the Concept of Communicative Rationality', in Cooke, Maeve (ed.), *On the Pragmatics of Communication* (Cambridge, MA: MIT Press, 1998) 198–231.

Hajnal, Zoltan, et al., 'Voter Identification Laws and the Suppression of Minority Votes' (2017) 79(2) Journal of Politics 363.

Hameleers, Michael, et al., Civilized truths, hateful lies? Incivility and Hate Speech in False Information—Evidence from Fact-checked Statements in the US' (2021) Information, Communication & Society, DOI: 10.1080/1369118X.2021.1874038.

Hans, G. S., 'Changing Counterspeech' (2021) 69 Cleveland State Law Review 749.

Hansard Society, *Audit of Political Engagement 15* (2018), https://www.hansardsociety.org.uk/publications/reports/audit-of-political-engagement-15-2018.

Hart, H. L. A., *The Concept of Law*, (3rd edition, Oxford: Oxford University Press, 2012).

Haselmayer, Martin, 'Negative Campaigning and its Consequences: A Review and a Look Ahead' (2019) 17 French Politics 355.

Hasen, Richard L., 'A Constitutional Right to Lie in Campaigns and Elections?' (2013) 74 Montana Law Review 53.

Heard, Andrew, 'Lies My Politician Told Me: *Friesen v Hammell* and the Nature of Election Fraud' (1997) 35(4) Alberta Law Review 1057.

Hicks, William D., et al., 'A Principle or a Strategy? Voter Identification Laws and Partisan Competition in the American States' (2015) 68 Political Research Quarterly 18.

HM Government, *Online Harms*, (White Paper, CP 57, April 2019).

Hmielowski, Jay D., et al., 'Talking Politics: The Relationship Between Supportive and Opposing Discussion With Partisan Media Credibility and Use' (2020) Communication Research, DOI:10.1177/0093650220915041.

Hochschild, Jennifer, 'Dimensions of Liberal Self-Satisfaction: Civil Liberties, Liberal Theory, and Elite Mass Differences' (1986) 96 Ethics 386.

Hor, Michael, 'Freedom of Speech and Defamation: *Jeyaretnam Joshua Benjamin v Lee Kuan Yew*' [1992] Singapore Journal of Legal Studies 542.

Horder, Jeremy, 'How Culpability Can and Cannot be Denied in Under-Age Sex Crimes' [2001] Crim LR 15.

Horder, Jeremy (ed.), *Ashworth's Principles of Criminal Law* (9th edition, Oxford: Oxford University Press, 2019).

Horder, Jeremy, 'Criminal Law at the Limit: Countering False Claims in Elections and Referendums' (2021a) 84(3) Modern Law Review 429.

Horder, Jeremy, 'Online Free Speech and the Suppression of False Political Claims' (2021b) 8(1) International and Comparative Law Quarterly 15.

House of Commons Select Committee on Home Affairs (4th Report, 1997–8), https://publications.parliament.uk/pa/cm199798/cmselect/cmhaff/768/76806.htm.

House of Commons, Digital, Culture, Media and Sport Committee, *Disinformation and Fake News: Final Report* (2019), https://publications.parliament.uk/pa/cm201719/cmselect/cmcumeds/1791/1791.pdf.

House of Lords European Union Committee, *The UK the EU and a British Bill of Rights* (12th Report of Session 2015–16), https://publications.parliament.uk/pa/ld201516/ldselect/ldeucom/139/139.pdf.

House of Lords Select Committee on Communications, *Social Media and Criminal Offences* (2014–15), https://publications.parliament.uk/pa/ld201415/ldselect/ldcomuni/37/3704.htm#a3.

House of Lords, *Digital Technology and the Resurrection of Trust* (Report of Session 2019–2021, HL Paper 77, 2020).

Hyde, Susan, 'Democracy's Backsliding in the International Environment' (2020) 369 Science (6508) 1192.

Jaggard, Edwin, 'Small Town Politics in Mid-Victorian Britain' (2004) 89 History 3.

Jay, Martin, *The Virtues of Mendacity: On Lying in Politics* (Chapel Hill: University of Virginia Press, 2010).

Jensen, Michael, 'Russian Trolls and Fake News: Information or Identity Logics?' (2018) 71 Journal of International Affairs 115.

Joint Intelligence and Security Committee (UK), *Russia* (HC 632, 2020).

Jones, Kate, 'Online Political Disinformation and Political Discourse: Applying a Human Rights Framework' (2019), https://www.chathamhouse.org/sites/default/files/2019-11-05-Online-Disinformation-Human-Rights.pdf.

Karanicolas, Michael, 'Subverting Democracy to Save Democracy: Canada's Extra-Constitutional Approaches to Battling "Fake News"' (2019) 17 Canadian Journal of Law and Technology 201.

Kasakowskij, Thomas, et al., 'Network Enforcement as Denunciation Endorsement? A Critical Study on Legal Enforcement in Social Media' (2020) 40 Telematics and Informatics 101317.

Katsirea, Irina, '"Fake news": Reconsidering the Value of Untruthful Expression in the Face of Regulatory Uncertainty' (2019) 10 Journal of Media Law 159.

Kettermann, Matthias, 'Follow-up to the Comparative Study on Blocking, Filtering and Takedown of Illegal Internet Content' (2019), https://rm.coe.int/dgi-2019-update-chapter-germany-study-on-blocking-and-filtering/168097ac51.

King's College Policy Institute, 'How British Moral Attitudes Have Changed in the Last 30 Years' (2019), https://www.kcl.ac.uk/policy-institute/assets/British-moral-attitudes.pdf.

Kirchmeier, Jeffrey L., 'The Illusion of the Fact–Opinion Distinction in Defamation Law' (1988) 39 Case Western Reserve Law Review 867.

Kirgis, Paul, 'Meaning, Intention and the Hearsay Rule' (2001) 43 William and Mary Law Review 275.

Kirk, Harry, *Portrait of a Profession. A History of the Solicitors Profession, 1100 to the Present Day* (London: Oyez Publishing, 1976).

Klonick, Kate, 'The New Governors: The People, Rules and Processes Governing Online Speech' (2018) 131 Harvard Law Review 1598.

Klonick, Kate, 'The Facebook Oversight Board: Creating an Independent Institution to Adjudicate Online Free Expression' (2020) 129(8) Yale Law Journal 2232.

Kofi Annan Commission on Elections and Democracy in the Digital Age, *Protecting Electoral Integrity in the Digital Age* (January 2020), https://www.kofiannanfoundation.org/app/uploads/2020/01/f035dd8e-kaf_kacedda_report_2019_web.pdf.

Laborde, Cécile, and Maynor, John, (eds), *Republicanism and Political Theory* (Oxford: Blackwell, 2008).

Lamo, Madeline, and Calo, Ryan, 'Regulating Bot Speech' (2019) 66 UCLA L Rev 988.

Lang, Andrej, 'Netzwerkdurchsetzungsgesetz und Meinungsfreiheit' (2018) 143 Archiv des öffentlichen Rechts 220.

Laski, H. J., *Studies in Law and Politics* (New Haven: Yale University Press, 1932).

Law Commission for England and Wales, *Criminal Libel* (Law Com No. 149, 1985).

Law Commission for England and Wales, *The Admissibility of Expert Evidence in Criminal Proceedings in England and Wales* (CP No. 190, 2009).

Law Commission for England and Wales, Research Paper, *Legal Challenge to Elections* (London: TSO, 2012).

Law Commission for England and Wales, *Abusive and Offensive Online Communications: A Scoping Report* (Law Com No. 381, 2018).

Law Commission for England and Wales, *Harmful Online Communications* (CP No. 248, 2020).

Law Commission for England and Wales; Scottish Law Commission; Law Commission for Northern Ireland, *Electoral Law: A Joint Consultation Paper* (LCCP 218 / SLCDP 158 / NILC 20, 2014).

Law Commission for England and Wales; Scottish Law Commission; Northern Ireland Law Commission, *Electoral Law: A Joint Interim Report* (London: TSO, 2016).

Laycock, David, *Populism and Democratic Thought in the Canadian Prairies, 1910 to 1945* (Toronto: University of Toronto Press, 1996).

Leiffring, Staci, 'First Amendment and the Right to Lie: Regulating Knowingly False Campaign Speech After *United States v Alvarez*' (2013) 97 Minnesota Law Review 1047.

Levin, Don, 'A Vote for Freedom? The Effects of Partisan Electoral Interventions on Regime Type' (2019) 63(4) Journal of Conflict Resolution 839.

Littler, Mark, and Feldman, Matthew, 'Social Media and the Cordon Sanitaire: Populist Politics, the Online Space, and a Relationship that Just Isn't There' (2017) 16 Journal of Language and Politics 510.

London School of Economics Commission on Truth, Trust and Technology, *Tackling the Information Crisis: A Policy Framework for Media System Resilience* (2018), https://www.

lse.ac.uk/media-and-communications/assets/documents/research/T3-Report-Tackling-the-Information-Crisis-v6.pdf.

Lowe, Robert, *Speeches and Letters on Reform with a Preface* (London: Robert John Bush, 1867).

Lukes, Steven, *Power: A Radical View* (London: Macmillan, 1974).

McClosky, Herbert, and Brill, Alida, *Dimensions of Tolerance: What Americans Believe about Civil Liberties* (New York: Russell Sage Foundation, 1983).

McGaughey, Ewan, 'Could Brexit be Void?' (2018) 29 King's Law Journal 331.

McGonagle, Tarlach, *Freedom of Expression and Defamation: A Study of the Case Law of the European Court of Human Rights* (Strasbourg: Council of Europe, 2016).

McMillan, Imara, 'Enforcement Through the Network: The Network Enforcement Act and Article 10 of the European Convention on Human Rights (2019) 20(1) Chicago Journal of International Law 252.

Mahoney, Kathleen, 'Hate Speech, Equality, and the State of Canadian Law' (2009) 44 Wake Forest Law Review 321.

Martí, José Luis, and Philip Pettit, *A Political Philosophy in Public Life* (Princeton, NJ: Princeton University Press, 2010).

Marwick, Alice, and Lewis, Rebecca, *Media Manipulation and Disinformation Online* (New York: Data & Society, 2017).

Massicotte, L., Blais, A., and Yoshinaka, A., *Establishing the Rules of the Game: Election Laws in Democracies* (Ontario: University of Toronto Press, 2004).

Mattinson, M. W., and Macaskie, S. C., *The Law Relating to Corrupt Practices at Elections* (London: Waterlow and Sons, 1883).

Mayer, William G., 'In Defence of Negative Campaigning' (1996) 111 Political Science Quarterly 437.

Media Legal Defence Initiative, *Freedom of Expression, Media Law and Defamation* (2015), https://www.mediadefence.org/wp-content/uploads/2020/06/MLDI.IPI-defamation-manual.English-1.pdf.

Miall, E., *The Suffrage or Reconciliation between the Middle and Labouring Classes* (London, 1848).

Mill, J. S., *On Liberty* (Gertrude Himmelfarb edition, London: Penguin, 1974).

Montgomery, Martin, 'Post-Truth Politics? Authenticity, Populism and the Electoral Discourses of Donald Trump' (2017) 16 Journal of Language and Politics 619.

Morris, Caroline, and Wilks-Heeg, Stuart, '"Reports of My Death Have Been Greatly Exaggerated": The Continuing Role and Relevance of Election Petitions in Challenging Election Results in the UK' (2019) 18 Election Law Journal 31.

Morris, Roger, and Heath, Mark, *Running Elections 2020* (4th edition, Stourbridge: APS books, 2020).

Mouffe, Chantal, *On the Political* (London: Routledge, 2005).

Muller, Jan-Werner, 'Militant Democracy', in Rosenfeld, Michel, and Sajó, András (eds), *The Oxford Handbook of Comparative Constitutional Law* (Oxford: Oxford University Press, 2012) ch. 59.

Murray, David, 'Protecting Our Elections: Examining Shell Companies and Virtual Currencies as Avenues for Foreign Interference', *Financial Integrity Network*, 26 June 2018, https://www.judiciary.senate.gov/imo/media/doc/06-26-18%20Murray%20Testimony.pdf.

Myerson, Michael L., 'Authors, Editors, and Uncommon Carriers: Identifying the "Speaker" Within the New Media', (1995) 71 Notre Dame LR 79.

Nash, Victoria, 'Revise and Resubmit? Reviewing the 2019 Online Harms White Paper' (2019) 11 Journal of Media Law 18.

NATO STRATCOM, *Internet Trolling as a Tool of Hybrid Warfare: The Case of Latvia* (2016), https://www.stratcomcoe.org.

Negrine, Ralph, *Politics and the Mass Media* (2nd edition, London: Routledge, 1994).

Nelson, Jacob L., and Taneja, Harsh, 'The Small, Disloyal Fake News Audience: The Role of Audience Availability in Fake News Consumption' (2018) 20 New Media & Society 3720.

Network Enforcement Act: Regulatory Fining Guidelines (2018), https://www.bundesjustizamt.de/DE/SharedDocs/Publikationen/NetzDG/Leitlinien_Geldbussen_en.pdf?__blob=publicationFile&v=2.

New Zealand Law Commission, *Ministerial Briefing Paper on Harmful Digital Communications: The Adequacy of the Current Sanctions and Remedies* (August 2012), https://www.lawcom.govt.nz/sites/default/files/projectAvailableFormats/NZLC%20MB3.pdf.

Norris, Emma, 'Manifestos Still Matter Even Though Their Promises Aren't Being Delivered' (2019), https://www.instituteforgovernment.org.uk/blog/do-manifestos-matter-anymore.

Oborne, Peter, *The Rise of Political Lying* (London: The Free Press, 2005).

Ofcom: *The Ofcom Broadcasting Code* (2009), https://www.ofcom.org.uk/__data/assets/pdf_file/0027/19287/bcode09.pdf.

O'Gorman, Frank, *Voters, Patrons and Politics: The Unreformed Electorate of Hanoverian England 1754–1832* (Oxford: Oxford University Press, 1989).

Ohlin, Jens David, 'Did Russian Cyber Interference in the 2016 Election Violate International Law?' (2017) 95 Texas Law Review 1579.

O'Leary, Cornelius, *The Elimination of Corrupt Practices in British Elections 1868–1911* (Oxford: Clarendon Press, 1962).

Parsons, Alex (2016), 'Free and Fair: Preventing Political Misinformation', https://research.alexparsons.co.uk/free-and-fair/free-and-fair.pdf.

Pennycook, G., Cannon, T. D., and Rand, D. G., 'Prior Exposure Increases Perceived Accuracy of Fake News' (2018) 147(12) Journal of Experimental Psychology 1865.

Perry, Ronen, and Zarsky, Tal, 'Who Should be Liable for Online Anonymous Defamation?' (2015) 82 University of Chicago Law Review Dialogue 162.

Peters, Michael A., 'The History and Practice of Lying in Public Life' (2015) 14 Review of Contemporary Philosophy 43.

Pettit, Philip, *The Common Mind: An Essay on Psychology, Society, and Politics* (Oxford: Oxford University Press, 1996).

Pharand, Michael et al., *Benjamin Disraeli Letters 1868: Volume X* (Ontario: University of Toronto Press, 2014).

Price, Zachary S., 'Our Imperilled Absolutist First Amendment' (2018) 20 Journal of Constitutional Law 817.

Privacy International (2019), *Submission to the House of Lords Select Committee on Democracy and Digital Technologies*, https://privacyinternational.org/sites/default/files/2020-03/19.09.20%20HoL%20Democracy%20and%20Digital%20Tech%20submission_final-1.pdf.

Rawlings, H. F., *Law and the Electoral Process* (London: Sweet & Maxwell, 1988).

Raymond, Allen, *How to Rig an Election: Confessions of a Republican Operative* (New York: Simon & Schuster, 2008).

Raz, Joseph, *The Morality of Freedom* (Oxford: Clarendon Press, 1986).

Renwick, Alan, and Palese, Michela, *Doing Democracy Better: How and Information and Discourse in election and Referendum Campaigns in the UK be Improved?* (London, University College London Constitution Unit, 2019).

Reuters Institute, *Digital News Report 2018*, https://reutersinstitute.politics.ox.ac.uk/sites/default/files/digital-news-report-2018.pdf.

Rini, Regina, 'Fake News and Partisan Epistemology' (2017) Kennedy Institute of Ethics Journal, https://kiej.georgetown.edu/fake-news-partisan-epistemology/.

Rix, Kathryn, 'The Elimination of Corrupt Practices in British Elections'? Reassessing the Impact of the 1883 Corrupt Practices Act' (2008) 123 The English Historical Review 65.

Rix, Kathryn 'The Second Reform Act and the Problem of Electoral Corruption' (2017) 36 Parliamentary History 64.

Robertson, Craig T., et al., 'Who Uses Fact-Checking Sites? The Impact of Demographics, Political Antecedents, and Media Use on Fact-Checking Site Awareness, Attitudes, and Behaviour' (2020) 5 The International Journal of Press Politics 217.

Romei, Annibale, *The Courtier's Academie* (1598).

Rose-Ackerman, Susan, and Palifka, Bonnie J., *Corruption and Government: Causes, Consequences and Reform* (2nd edition, Cambridge: Cambridge University Press, 2016) Introduction.

Rowbottom, Jacob, 'Lies, Manipulation and Elections—Controlling False Campaign Statements' (2012) 32(3) OJLS 507.

Saunders, Robert, 'The Politics of Reform and the Making of the Second Reform Act 1848–1867' (2007) 50 Historical Journal 571.

Scanlon, Thomas, 'A Theory of Freedom of Expression' (1972) 1 Philosophy and Public Affairs 204.

Schnadhorst, Francis, 'The Caucus and its Critics' (1882) 12 Nineteenth Century 23.

Schroeder, Ralph, 'Digital Media and the Entrenchment of Right-Wing Populist Agendas' (2019) 5(4) Social Media and Society 1.

Schultz, Wolfgang, 'Regulating Intermediaries to Protect Privacy Online—the Case of the German NetzDG' (2018), https://www.hiig.de/publication/regulating-intermediaries-to-protect-privacy-online-the-case-of-the-german-netzdg/.

Scottish Ministerial Code: *A Code of Conduct and Guidance on Procedures for Members of the Scottish Government and Junior Scottish Ministers* (Edinburgh: Scottish Government, 2018).

Seidenfeld, Mark, 'A Civic Republican Justification for the Bureaucratic State' (1992) 105 Harvard LR 1511.

Select Committee on the Operation and Effect of Corrupt Practices Prevention Act (1854), *Report* (House of Commons, 22 May 1860).

Sellers, Joshua S., 'Legislating against Lying in Campaigns and Elections' (2018) 71 Oklahoma LR 141.

Seymour, Charles, *Electoral Reform in England and Wales: The Development and Operation of the Parliamentary Franchise 1832–1885*, first published in 1915 (London: David and Charles, 1970).

Shauer, Frederick, *Free Speech: A Philosophical Enquiry* (Cambridge: Cambridge University Press, 1982).

Shauer, Frederick, and Pildes, Richard H., 'Electoral Exceptionalism and the First Amendment' (1999) 77 Texas Law Review 1803.

Shuckburgh, E. S. (ed.), *The Letters of Cicero* (New York: Palatine Press, 2015).

Simester, A. P., 'Why Distinguish Intention from Foresight?', in A. P. Simester and A. T. H. Smith (eds), *Harm and Culpability* (Oxford: Oxford University Press, 1996) 71–101.

Smith Pfister, Damian, 'Public Sphere(s), Publics and Counterpublics', in Cloud, Dan L. (ed.), *The Oxford Encyclopedia of Communication and Critical Cultural Studies* (Oxford: Oxford University Press, 2019) ch. 93.

Sobell, J., 'A Theory of Credibility' (1985) 52 Review of Economic Studies 557.

Spano, Robert, 'Intermediary Liability for Online User Comments under the European Convention on Human Rights' (2017) 17 Human Rights Law Review 665.

Spencer, John, 'Criminal Libel: The Law Commission's Working Paper' [1983] Crim LR 524.

Sunstein, Cass, *Republic 2.0* (Princeton, NJ: Princeton University Press, 2007).

Sunstein, Cass, *Liars: Falsehoods and Free Speech in an Age of Deception* (New York: Oxford University Press, 2021).

Tambini, Damian, 'The Differentiated Duty of Care: A Response to the Online Harms White Paper' (2019) 11 Journal of Media Law 28.

Tetlock, P., *Expert Political Judgment: How Good Is It? How Can We Know?* (Princeton, NJ: Princeton University Press, 2005).

Theil, Stefan, 'The Online Harms White Paper: Comparing the UK and German Approaches to Regulation' (2019) 11 Journal of Media Law 41.

Thomas, A., 'The System of Registration and the Development of Party Organisation 1832–1870 (1950) 35 History 81.

Thompson, Debra, 'An Exoneration of Black Rage' (2017) 116(3) The South Atlantic Quarterly 457.

Thompson, James, *British Political Culture and the Idea of 'Public Opinion', 1867–1914* (Cambridge: Cambridge University Press, 2013).

Tirell, Lynne, 'Toxic Misogyny and the Limits of Counterspeech' (2018–19) 87 Fordham Law Review 2433

Toms, Michael, and Weeks, Jessica L. P., 'Public Opinion and Foreign Electoral Intervention' (2019), https://web.stanford.edu/~tomz/working/TomzWeeks-ElectoralIntervention-2019-08-13i.pdf.

Tóth, Gábor Attila, 'Authoritarianism', in Grote, Ranier, et al. (eds), *Max Planck Encyclopedia of Comparative Constitutional Law* (Oxford: Oxford University Press, 2017) ch 02.05.

Twitter, *Civic Integrity Policy* (2021), https://help.twitter.com/en/rules-and-policies/election-integrity-policy.

Tworek, Heidi, 'An Analysis of Germany's NetzDG Law' (Working Paper, Transatlantic High Level Working Group on Content Moderation Online and Freedom of Expression) (2019) https://pure.uva.nl/ws/files/40293503/NetzDG_Tworek_Leerssen_April_2019.pdf.

UN Special Rapporteur, *Report on the Promotion and Protection of the Right to Freedom of Opinion and Expression* (2015), https://webcache.googleusercontent.com/search?q=cache:0YYYHOnWVhQJ:https://www.ohchr.org/EN/HRbodies/HRC/RegularSessions/Session29/Documents/A.HRC.29.32_AEV.doc+&cd=1&hl=en&ct=clnk&gl=uk.

Valentino, Nicholas, et al., 'Election Night's Alright for Fighting: The Role of Emotions in Political Participation' (2011) 73(1) Journal of Politics 156.

Van Bavel, Jay J., and Pereira, Andrea, 'The Partisan Brain: An Identity-Based Model of Political Belief' (2018) 22 Trends in Cognitive Science 213.

Véliz, Carissa, 'Online Masquerade: Redesigning the Internet for Free Speech Through the Use of Pseudonyms' (2019) 36 Journal of Applied Philosophy 643.

Vilmer, Jean-Baptiste Jeangène, et al., *Information Manipulation: A Challenge for Our Democracies* (2018), https://www.diplomatie.gouv.fr/IMG/pdf/information_manipulation_rvb_cle838736.pdf.

Vivyan, Nick, Wagner, Markus, and Tarlov, Jessica, 'Representative Misconduct, Voter Perceptions and Accountability: Evidence from the 2009 House of Commons Expenses Scandal' (2012) 31(4) Electoral Studies 750.

Volokh, Eugene, 'The First Amendment and Criminal Libel Law' (2019), https://reason.com/2019/04/10/the-first-amendment-and-criminal-libel-l/?itm_source=parsely-api.

Vosoughi, Soroush, Roy, Deb, and Aral, Sinan, 'The Spread of True and False News Online' (2018) 359 Science 1146.

Wagner, Ben, et al., 'Regulating Transparency? Facebook, Twitter and the German Network Enforcement Act' (2020), https://www.researchgate.net/publication/338802975_Regulating_Transparency_Facebook_Twitter_and_the_German_Network_Enforcement_Act/link/5e2b217292851c3aadd7b7f5/download.

Wakefield, Edward Gibbon, *England and America: a Comparison of the Social and Political State of Both Nations* (New York: Harper, 1834).

Waldron, Jeremy, 'Judges as Moral Reasoners' (2009) 7(1) I-CON 1.

Warner, Michael, 'Publics and Counterpublics' (2002) 14 Public Culture 49.

Weale, Albert, *Democracy* (2nd edition, Basingstoke: Palgrave MacMillan, 2007).

Weber, Max, 'Objectivity in Social Science and Social Policy' (1904), in Shils, Edward A, and Finch, Henry A, (eds and trs) *Max Weber on the Methodology of the Social Sciences* (Illinois: Free Press of Glencoe, 1949).

Weber, Max, *Science as Vocation* (1919), http://www.wisdom.weizmann.ac.il/~oded/X/WeberScienceVocation.pdf.

Williams, Bernard, *In the Beginning was the Deed* (New Jersey: Princeton University Press, 2005).

Williams, Faye H., 'Voting Barriers: Strategies for Removing Obstacles to the Black Ballot' (1972) 2 Black Law Journal 164.

Wischmeyer, Thomas, 'What is Illegal Offline is Also Illegal Online' – The German Network Enforcement Act 2017,' in Petkova, Bilyana, and Ojanen, Tuomas (eds) *Fundamental Rights Protection Online: The Future Regulation of Intermediaries* (London: Elgar, 2019) 28–56.

Wolchover, David, and Robinson, Amanda, 'Is Brexit a Russia-backed Coup?' (24 January 2020) NLJ online (https://bit.ly/2QYl2Ao).

Index

For the benefit of digital users, indexed terms that span two pages (e.g., 52–53) may, on occasion, appear on only one of those pages.